THE HIDDEN PARTY

Life is a breath
Living on an endless fast lane.
Humans are but for a time,
Nothing remains with humans forever.
Therefore the living is
THE MEMORY
That which affects humans in the cycle of life.
The never aging, never fading is but only
A gift offered to future generations.
August 2014

Disclaimer:

This book is based on true experiences of the author who was a freedom fighter with the Eritrean People's Front for The liberation of Eritrea. The book narrates the activities and the history of struggle; all names and nicknames mentioned in the narration are trued representations. The author has mentioned the names and nicknames in a clear and unambiguous manner, remaining true to the spirit of a history in which he was part. In disclosing his experiences, the author apologizes in advance for what might follow of uneasiness or harm to anyone. Neither the publisher nor the author bears any responsibility for comments by, or contents of, other parties regarding this work.

A Short Note from the Author

This book is a revised edition of the Tigrigna version published earlier. I was pleasantly surprised by the number of very encouraging comments I received from readers of the Tigrigna version. Readers expressed astonishment and disappointment at the very fact of there being a secret party within the EPLF known only to a select few who had sworn an oath of secrecy. When this was revealed in 1994 in the 3rd congress of the EPLF in Nakfa soon after liberation, there was general shock and disappointment by members of the EPLF, the vast majority of whom knew nothing about the party's existence. And they were intrigued—and felt a sense of alienation—at being outsiders of the organization for which they committed their life and fortune.

In this respect it will probably be useful to this book by reading the Postscript first. This would enhance the sense of wonder in the reader's mind and perhaps even help explain, if not justify, the origin and purpose of the Secret Party.

—*Tsegu Fessahaie Bahta*

THE HIDDEN PARTY

My Personal Experiences in the Eritrean Struggle

Tsegu Fessahaie Bahta

Foreword by
Bereket Habte Selassie & Dan Connell

THE RED SEA PRESS
TRENTON | LONDON | NEW DELHI | CAPE TOWN | NAIROBI | ADDIS ABABA | ASMARA | IBADAN

THE RED SEA PRESS
541 West Ingham Avenue | Suite B
Trenton, New Jersey 08638

Book design: Ashraful Haque
Cover design: Lemlem Tadesse

Library of Congress Cataloging-in-Publication Data

Names: Bahta, Tsegu Fessahaie, 1954- author.
Title: The hidden party : my personal experiences in the Er-
    itrean struggle / Tsegu Fessahaie Bahta.
Description: Trenton : Red Sea Press, 2019. | Includes index.
Identifiers: LCCN 2019000295| ISBN 9781569025192 (hb) |
    ISBN 9781569025208 (pb)
Subjects: LCSH: Bahta, Tsegu Fessahaie, 1954- | Hezbawi
    genbar harenat Eretra--History. | National liberation
    movements--Eritrea--History. | Soldiers--Eritrea--Biog-
    raphy. | Eritrea--History--Revolution, 1962-1993--Person-
    al narratives. | Eritrea--Politics and government-- 1962-
    1993. | Eritrea--Politics and government--1993-
Classification: LCC DT397 .B34 2019 | DDC 963.5071092--
    dc23
LC record available at https://lccn.loc.gov/2019000295

DEDICATION

This book is dedicated in memory and honor of those who fell in the struggle to realize the freedom and independence of the Eritrean people, to the martyrs Isaac Rezene, a friend and a comrade; Afwerki Teweldemedhin (aka Bureaucracy), Rusom Teklemariam (aka Tarzan), and other dedicated fighters whose stories have not been told yet, for those who worked inside the belly of the enemy carrying out intelligence activities in Asmara and Ethiopian cities, and were executed in enemy prisons and in the outskirts of Asmara in Qushet.

To those who are languishing in the ravines of Ella-Ero and other PFDJ prisons, and who are suffering and dying, the senior leaders of the Eritrean revolution, journalists whose only crime is being voice of the voiceless, and all those who pursued a non-violent struggle for change.

To all those, who at this time and age, have become shooting targets for the PFDJ on the border areas, or lost their lives in the desert of Sinai where their body parts was extracted, or the youth who are drowning in the Mediterranean Sea.

To the memory of my three martyred brothers, my friends and comrades: Isaias Fessahaie, Amanuel Fessahaie, and Mussie Fessahaie.

To all those who fell and became handicapped in the struggle to realize the independence of Eritrea, and to all the children of martyrs.

To my beloved children whom I left behind in Asmara Eritrean because of the unjust PFDJ regime, Pitias Tsegu, Aman Tsegu, Selam Tsegu; to the memory of my parents who raised me to participate in the making of history and in whose funeral I couldn't participate, my late father Memhir Fessahaie Bahta and my late mother Weizero Besrat Habteselassie.

TABLE OF CONTENTS

FOREWORD

By Dan Connell

Eritrea—an Italian colony from 1890 to 1941 and then a British protectorate before it was joined with Ethipia in a federatin in 1950 and was then annexed by Ethiopia in the 1950s—won its de facto independence from Ethiopia in May 1991 when the Eritrean People's Liberation Front (EPLF) defeated the Ethiopian army and helped an allied guerrilla movement within Ethiopia oust the Ethiopian dictator, Mengistu Haile Mariam, who today resides in Harare, Zimbabwe. In April 1993, the EPLF-led government, acting with Ethiopian approval, held a UN-monitored referendum on the territory's status. The outcome was an overwhelming vote for sovereignty (99.8 percent). This was quickly followed by formal recognition of the new government by the United States, among others, and by Eritrea's acceptance as a full member into the United Nations. At that time, there was great optimism about Eritrea's prospects for democratic development among most of its citizens and within the international community.

Relations between Eritrea and Ethiopia appeared friendly after Eritrea's independence, but a legacy of rivalry and tension remained. After a series of disputes over economic policy in the mid-1990s and a number of armed incidents along the two countries' as-yet-undemarcated border, war broke out in May 1998. There were three rounds of fighting involving more than a half-million soldiers on both sides—May-June 1998, February-March 1999, and May-June 2000—before a truce went into effect. UN peacekeepers were deployed in November 2000. On April 13, 2002, an international Boundary Commission set up to adjudicate the dispute issued its binding verdict. Both states nominally accepted, but Ethiopia would not allow the UN to proceed with demarcation, claiming the outcome unfairly favored

Eritrea, and Eritrea refused to engage in negotiations. As a result, hundreds of thousands of soldiers are still deployed along the frontier.

For more than a decade, the two countries have been in what they call a state of "no-peace-no-war." Meanwhile, both have tried to subvert each other by supporting opposition groups, some of them armed, and by waging proxy wars in neighboring states, notably Somalia. Major clashes between the two countries occurred in June 2016 when heavy fighting erupted near the town of Tserona. Though it subsided after a day, the incident highlighted the potential for renewed war at any time. Meanwhile, the government of Eritrea has acted ruthlessly to suppress internal dissent by arresting individuals suspected of disloyalty and using extra-judicial procedures and punishments against political opponents and religious dissidents, including torture, according to leading human rights groups ranging from Amnesty International and Human Rights Watch to the United Nations. What brought about this remarkable reversal? Or was it a "reversal" at all?

Colonel Tsegu Fessahaie Bahta's personal account of the role of the secret party within the victorious liberation front up to and after independence makes a convincing case for the view that the seeds of the present autocracy were planted decades ago, even if they took years to germinate and renewed war to burst into full view. But his memoir gives us far more than an inside look at the history that brought Eritrea to this point; it provides a remarkable insight into the mechanics of the movement that now rules the country and the ways that history shapes the post independence political landscape.

High Hopes & Dashed Dreams

The political culture of Eritrea's ruling party has always been an authoritarian one, predicated upon secrecy and the arbitrary exercise of absolute power by a small number of people making decisions in secret. The EPLF was controlled throughout its 20-year existence by a clandestine Marxist-Leninist core known as the Eritrean People's Revolutionary Party (EPRP),[1] headed by Isaias Afwerki, who was nominally second-in-command in the front but who actually ran it through his party post. In practice, the party drafted the EPLF's program, selected its leadership slates prior to elections, and,

---

1   EPRP should not be confused with the Ethiopian People's Revolutionary Party (EPRP) which has been efunct for over two decades.

unbeknownst to the front's non-party members, managed its affairs on a day-to-day basis, from determining its military strategy to overseeing its civilian mobilization and running its extensive social services and economic operations.

The government apparatus set up in 1991 was almost exclusively comprised of EPLF guerrillas appointed by the president or his subordinates. Most high officials had been members of the secret EPRP, and many had ties to the national security apparatus. Though the party was officially disbanded at the end of the war, the leadership continued to meet in secret to manage the transition to statehood up to the point in 1994 where Isaias reorganized his inner circle and the EPLF was renamed the People's Front for Democracy and Justice (PFDJ). During this time, non-party members in the EPLF and people who had supported the independence movement in exile were encouraged to participate in the reconstruction of the country but were kept at arm's length by the inner circle. From this point forward, officials down to the level of village administrators were selected by the top leadership of the ruling party and, like the new government, were managed by former guerrillas in civilian clothes who reported to their former commanding officer, the country's unelected president.

The National Assembly, which only met when called into session by the president and was dominated from the outset by the PFDJ central council, quickly became a rubber stamp for proclamations drafted in the president's office. However, it has not even convened a formal session since 2002. Today, the judiciary, too, lacks independence and is routinely bypassed through a system of "special courts" and clandestine prisons that hold thousands of suspected dissidents.[2] The result is a facade of institutional normalcy that masks a remarkably efficient tyranny. Now, as during the struggle, hidden networks are far more important than visible institutions. In this and other respects, Eritrea functions less as a modern state than as a guerrilla movement headed by a single charismatic figure holding a "liberated" zone.

The continuing hostilities between Ethiopia and Eritrea have provided the government in Asmara with a rationale for blocking all moves toward democratization and suppressing all criticism of the political leadership. The limited debate that was tolerated between

---

2   The Chief Justice, a respected lawyer – revolutionary, was dismissed by the President.

1991 and 2000—a period that saw the appearance of a vigorous private press—came to a crushing halt with the September 2001 jailing of top government officials identified with the dissident Group of 15 (G15). The G15 had privately submitted a letter to the president calling for democratization and published it when he was unresponsive. The 2001 crackdown was consolidated over the following year through a program of party-run seminars and selective arrests, and it set the tone for the years since.

The Constitution, ratified in 1997, was never implemented. Freedoms of speech, assembly, press, and religious practice—promised in the Constitution—were and remain sharply restricted. National elections have been repeatedly postponed. No other political organization apart from the ruling liberation front, the PFDJ, has been permitted. Nor are nongovernmental organizations permitted unless they are directly controlled by the party, and no demonstrations of protest are allowed. Unsanctioned churches have also been forcibly closed since 2002. Today, the country languishes under one-man rule—that of Isaias Afwerki—and a small group of people drawn from the armed forces, the security apparatus and the secretariat of the PFDJ, which maintains a system of informers that reaches into every village and town through a network of party-run neighborhood committees called kebeles and monitors Eritreans in the diaspora through similar means.

From the middle of 2001 to 2002, as the crackdown was unfolding, I visited Eritrea four times. On each visit, I was struck by how much the atmosphere had changed since prior visits. Long-time confidants refused to criticize the regime in public places, even in whispers, for fear they might be punished. Nor would they do so on the phone or in emails, as they believed all communication was monitored. Their anxieties were enhanced by the manner in which arrested dissidents were treated. People who questioned the policies of the regime simply disappeared, including those who merely voiced such views to friends in public places and were overheard by government supporters and reported. No formal charges were brought against them, and no one had access to them once they were imprisoned (even their families). The lack of clarity on what would get one arrested engendered a pervasive terror of the authorities and a growing mistrust of friends, neighbors, co-workers and others. After I criticized these practices in an interview with an externally-based Eritrean website, Asmarino.com, I was ordered to leave the country.

I have since then interviewed hundreds of Eritreans who described being detained, abused, and tortured. Few were prominent in oppositional organizations; most simply voiced critical opinions, often in public "seminars," and were reported for it or participated in banned meetings or religious services. Some were incarcerated in shipping containers in the desert lowlands or on islands in the Dahlak Archipelago where they were beaten and held for long periods with inadequate water and food; others were held in warehouses or underground cells, some sited within towns and cities but invisible to passersby. Refugees told me disturbing stories about torture used on political and religious dissenters, including the "helicopter" in which the victim is stripped of his clothing, tied with arms behind his back, and either laid on the ground face down or hung from a tree and left for several days and nights. Such treatment is routine for those caught trying to escape. This is what it has come to.

The key to understanding why it has done so and how it works lies in an examination of the secret party—then and now.

The Inside Story

Tsegu opens with a deeply personal account of his early experience in the "field"—short for battlefield but connoting much more than just a place where people fought. The field, medda, was as much a state of mind as a physical place, the rarified world of the guerrilla fighter, with all its privations, camaraderie, sacrifice, self-effacement, shared conviction, individual courage, and organizational discipline, much of it the product of the party whose fundamental aim was to remold the fighters into what its leaders saw as the new Eritrean. The results were impressive but also unsettling. What was not always obvious was the level of control behind what we saw from the outside and the extent of the coercive apparatus that imposed it.

Tsegu immerses us in the details of life within the EPLF in the mid-1970s, giving us a visceral feel for what it was like to be there, from his training and early "political education" in the Sahel mountains to his assignment to the front's security department, HalewaSewra (Shield of the Revolution), then headed by Solomon Weldemariam, one of the party's enforcers who would soon run afoul of Isaias and be imprisoned as an alleged leader of a dissident movement dubbed yameen (rightists). The time was 1975, but Tsegu had been a clandestine member of the front inside Asmara, the capital, since 1972.

He was not yet a member of the party at this point, but he was surrounded by party cadres without knowing it.

Tsegu was initially assigned to guard prisoners: not Ethiopian POWs but EPLF fighters suspected of being spies, abandoning their posts, embezzling supplies, engaging in acts of homosexuality, expressing deviant political views—one or another of a grab bag of crimes and heresies, some political, some social. Deviation from the party line in thought or deed was the operative concept. His account of this period, during which he was introduced to the welter of rules and policies that governed fighter behavior and the methods by which the front—actually the party—administered and punished those deemed guilty of infractions, reveals a lot about the character of this movement and the people who led it. Many of the names of those he encountered within the security framework will be familiar to Eritreans, as they are at the center of the heavily securitized state the movement produced later.

Three years on Tsegu is inducted into the party by his political commander, Estifanos "Bruno" Afeworki, a cadre of the EPRP and a member of the EPLF's central committee who is today Eritrea's ambassador to Japan. Chapter Two provides us with an inside view of how both the front and the party functioned at a crucial point in their intertwined history, six months after an all-out Soviet intervention on the side of Ethiopia that forced the Eritreans to retreat from large swathes of captured territory while also isolating them from many countries and political movements they had seen as natural allies. It was enough to make anyone paranoid, and it certainly heightened such tendencies within EPLF and its clandestine party leadership, already so inclined. Tsegu's descriptions of the ways people were wrongly accused of being traitors, coerced into making false confessions and punished unmercifully are instructive, not only for an understanding of this period but for what they presaged for later.

The next chapters recount his experiences in the 1980s with a mix of fascinating insights into such things as the contest among rival liberation fronts—Eritrean and Ethiopian—over the obscure frontier community of Badme, the practice of interrogation of suspected traitors and dissidents, the treatment of POWs, and the party and front's successive congresses in 1987 when major changes in leadership took place. The EPRP congress was where all major decisions were taken. That of the EPLF was where Isaias came out of the closet as the front's official leader, mirroring his long-standing role within the party, and where he surrounded himself with hard-line loyalists like General Abraha Kassa, who today runs the national security service.

After the war was won in 1991, the security services—operating under the command of party leaders, not the liberation front—set out to "eliminate" traitors in Ethiopia and other neighboring states, Tsegu tells us. Isaias took this approach rather than capturing and arresting them because he wanted to avoid trials in which secrets might be exposed that he wanted hidden from the public. A committee was set up to determine who and what would be investigated that was chaired by Simon Gebredingel, a prominent member of the Intelligence and Security Department who would go on to become another key figure in Isaias's inner circle. Again, the approach to dissent and difference is instructive, as it would be replicated on even larger scale after 2001. Tsegu had a bird's-eye view of this round as one of five mid-level managers in the department.

His account of the party's third and last congress at the end of 1993 is one of the most revealing sections of the book, for it was here that Isaias carried out the crucial maneuver in a rolling coup d'état that would less than a decade later leaves him the unrivaled strongman atop a tightly controlled one-party police state. The highlight, according to Tsegu, was Isaias's statement that the movement's leadership was "rotten"—that it had "lost direction and couldn't lead." The only solution was to replace it with "new blood." And he had already composed a list of who ought to be included.

Key leaders from the independence war were then shunted aside or demoted, while others lower down the chain of command were elevated, including several who had come into the party through diaspora-based organizations in the United States and Europe and had proven themselves loyal to Isaias while avoiding the rivalries, friendships and intrigues, real or imagined, that Isaias perceived among older veterans.

The front's third congress a few months after that of the party was an anti-climax as all the major decisions had by then been taken and the new leadership already selected. Afterward, Isaias moved to further isolate those he suspected of disloyalty, freezing or demoting them or sending them on diplomatic missions abroad where they could not cause trouble or impede his consolidation of power. It was at this congress that the existence of the clandestine People's Party was announced for the first time to non-party members of the front, shocking many of them, even as they were told it had been dismantled and was now a relic of the liberation front's history.

Tsegu is convinced that Isaias took this opportunity to launch a new secret party. I'm not totally convinced there is a formal organization, but he makes a compelling case for it, and all the signs are there of some version of it. There can be little argument over the fact that the method of operation of the government today, in terms of where and how power is exercised, is little different than that of the liberation front when it was secretly run by EPRP, which is the main point. Now, as then, a secretive inner circle makes the key decisions in all matters of substance and is accountable to no constituency, public or otherwise, other than the boss, Isaias.

Whether they meet as an organization, as the EPRP did, and select their own leadership, hash out differences in policy and program, and function within a more or less defined hierarchy or they simply constitute a network whose members are known to one another but selected and managed by Isaias is beside the point. What Tsegu's account makes clear is that whatever the extent of current participation by a chosen few, their enforcement of decisions made at the top of the pyramid relies on a toxic combination of deception, fear and intimidation in which violence always lurks below the surface calm. As a consequence, the country's political culture has been deeply warped—so much so that many Eritreans now take it as normal and either deny it or find ways to rationalize it so long as it doesn't affect them directly. Under these circumstances, more will have to change in Eritrea than merely the man at the top if the nation is to heal itself. Getting the truth out is a necessary part of that process. Tsegu's book is an important step.

Gloucester, Mass., USA, 4 July 2016

FOREWORD

By Bereket Habte Selassie

Tsegu is the son of my beloved older sister, the late Besrat Habteselassie. Since his childhood, Tsegu was hot tempered and his aunt, Hanna, worried he might grow up to become naughty and troublesome. She was right; though he was not that bad he became a tenacious debater who would not sway from his position. When he started high school, after he matured by experience and education, he was influenced by the prevailing situation in our country and transformed his character from a troublesome boy to a furcious debater. At his early age he worked as an underground member of the Eritrean People's Liberation Front (EPLF) inside the belly of the enemy, and later joined the field to struggle. I am honored and proud of him for being one of the fighters who accomplished his obligation to his country by being part of the struggle for the independence of Eritrea.

This book sheds light on the national struggle, and the complicated life and difficulties and sufferings that Tsegu went through.

This book focuses on three aspects:
1. As its title suggests, he has exposed and analyzed the roots of the secret party that baffled many people, the tool that enabled the tyrant to block the path towards democracy that our people struggled for, thus documenting it for posterity.
2. He contributed in explaining through his experience, the detailed history of the Eritrean revolution and that of his fellow fighters, in order to pass it to the post independence generation and thus provided a clear narrative.
3. His third contribution concerns his writing style. From the beginning to the end, in each chapter of this book, be it the

arrangement of words or their use to express ideas, it is graced with a unique writing style.

Therefore, I welcome the contribution of Tsegu, and I say "Kudos nephew" expressing my happiness and gratitude; and I wish readers enjoyable and insightful moments with the book.

Bereket Habte Selassie
Distinguished Professor of African Studies and Law
University of North Carolina at Chapel Hill

PREFACE

Firstly, I thank God for keeping me healthy and alive to pass on this history. The contents of the book are true narrations sourced from my own memories. I started to write this book in 2005, but since it was not possible to publish such truths inside Eritrea, I wrote it in the form of fiction. However, since the regime would not tolerate the basic right of self expression let alone private teashop conversations, I decided to keep away from potential risks and instead chose to wait for an opportune time to write it.

And now, since time is of the essence I raised my pen again and continued to pursue the fiction mode. However, since the reason for deciding to make it a fiction was eliminated, I chose to rewrite it as a true narration. In such a time that I am recording my memoirs away from my country, without access to certain documents, and I could not reach individuals who participated in certain activities, even with the existence of situational hindrances that prevent me from presenting the stories in full, I decided to step over incidents that had faded from my memory and instead focused on documenting what remains as vivid memories in my mind to preserve the integrity of our history.

What I have presented in this book is by no means final or an infallible truth; thus I appeal to all those who participated in the journey of the struggle, depending on their individual experiences and knowledge, to provide additional information, criticisms and corrections, and I hope that in a free Eritrea of the near future, I will represent it in full and in an improved manner, and I pray to God to give me long life and health.

My plan was to present this initial book in a more detailed and comprehensive manner. However, given the current precarious situation, I am presenting only what I considered timely and urgent out of the comprehensive story. Since the EPLF's external experience of struggle was in collaboration with known foreign entities, it is not difficult to get the details from these. However, to expose the roots and extract the truths from the secretive operations of the EPLF, it is important to find those who were present and have firsthand experience in certain activities. Therefore, now that the time has come, I am able to present to the reader what I observed and I could discern from close up position regarding the activities of the EPLF.

In this book, I have presented the major characters --patriotic fighters, martyrs, famous spoilers, etc--in their actual names. However, there are some whose names I could not fully remember due to the length of time, and I have represented them with either their nicknames or by the specific roles they were assigned to.

The contents of this book focus on what has not been talked about enough and secret operations that were curtailed from the rightful owner of the experience, the Eritrean people, the secret party that existed within the EPLF that helped to usher the independence of Eritrea. The secret party was first called Eritrean People's Revolutionary Party and then renamed the Eritrean Socialist Party; my narration focuses on the tool of its operation, the organ that is known as Halewa Sewra, the security of the revolution.

My experience in the struggle begins with my secret affiliation with the EPLF in 1972. Later on, in 1975 I joined the struggle and I was assigned to the security unit known as Halewa Sewra. In 1978 I became a member of the secret party and joined the secret activities of the EPLF.

Though the entire covert and overt struggle was to realize the independence and liberation of Eritrea, at a particular stage, the train was derailed, the liberation struggle was hindered, and the Eritrean people headed towards destruction.

Undoubtedly, the secretive techniques that we used in pursuit of independence and freedom had a big role in the independence of the country. But independence without liberation is not complete. The foreign oppression is now being replicated on our people by our compatriots who claim to have brought about independence but are now leading the country to destruction. And now, by identifying the one who has usurped the people of power and by knowing that he is determined to annihilate our people and in order to contribute towards preventing this impending destruction, I humbly present to my people what the secrets I witnessed within the EPLF.

There are many heroic deeds of mythical proportion that are unfortunately not told or documented as yet. Just as I have presented a book, I appeal to all those who passed through the experience to present their narrations so that the history of our struggle doesn't evaporate to nothingness. I appeal to all the initiators and actors of the revolution to document their knowledge and experience and pass it to the next generation and show them the way; and I call on the new generation to find a way to own and lead their country. I appeal to them to carry the good experiences of the old generation who have completed their role after independence, and to discard the old ELF-EPLF rivalry because its time is over, and has become museum piece.

Tsegu F. Bahta,
August 2014

GRATITUDE

It has been a while since I thought of writing this book. Though I tried to write some parts of it when I was in Eritrea, the situation didn't allow for the presentation of naked facts. Since the Isaias regime doesn't recognize or respect the right and freedom of expression, I chose not to present incomplete information; I suspended my writing and waited for the opportune time.

After I left my country, staying in a place far from the reach of the regime that doesn't allow the freedom of speech and expression, I was able to write what was kept in my mind in the way that I chose. I very much admire the freedom of expression that I found; after I unloaded the worries that I had, I felt good. The country for which I struggled for many long years and ushered its independence didn't give me that opportunity; but a country where I live as an alien enabled me to enjoy freedom of expression--that made me contemplate, and I wouldn't like to pass over that without expressing my gratitude.

In my place of exile, though the restraints of writing what I wished to was eliminated, yet survival remained a struggle of its own. I challenged the struggle of survival, and I found time to write the book, and for that I thank God.

I honor and respect my Uncle Professor Bereket Habte Selassie for his encouragement and for his moral support in writing the book. I would also like to express my immense gratitude for the invaluable editorial assistance and polishing of the Tigrignia and the English versions. Though an octogenarian, his tireless efforts to help others has provided me a life-lesson; I pray he is blessed with health and long life.

I would like to express my heart-felt thanks to Mesfin Hagos former Minister of Defense, EPLF Politburo and PFDJ Executive Committee member for his recommendations and suggested corrections after he reviewed my Tigrigna verision of the book.

I thank Brigadier General Tekeste Haile for several issues that he confirmed for me.

I have limitless respect for Semere Habtemariam and Saleh Gadi Johar for the editorial assistance they offered me in finalizing the Tigrigna version, and I thank them very much. This true narration that is being presented was initially presented as a work of fiction and Semere, after seeing its depth suggested to me to present it as a true narration thus enabling me to make major changes in it; and Saleh Gadi Johar who designed the Tigrigna version book and its cover, and who also helped me in translating the book into English--I thank them both very much.

My profound thanks to my uncle Elias Habte Selassie with whom I have had the great luxury of working together in finalizing editorial work of the English version when he was visiting us in Washington, DC and the constructive and critical comments and suggestions he made on the final draft.

This book could not have been written without the generous assistance of countless individuals who shared their knowledge and expertise. To all of you, I extend my deep appreciation.

Chapter 1. JOINING THE REVOLUTION

1.1 Origin, Growing Up and the March to the Revolution

I was born in a family that adored progress and development; and I discovered that revolution is the widest avenue of change. As I became an adult I started to hear the cries of my people, and I became part of the Eritrean struggle that lasted for over thirty years. The struggle did not only etch in stone the Eritrean patriotism that the enemy was determined to destroy, it also gave me an invaluable life experience and eventually formed my character. Indeed, I was a fighter, and I am a fighter. But the main course of the stream of my life, that many tributaries later joined, has its source in the way my parents had raised and nurtured me.

Like Methuselah, my grandfather Bahta was blessed with longevity. He grew up in the village of Geremi, in the northern outskirts of Asmara, and died at the age of 102. That day sitting in the front yard, he had told his wife Lemlem that he was going to the hall to rest a little; he died upon putting his head on the bed without any suffering. All his peers had died and only one man who lived across from his house remained from his generation. About an hour before he died, my grandfather heard about the death of his only remaining peer; maybe then he was sad and didn't like to be left alone; he did not wait for long in following his friends.

At that moment during the day, enemy artillery bombs that were fired from the confines of Asmara were falling in the areas were the Eritrean fighters took position, the residents of the villages stayed in a far and safe place together with their animals. But Ato Bahta, who was living his twilight years, after his eyesight deteriorated and his body was weakene stayed behind in the village engulfed by the noise of the bombardment. He murmured, "bad times, we reached an age where the sound of trumpets and drums is replaced by cannons and bombs. May God have mercy on us!" With such words he left this world, and went to a faraway place.

A few weeks before he died, my grandfather met his grandson Amanuel Fessahaie, a fighter from the military units of the Eritrean Peoples' Liberation Front (EPLF). Amanuel never returned after he joined the revolution. He sat with him at the entrance to his house and asked him, "listen son, you have enough guts that make your mothers proud, you lack nothing on that. But, do you think you will be able to confront the power of all the artillery and tanks, and win?" He added, "They have too much steel and metals!"

Amanuel replied with confidence, "It's not steel and metals that bring victory, if we maintain our principles, nothing will prevent us from being victorious. In the history of a struggle, the decisive factor is the human being who decides to sacrifice his life for the sake of his people." He added, "You See grandpa, a lot of things was accomplished in this world..." He then realized he was speaking to a very old man, "nothing is undoable." He didn't say more.

"What is principle, what language is that? Do you mean guts?" In surprise he added a blessing, "alright son, may you be able to do that."

Amanuel digested the wise words of my grandfather and said, "Yes, it's a grand scheme that requires a lot of abilities." He repeatedly told that to himself, maybe he wanted to keep the words secured in his heart.

To many of those who were observing the process from afar the vision of liberation was hazy and beyond imagination, they could not predict its outcome. But for Amanuel a man who could see the freedom beyond the far and foggy horizon and for all those who were closely following developments and were ready to pay the ultimate price with conviction, even when the struggle appeared long and arduous, it was clear that one day it will be reality.

Though my grandfather and the other old man who died early in the morning, and according to tradition they should have been buried during the day, it was not possible to bury them during day time because of the ongoing bombardment, and instead they were buried late around sunset.

Two years before my grandfather Bahta Tsegu died, I stayed with him in the village of Geremi for three months until I joined the EPLF in 1975. At that time, the Ethiopian Navy Commandos were strangulating the youth with piano wire, and most of the youth either flooded to the fronts or left in droves to exile. I was working with the clandestine secret cells of the EPLF in Asmara, but after I was exposed and couldn't stay anymore, I fled through Derfo and followed the trail of my three brothers.

The Zero 6 Unit of the EPLF ("06") was in charge of communication with clandestine cells in Asmara, and when the situation inside the city worsened, they made me stay with my grandfather to give support and to organize the youth in the environs of Asmara. It didn't take me long to implement that directive. I watched the fighters entrenched around the village with their Kalashnikov rifles fighting the enemy, and during the night they would sit on the hay stacks and clean their machine guns, or assemble the people in secluded places to educate and organize them; I yearned to be at their level to educate my people and be able to sacrifice my life on their behalf. Within fifty-days I formed five cells in the surrounding area and many youths started to flood to the ranks of the revolutionaries.

In 1972, I was at the Prince Mokonnen High School when I first became a member of the EPLF clandestine cells. In that time, leaflets were circulated and talks about the differences between the ELF and EPLF started to be raised within the student movement. In that situation, though I didn't have deep knowledge, the leftist ideology had an influence on me; I was watching my elder brothers read Marxist Leninist books that I also began to read occasionally, particularly my immediate elder brother, the martyr Amanuel, who was a gifted artist. His hand drawn posters of Che Guevara and other leftist revolutionaries adorned the walls of his room. And in discussions with my peers, the EPLF was characterized as a leftist organization; it didn't take time for Mebrahtu Zewde, a member of the mass organizations working secretly, to meet with me and friends and recruit us to the cause.

The villagers bitterly complained to my grandfather that I was agitating their children. People always watched me swagger around the villages donning the then modern Asmara fashion, wearing bell-bottom pants and tight shirts, walking about the countryside with my afro hairdo; my grandfather didn't like my swagger. One day, he remarked, "What's with your disheveled hair!" He didn't approve of my behavior, "a grown up man, what are you doing here?" As if I was

3

aware of his remark beforehand and was already prepared for it, I quickly replied, "instead of the Amhara slaughtering us while we sit, I thought getting away from their sight would enrage the devil." It seemed he was expecting that type of reply. He continued his interrogation and said, "Then, if you are a man act like one, do the appropriate thing." Since I knew very well that he doesn't like beating around the bush, I went ahead of him and said, "Don't you think those who left are enough!" I tried to defuse the heated discourse because three of my brothers had already joined the front.

"In this village people think you are the main EPLF person." I recognized the concern in his voice and strongly denied it, and I said "not at all." I don't think he believed me; he sounded sure that I would go to the field, and continued his interrogation, "Are the ELF okay? The EPLF accuses them saying they feed on eggs." Recognizing his smart attempt to find proof, and in order to deny him that, I said, "They were spending their time with you grandpa." He discovered that I understood his tricky question; he squinted his right eye and held his cane with the right hand, "even in Asmara they are doing that" and thus he shed more light to what I already knew clearly. Since it was not the right time to speak all the truth, even with close relatives, I went ahead of him and asked, "What is their differences grandpa?"

"You are young, son, you don't know them very well, but we have seen many governments since the Italians, and these revolutionaries, we will see them when they ascend to the watch tower of authority." He changed the topic and added, "now go and eat your lunch, son." It seems he was concerned that my youthful heart will not understand what he said. But I was surprised by the word 'WALA' that I never heard before. Immediately I asked him, "What is a watch tower grandpa?"

"To protect his farm from being eaten by birds, a farmer builds scaffolding and stands there with a sling to guard it. And those who say they will liberate their people while they kill each other, you will see them in reality when they ascend the scaffolding, my son. As for me, I don't think I will see that." He supported himself on the cane that he held in his right arm and raised himself from his seat, and made an excuse, "the sun has become scorching; let me go inside the house and rest." I asked him as I followed him to the house, "what are they fighting about grandpa?"

"Listen my son Tsegu, your father didn't name you Tsegu in vain; whose character do you think you inherit? My father Tsegu, after whom you are named, was a very observant and intelligent man; he was a wise and dignified man who would not rest unless he digests everything. But now, son, let's leave the conversation for another time, I have to rest." He climbed and lied down on his bed.

I was restless because he didn't answer my question. After lunch, I peeked into his room; he was still sleeping and I left for the coastal area to take care of my organizational tasks. I didn't return to the village after I finished my task, but I headed to the campaign of liberation to which I embarked at the outset; I followed the path of my friends and brothers. Regardless of whether I would eventually return or not, I left without bidding my grandfather and my parents goodbye, and after that their images remained transfixed in my mind. Subsequently I joined the revolution.

Though my father was born to a farming family, he left his village and went to Asmara at a young age living behind him the life of a shepherd, attending to sheep and goats. Influenced by his uncle, who was a pastor of the Lutheran Church, soon after his arrival in the city, he abandoned the Orthodox faith of his ancestors and became a protestant. Encouraged by the support of the clergy, during the Italian period he went to school and studied until grade four, followed by a study of Italian and English languages, and some skill training, and he was relieved from the tough life of the peasants in the countryside. He expanded his experience and on the job training and advanced as far as becoming the chief of the medical store in Mekane Hiwet hospital, formerly known as Ospedale Regina Elena, where he worked until he retired. Before he started to work in the hospital, he was a school teacher, and later director of different schools and he has contributed immensely to the advancement of educational opportunities in Eritrea during the period of British Military Administration, 1950 to 1962.

Memhir, which in the Tigrigna language means teacher, Fessahaie Bahta had gradually developed a very close relation with the Eritrean Lutheran Church. From the time he became an ordinary member of the congregation, he was involved in and contributed to the administration of the church and in evangelical work, and owing to the close relations that he had with the clergy; he eventually married to a daughter of one of the Lutheran Church leaders. The honorable father of my mother Weizero Besrat was born to a family of farmers whose father was initially an Orthodox Christian priest. However, when the Lutheran church entered Eritrea, he was among the first people who studied the new faith and became a devoted follower of the Lutheran church and as a pastor.

Qeshi, pastor, Habteselassie Gilwet, on whom the Swedish Lutheran Mission impressed the importance of education, sent several of his sons to attend schools in Asmara, to Ethiopia and beyond and enabled them acquire necessary education to become successful people. But his daughters, who according to the social tradition of the time, were married off young and couldn't attain much education, he made sure they got the opportunity to have literacy classes and to be trained in home economics such as sewing and tailoring, as well as needle works and handicrafts at the Swedish Mission School in Beleza. My mother was a calm and wise woman, and many of her siblings often sought her advice whenever the need arose. One of her younger brothers invoked a saying when he describes her, "Wisdom is superior to education," and he says that no one in their family was blessed with her kind of wisdom and intelligence.

Kentiba Gilwet, my mother's grandfather, was a highly respected and appreciated man of his generation and as one of the prominent elders in his district he was often consulted and involved in the resolution of community related conflicts. It is said that his son, Qeshi, Pastor, Habteselassie, often accompanied him in the village assemblies thereby gaining knowledge and experience in the art of adjudication and management of meetings and resolution of disputes; added to that he also acquired the art of public speaking and preaching skill that he gained from the church. His influence went beyond the confines of the village and spread to the surrounding villages of the region.

Therefore, my parents, given their family background and leanings, were not only appreciative of modernity, but encouraged and struggled for it. This Lutheran family raised nine children with care and love. I was in the middle among four sisters and four brothers. Except the youngest boy of the family, Paulos, the rest of us four brothers followed each other in the quest for the realization of the Eritrean people's dream and joined the revolution. Isaias, the eldest studied and graduated in Pharmacy at Haile Selassie I University in Addis Ababa, and joined the movement after working for a few years. Amanuel was a second-year engineering student in the university when he joined the movement in 1974, and I was enrolled as a first year student while Mussie was in high school; we all three interrupted our education and joined the front to help accomplish the grand mission of political change in Eritrea.

I left from the home of my grandfather through Derfo[3] and joined the movement, and once there, I reported to the Zero 6 Unit members in the area about my activities; having done my reporting I wanted to go to Sahel as soon as possible for training. But the trip to Sahel was not that easy. I had to wait until more people came to make a bigger group. In Derfo, even though I made efforts to participate in the day to day activities of the fighters, my lack of experience made it difficult to carry out the chores. But since I used to meet most of the fighters in that unit when I used to sneak out of the city, I was given support of the unit members.

Derfo, which can be seen in the distance from Mai Dbnet in the edges of Asmara, is a small impenetrable village in the northern coastal region positioned on the foot of a mountain range with sharp edges. A river passes through and cuts it into two and on the banks are a few gardens. When I was in Asmara I used to go to Derfo at least once a month and I know the place very well. Also, my maternal relative Aboy Abraham Tsadiq, a member of the mass organizations lived there and occasionally he provided me with food and other small things that I needed.

It was in Derfo that I became aware for the first time in my life of the nature of the problems that I will face in the journey of the struggle. Most of my friends who had joined the struggle ahead of me are either in the Front or were already martyred; still some went into exile. I left only a few of them to struggle from inside the belly of the enemy in Asmara. Soon, I realized that the colleagues who will accompany me on the revolutionary journey will be people that I don't know and who will be assigned by the leaders in charge of the EPLF.

The members of Zero 6 unit in the Derfo valley area were facing difficulty in replacing a number of people whose secret membership in Asmara was being exposed. But since what they accomplished by staying in the belly of the enemy in Asmara was by far of greater risk and of greater importance than the activities of the field, it was decided by the Eritrean Peoples' Liberation Front (EPLF)that they must continue to stay and operate inside the city. In an attempt to find a solution for the difficulties that could be faced by the clandestine cells, a member of Zero 6 Unit looked at the people around and asked me in a soft voice, "Listen Tsegu, how do you think the task you left behind in Asmara will continue? There are a lot of gaps, why don't you

---

3   Derfo, a small village on the Windy road towards the portof Massawa.

go back?" I looked him in the eye, and in an angry tone I replied, "Why would I go back?" Fessahaie Afro wanted to calm the situation and said, "See, boy! The situation is becoming tighter, particularly since the navy stranglers have denied us space to operate."

I realized why he said that but since I didn't have other chances, I stood firm in my position, "So, what do you want me to do now?" A member of Sebhat Ephrem's squad interjected and made a stinging remark, "It's martyrdom in the field and it is similar martyrdom in the city, do you wish to be buried in a lush green grass or what/" I was annoyed by his remark but before I could say anything, Weldenkiel Abraha scolded him by saying, "then why don't you return to the city if martyrdom in the city and the field is the same? Why did you build a trench here, isn't it to defend yourself? Fessahaie Afro is asking Tsegu to find out if he can build a trench inside the city, and he knows what is possible, don't disturb him." By saying that, Weldenkiel gave me a green light to join the struggle. I liked what he said and comforted myself, and uttered, "That is a palatable talk."

Afro didn't seem he wanted to let go of the issue and said, "Then let him stay here for a while to help establish link with the cells inside Asmara." Weldenkiel asked, "How long has it been since Tsegu arrived?" I didn't give Afro a chance and I replied, "Three months." I added, "even those in the village were already introduced to those in the city... please leave me alone." I realized that I had replied before I was asked; in embarrassment I scratched my head. Luckily, he ended the conversation, "all right then, let's move on to our positions," and we all returned to our defensive positions for the night.

I started to talk to myself, "why are they causing me trouble and why don't they just see me off! Am I supposed to play hide and seek with the navy stranglers, how I would operate and if I go back, they will certainly catch me. If not, it would have been better in the city than feeding on bread that looks like it was made of manure... and then what's with the "Tof" guy (messenger boy), the member of Sebhat Ephrem's accompanying squad! If I go back, who would tune the fiery eyed Kalashnikov! There is no turning back." I went on deep reflection... "And why is that talkative Tof mentioning lash green death and street death; what a despicable country boy." I steered so many thoughts in my mind as I returned to my position.

I tried to spread my blanket on the rocky surface to sleep, but my eyes wouldn't close. Then I covered myself with the blanket and lighted a cigarette that Aboy Abraham Tsadiq bought for me, the messenger boy smelled it and came, "you spy! I think you are on a spying mission, you light a cigarette in the dark, and do you want to alert the enemy?" I was stunned, and told him, "C'mon, it's concealed inside the blanket, how on earth can the enemy see it?" He replied, "All right then, let me have a puff or two." Surprised, I threw the cigarette at him. He picked the fag and he covered himself with his blanket and blurted, "Damn, why don't you hand me the fag in a nice way!" I replied, "Damn you, why don't you ask in a good manner? Now leave me alone, I want to go to sleep." I lighted another cigarette to enjoy it alone and continued conversation with myself.

When I left my house in Asmara on my way to the countryside, I brought along some Marxist books that were sent from Addis Ababa, destined to the field. But since I had to pass through the checkpoint in the outskirts of Asmara where the soldiers conducted strict searches, I had asked my mother to hide it in her basket with other things and carry it for me to the village. My mother, who was afraid I would face risks in her presence if I was to be caught, was prepared to do anything for me and wanted me to move out of the city. The Derg cars that moved near our house were so many. But considering her age, she was not suspected and she put the books together with vegetables and smuggled the books out. One day, hoping to see her wishes are accomplished, she said to me, "Tsegu, my son, I know the night will not pass for you without books, but now, I don't want to see bad things happening to you in front of my eyes. Why don't you silently go to your grandfather's house in the village?" She didn't know I was already planning to go even further to join the revolution. Maybe she feared I might feel bad, "We are passing through a bad period son, had it not been so I wouldn't want you to be away from me even for one night." She encouraged me in a motherly way, and went on to say "I lost your brothers and now I don't want to lose you. I will bring the supplies you need to the village myself every few days, and your reading materials are already there." She ended the topic without me adding more.

I hoped to find the books that I sent to Derfo. Remembering what I told my mother, deceiving her in carrying the books, I said to myself, "it's better to read instead of talking to the messenger boy," I continued talking to myself while I smoked and prayed for sleep to overcome my bodily fatigue. After a lot of tossing and turning, when I hadn't slept enough, I was awoken by a finger click over my head just before dawn. A voice told me to fold my blanket and to follow him and I did. And with half closed eyes, I left the night location and went to the place where we spent daytime. When I reached there, I asked Tekle Wedi Lbbey, "listen, where are the books that I sent?" Sarcastically he said, "The books that your mother brought?" He knew how I managed to smuggle them out. I told him I didn't sleep a blink. Tekle Wedi Lbbey understood my situation, and sympathetically said, "Do you think it is convenient to read in a defensive position, at night?" Pushed by my hunger for reading, without caution, I said, "If I find a small flashlight like the one you have, why wouldn't it be convenient?" I have seen him reading under his blanket. He redirected the topic, "if you will be careful, I can get you a flashlight, but you will not keep it once you go to the training camp." He added to my worries.

"Can we have cigarettes in the training camp? I can do without a flashlight." He replied, "you will leave all the luxury things here, there is no cigarettes or flashlight during training, there, you only have to hold your guts tight, importantly, you have to learn how to cooperate with your colleagues," the guide has told him that I threw a cigarette at him. I understood the nuances of his remark, and because I couldn't swallow the criticism he threw at me, I said, "Listen Tekle Wedi Lbbey, how can you bear someone calling you a spy when you have come to join the struggle while at the same time he was begging me to give him a cigarette?" He was not interested in my reply, he advised me, "listen, a revolution is like a shopping basket which holds everything put in it, and in the movement you will need to be careful and be always attentive."

His words rang in my ears; I couln't sleep thinking of the Tof guy: one time he mocks me if I want to die in a lash green grass and another time he calls me a spy, for what? Indeed, the unit is no better than the shopping basket. I told Tekle Wedi Lbbey, "Okay, I want to visit Aboy Abraham Tsadiq, I will come back soon." I left hoping to get some decent breakfast.Tekle Wedi Lbbey was fond of me because while I worked in a clandestine cell whenever I observed a movement of the enemy, I used to immediately go to Derfo and meet him in person myself or send a member of our cell to warn the fighters. This was particularly so after the attack which took away the lives of the dedicated fighter Alem and his colleagues in Mai Dbnet. I had tried to convince them to give me a PRC radio (a portable radio communicator) in order to have the possibility and assurance of communicating vital information in a timely manner. However, at that time the Derg had already introduced Radio Direction Finder equipments with which they attempted to trace the EPLF's radio communication system thereby hampering the communication line between Asmara and the EPLF which resulted in a decision to limit the number of radios that were available for the cells in the city and hence I was unable to obtain one. That is why the face-to-face meeting became more frequent. Tekle Wedi Lbbey allowed me to visit my relative but warned me not to be late and he accompanied some mass organization members who just arrived from Asmara and took them to a secluded place for the usual debriefing.

I found Aboy Abraham near his house as he returned with his animals, and we went in together. He asked me to check for eggs at the barn if hens had laid some eggs in which place I found some that we cooked and ate breakfast. Aboy Abraham said, "So it is now time to join your brothers but your mother will be extremely sad because losing four children from one family is not easy!" He knew the situation in Asmara is not healthy either, but since I was determined, he advised me to recognize that there are many ups and downs on the way.

Aboy Abraham asked if I could name some people who would cooperate with the EPLF in Asmara. I didn't like the question, I ended the topic by telling him that I have been out of Asmara for more than three-months, and that those who worked with me were already out, and that I have already reported about it to Tekle Wedi Lbbey. Understandably Aboy Abraham needed people to cooperate with him since he used to frequently go to Asmara on urgent matters. But since affairs of the mass organizations were strictly secretive, names and other information could only be released in a formal way, and people were only introduced in that manner.

He dropped a carton of cigarettes on my lap, and said "enjoy it with your friends". I was silent for a while and then I said, "Okay then, and please explain the situation to my mother..." He interrupted me, "She wanted to send you abroad," I stood up, "I know, but our plans differed." He knew I had made my final decision, "True, my son, but she thought your brothers were enough, even with the cooperation of all, the struggle is not easy... all right now, return to your colleagues, and don't be late." He saw me off.

I returned to my place but Tekle Wedi Lbbey was not back yet, I told the day's cook, "If Tekle Wedi Lbbey wants me tell him I am sitting under the sycamore tree." He suggested that I go after I had breakfast; I told him I was not hungry and I left. I spread my blanket under the tree and as soon as I lay down, I went into a deep sleep.

After a while I heard shots and woke up. I went to the cooking area and found Tekle Wedi Lbbey and asked him about the shots. He told me it was our colleagues who were hunting.

"Tsegu, you are lucky, one of those mass organization members came from Asmara last night using a flashlight, I took it away from him it means I found a reading aid for you". He gave me the flashlight. I was happy and took a packet of cigarettes from my pocket, "here you are, take it." Since he was always close to Asmara, he said, "keep it, you will need it in Sahel, I am always close to the city and I will always find some...you do not want to stay here any longer...you will remember me when you see the angry mountains of Sahel." He gave me back the packet...he had wished to keep me around the area to work with the unit.

He handed me a book, Anna Karenina by Leo Tolstoy, which I had asked him for, and I was very happy. I was still talking to Tekle Wedi Lbbey when the cook called for group lunch, we sat down to eat but after I picked a bite, the food was finished before I could take another bite.

Tekle Wedi Lbbey was sarcastic, "all right, now you can go and eat your book... why didn't you eat?" I replied, "It was so hot, but the messenger boy must have a freezer inside his mouth, I was cooling the first bite in my hand when at a glance the food was gone. It was not taste food anyway; it was food made of chaff." Tekle Wedi Lbbey reached for his bag and took out a sandwich that a member of the mass organization gave him, my saliva ran and I wanted to snatch it from his hands. He said, "Wouldn't you rather stay here with us and eat sandwiches?" he handed me the sandwich. I replied, "And who will fine tune the fiery mouthed Kalashnikov?" I expressed my wish. Tekle Wedi Lbbey, asked me, "is it because you heard gunshots that you decided to join the struggle..." He corrected himself, "I mean you were already struggling!" I replied, "It's not the gun shots or reading books that brought me here, do you think the wires of the navy commando stranglers is easy, I decided to join because I want to pay them back. I will not stay here, never." He joked, "Then you need to take along a freezer that you can put inside your mouth..." I interrupted him laughingly, "No problem, I can borrow your freezer... I will get used to it all" I noticed the cook who was attentively looking at us;" we will even get used to the messenger boy, and am I not right?"

I was born in the Asmara neighborhood of Emba Galiano and lived there with my parents until I left to join the front save for a brief period of two years that I stayed in Edaga Hamus during which time our prefab house in Emba Galiano was demolished and rebuilt and the brief stay in Addis Ababa, Ethiopia. The Emba Galiano area was my home. The love I had for my peers is still in my memories. Being a protestant it was natural that I go to the Lutheran Elementary School at Edaga Hamus. I studied there until I reached the fifth grade, but in the sixth grade, in order to attain higher grades for the major examination, I had to join one of the best public schools, I went to Bet Gerghis, Saint George, school where I studied until the eighth grade. I achieved a good grade at the eighth grade examination, and even though I got a scholarship in Santa Familgia where I could finish my high school within three years, but because the reputation of Santa Famiglia was so bad and there was a saying which goes: "a bad bull to the slaughterhouse, a bad worker to the railways, a bad student to Santa Familgia," I abandoned that school and joined the Prince Mokonnen High School.

In my youth, I was very social and liked to chat and joke and at the same time I was also unruly. I would leave home early and spend the day playing football with the neighborhood kids. I would skip lunch and then eat snacks. Later on, I would stay with my friends talking and joking until late, and only entering into the house just before my father arrived from work in the evenings and I would pick a book and pretend that I have been reading all day. But since I was gifted and receptive of education, I often retained what I heard from the lectures.

When I was in eighth grade, I fell in love with a schoolmate named Medhin and I valued her above all students. I was only fourteen and our relation was limited to spending time together and chatting, though we dreamed of a serious long term relation in the future. However, after we went to high school, Medhin went to Haile Selassie Secondary School while I went to Prince Mokonnen High School and as a result of such separation our relation died out. At Prince Mokonnen School I observed a few girls but I was spending most of my time with my friends: Abraham, Chipola, Araya, and Asgedom Chera. I used to spend most of the time playing football and other types of entertainment. I later started to play Bigfoot at Men'esey (youth) Teashop, and sometimes I started to go with my friends to local beer houses (Enda Siwa).

My friend, the martyr Goitom used to say, "An 'A' student becomes a good professor and a 'C' student becomes a good lawyer."

To be a lawyer you have to learn the culture of the society, to get deep into it and interact, and that doesn't allow for too much time to read. In the explanation of the lazy, in order to see the world in a wider sense, and to experience it in real life; that prevents you from applying what you read because you put the culture and tradition of a society into consideration. Chances are very narrow to get an 'A' while spending too much time with the people. But the efforts exerted to become a professor, since you learn by studying and memorizing, chances for getting an 'A' are wider.

When we were young, we used to make excuses to play and entertain ourselves; we went to local beer houses to have fun as youth and we didn't dream of becoming lawyers, and that we had to go to the local beer house to learn about our culture and tradition. As a matter of fact, both the good and the bad frequent local beer houses: those who get drunk, and those who chat and leave, it was not a place where a narrowly defined type of people gather and it was also not a place where you do not observe or learn serious matters either.

One day we won a football game in Edaga Hamus and we went to a local beer house known by its owner Adey Demeqesh to celebrate. We were drinking and talking about sports when I asked Goitom, "Where did you get the statement that you made about a 'C' student becoming a lawyer?" He sounded serious, "the job of a lawyer starts here, because after talking and drinking in places like this, you do not get time for books. But here, if you discuss about culture and tradition, everything goes fine with beer, you do not lose, and at least you go home with a 'C' grade." I was aware his answer was that of an intoxicated person, and I made it worse, "since when did you finish drinking your cup?" Chipola interjected, "She served him with a cup which has a hole at the bottom," he wants someone to finish his cup for him". Goitom smiled to that. "See! Even Chipola started to be a lawyer, when he couldn't even finish his cup; he put a hole in mine." I laughed and added, "Today he was being tricky because every time they feel his cup, he tips it and he makes Adey Demeqesh's daughter tired, cleaning the floor after him." He was sloppy.

A youngster who sat across from us liked our conversation and said, "People who lack a system and a set of laws really need lawyers, but surprisingly, sometimes may be it is the drinks or the anger, everyone speaks casually, not aware of what they are saying, everyone elevates himself to a level of a lawyer, and for what? We are on the edges of death; why would we need a lawyer?" He looked at the ladies of the house and said, "Gual Demeqesh, give me some more siwa (locally brewed beer), and give this group with Tsegu more drinks." Chipola looked me in the eyes, "Boy, you refuse to get off my back; those who are addicted to siwa can keep drinking, but leave me alone." I replied, "Particularly you, siwa doesn't go well with you, it makes you bark like a dog." The young man got excited, he liked our jokes and discussion and he asked the owner of the beerhouse to play a song by Yemane Barya.

Gual Demeqesh was happy because her joint was doing well; immediately she played the recorded music entitled "Wedebat A'adey" by Yemane Barya, and recognized the song was fit for the occasion. She picked her beer kettle and started to fill our cups, she was reluctant when she reached to Chipola's cup and remarked with a smile, "and now you will tip your cup over like always?" As if it was prescribed for him by a doctor, he picked his cup to be filled with the rest of the cups. The young man continued to sing loudly along with Yemane's tape; we followed suit, and the house become merry and noisy.

A few elder people who were quietly chatting and drinking in one corner waited until we finished singing and one of them reprimanded us, "my children, why don't you manage to have good manners, you are witnessing the times, it is bad." He asked the young man, "What's your name, whose son are you?" It was obvious he was the one steering it all. The young man said he is known as Mebrahtu Zewde. They were silent; one of them whispered to his friend and told him he didn't like the name; it resembles an Ethiopian name.

We ignored the advice of the elders and continued singing, "death awaits you whether stretched out or sitting down in discomfort, isn't it better to go to the coast for one year!" The man said, "listen sons, my name is Balambaras Gebrihiwet, I have children your age, just like I don't want anything bad to happen to my children, I do not want your parents to see anything bad happening to you--cool down, the ears of people have grown antennas and are deployed everywhere, but you don't seem to realize that."

Chipola was the one who heard one of the men whispering to Balambaras. He looked at him, "You are right Aboy Balambaras, youth and drinks make you commit mistakes, and as they say, 'one who is up to something bold doesn't even consult his mother.' It's the recklessness of youth, my apologies." Balambaras was calmed and said, "Well done son, you respected us, may you get respect from your children." The gentlemen then changed the topic of discussion and began talking about the Italian invasion of Tripoli during WWI. "There was no law then, the law was one's own stick, law of the jungle! Everyone is left to depend on his own devices, his own muscles, but now you are speaking about lawyers who gets an 'A' or a 'C', and we are just listening to you." Just like Chipola said, young age and drinks made Mebrahtu Zewde confident, he blurted out and asked, "and what laws do we have now, Balambaras? Aren't they threatening us when they say 'whoever refuses to submit feed him a bullet'? Tripoli was a well known reality, but how do you describe the situation in our country now?" It seemed he emptied what was kept in his chest. Balambaras was enraged, "son, why do you stay in the edges recklessly and run your mouth?" There is a saying, "'A man who wants trouble marries a fiddler's daughter.' If you know the situation to be that bad, then why are you running your mouth?" It is the young age and drinks that made Mebrahtu Zewde confident. He stood up, "if it is necessary, we will cut the ears with antennas; these old-timers wouldn't let us enjoy our drinks, let's go to Enda Wegihula" (dawn beerhouse.) Aboy Balambaras was astounded, "son, there are no beer houses that usher dawn, they only bring about darkness." He turned to his friends.

Mebrahtu Zewde lived in a small rented house. He was recruited by the EPLF at a very young age and he was in charge of coordination of communications, organizing recruits and seeing off the youth who were joining the revolution. When fighters come to the city for different purposes, he received and hosted them, and made the necessary security and guard arrangements for them. Once in the late of 1972, after monitoring me and my friends, he asked us to be organized in cells and work in the city. The first question I asked him was to which organization he belonged; he told me he worked for the Eritrean People's Liberation Force, and I accepted his call without hesitation.

I have several times observed Mebrahtu Zewde returning from the front to Asmara covered in dust, and I had strong suspicion that he was a member of the clandestine part of the revolution. Hence, I did not suspect him to be an agent of the enemy. Especially when I noticed the people who frequented his house dressed differently than the rest of the city dwellers, they looked like country folks dull and unlike city dwellers their faces not well oiled. That is why I didn't hesitate when he showed interest to recruit me, on the contrary I felt proud. He said he will give us new recruits instructions on how we are supposed to be organized and to start our clandestine activities. Abraham and I were over-excited with joy because what we used to hear about has become a reality. We were anxious and restlessly waited for instruction and assignment of tasks.

After we left Gual Demequ's local beerhouse, Mebrahtu Zewde headed towards Emba Galiano, whereas Abraham, Goitom and I got into Araya's taxi at Pharmacia Hamasien and headed left towards Enda Wegihula local beerhouse in the Acria neighborhood of Asmara. Araya used to drive his father's taxi after school hours and on this particular evening he dropped us at Wegihula's place and said, "You go ahead but I will return soon after earning some money" and he left. Gual Wegihula displayed her white teeth and a big smile when she received us, scanning our faces one after the other. She asked, "Where did you leave the boss? Do you want strong beer or light?" She started to take care of business.

Goitom replied, "Araya will come soon. Is the hard beer fresh? If it is, give me one." The rest of us ordered the usual light beer and continued our conversation.

Gual Wegihula sat close to me and started to talk about Wedi Shifa, a friend of Araya; she mentioned some places around her house and raised the name of Mai Dbnet. I suspected she might be a clandestine member of the EPLF. Mebrahtu Zewde knew the surrounding of Enda Wegihula very well since it was on the northern outskirts of Asmara through which he used to go to Derfo. A while earlier he has indicated that he wanted to join the field soon, "I hope I will not have to go down to Mai Dbnet."

Goitom gushed the strong siwa down his throat and jokingly said, "You seem to have forgotten about the person with the vest," mocking Abraham about a certain girl that he fancies; and following Goitom's remarks, Abraham cleared his throat using the voice that was perfected during his time at the 'Setawiyan Catholic Seminary' in Asmara where he was trained to become a deacon of the Catholic Church, he sang, as follows: "donning a Gilet, I saw Hiwet from afar, since that day she dwelled in my heart." This was a song which expressed his romantic wishes about a certain girl classmate of ours. I recall us, his friends, we finished the soles of our shoes accompanying him as he followed her everywhere; every time we asked him to talk to her, he won't dare. But he comes here and irritates us by repeatedly calling her name: Hiwet, Hiwet... and we told him, "now this is your last chance, if you do not ask her, we will never run after her with you like before." Abraham had not finished singing when Araya came and peeked to the inside through the curtain.

"Hello pals, now you have also brought the memory of Hiwet with you here to Acria, sing another song for us to give us energy and you can sing for Hiwet back home down to Emba Galiano... did you drink enough by the way? You are welcome pals--what is the bill?" He took all the coins he had collected from driving his taxi, and set aside some of it, saying, "this is for the boss," meaning his father, while he set aside other coins, and said, "This is for us to enjoy tonight." As soon as she saw the money, Gual Wegihula's face radiated and she started to hug Araya. She must have thought what the group ordered that night will not be recorded on ice, but paid in full. She blurted, "Let's first settle what you owe for the old drinks before it gets confused with the coming drinks."

Goitom found the bill incongruous, "what are you saying dear sister!" Gual Wegihula raised her voice and reminded him, "Listen, there was unpaid account for what Tsegu and his group of friends drank last time, it was meant to be written on ice...don't disturb me for nothing." He looked at me and murmured, "we brought a problem to ourselves... okay, then give me one drink and record it on ice." I pretended I didn't have an argument with her and in an attempt to change the topic I remarked, "Ignore her Goitom, so much was recorded on ice."

The next morning, Abraham and I arrived late in school when students were already assembled ready to enter their classes. We knew we will be punished, and to make it worse, we started to sing a rock song by Rare Earth, and we joined the assembly singing the song, "I just want to celebrate...," A lady classmate joined us in the singing. We continued singing and attracted all attention to ourselves. From then on, we brought the young lady into our student clique, and started to take her along to places like Balambaras Teashop and even to Mama Hippie's beer house.

From that time on we nicknamed her "celebrate". Celebrate liked me and she didn't want to be separated from our group. Even in the evenings after school, I walked in town with her and her friend, Azieb Gual Negga. We were shocked to learn that her boyfriend stabbed and killed Azieb Negga at the Bar Awash in Campovuollo which belonged to her aunt. Our friendship with Azieb Gual Negga was cut short by the sudden and terrible incidence of her death. I remember, a short time before her death, we spent an evening in Celebrate's house, and

Azieb Gual Negga who missed her boyfriend left us after saying, "I am jealous of your chats, I miss Bereket." A few days later Bereket stabbed her to death. Celebrate and I couldn't bear the death of Azieb Gual Negga. What led to her death was a new and strange circumstance; we heard later that it was related to consumption of Hashish by her boyfriend. It is commonly held belief at the time that in order to sway the youth from politics and make them forget about the national struggle, the Ethiopian government encouraged the consumption of Hashish among the youth with a plan to lead them into entertainment and away from the national struggle.

A week after we talked with Mebrahtu Zewde, he waited for us in our neighborhood and notified us that we will start to work and he gave us instructions. The first task was related to the student strikes; we were supposed to agitate the students in order to cause the closing of all the high schools. For the second task he gave us names and details of three people who were suspected of being involved in the distribution of Hashish; we were supposed to follow and monitor them, and also pass a warning to them. Thus we started our active but clandestine role.

Abraham and I didn't ask for more instruction on what we have to do. We were already part of the student movement and we knew what needs to be done. On a Sunday afternoon, we found bulletins plastered on the walls of Prince Mokonnen High School, that were accusing Ato Sewasuw, who was the Ethiopian director of the school, of denigrating Eritreans students by saying that they are used to leftover Italian bread crumbs, and as a result of student campaign he was removed from his position, but to our dismay only to be replaced by a director who was no better than him in the management of the school. And, since the new appointee did not run the school to our liking we also campaigned to get him removed. Our strategy was that if he is not replaced, we will not attend classes. On one Monday morning, students found the bulletin on the walls and distributed elsewhere; this way we made sure students remained away from classes.

We went to the Point Four Technical School and joined those who were leading the movement there; we agitated the students not to attend classes. Then we went to Haile Selassie Secondary School, but we found the school in chaos and police commando forces had encircled it in search of the ring leaders of the movement. We escaped the place and were on our way to our neighborhood when close to Itege Mennen Hospital, formerly Ospedale Regina Elena, and we saw

Abraham who was caught by the Commando force and along with other students were put in jail. After a few days in jail the students were admonished and released after they were given strict warning. On that day around Santa Familgia, Kifle Bargano, the director of Point Four Technical School was hit by stones that the students who were organized by Mebrahtu Zewde hurled at him. The director was hurt and his car was damaged but those who hurled the stones were not identified.

After Abraham was released from jail, and in order to continue our task of monitoring the people whose names were given to us, we managed to introduce ourselves to Asmerom 'Hagereseb' and Dermas, and we started to study their movements closely and investigate them. They were both fun loving guys but we found no evidence that would confirm the suspicion of drug peddling and on the contrary we found out they were patriots and we took the opportunity to recruit them. They accepted our call without hesitation, together with a third friend of theirs named Iyob Halibay they joined the EPLF in the field.

Towards the end of 1972 and the beginning of 1973, almost all students stopped going to school after refusing to pay the high school leaving examination fees. It was a time that many youngsters flooded the field. At that time, Mebrahtu Zewde, gave us more tasks, he instructed us to look after fighters who came from the field, and to host them in a secure place. The fighters were accompanying those who were joining the field from Asmara and Addis Ababa through Acria and Mai Dbnet. The fighters were kept in places that the enemy would least suspect, to the extent they stayed in the heart of Emba Galliano's police camp, and they were kept in strict condition to avoid any risk of being exposed. Since the movement of the enemy was being thoroughly monitored, the fighters were accomplishing their mission without difficulties.

In that situation, the martyred Wedi Qeshi and Mebrahtu Zewde, the most senior and important members of the secret cell mass organizations, went to Derfo to join the front in the field while Abraham and others were waiting in line to leave. At around that time in the year 1973, the connection between the city cells and the field was disconnected as a consequence of a conflict that arose inside the EPLF. This was because the EPLF Units that were stationed in the highland were pulled to the rear base in Sahel to help resolve the internal conflict within the EPLF. It was starting from 1973 up to 1975 that many young Eritreans left through Asmara and others through the field and Sudan heading to life in exile. I also left for Addis Ababa and finished 12th grade at theAqaqi Beseqa Adventist School. During that time the Military Junta known as the Derg had just deposed Emperor Haile Selassie and took over government authority. The Derg introduced a program called "Edget Behbret", literally meaning Development through Unity, and sent all students to the country side to undertake literacy campaign as ploy to weaken the student movement. I did not want to participate in the program of the Derg and instead returned to Asmara. After registering at the Asmara University I went down to Derfo and renewed my connections with the EPLF, and started to work full time with the clandestine mass organization inside the city.

After I returned to Asmara, I started to work closely with Fitsum Se'are, Ephrem Asmelash and Michael Haile 'Barba', all martyrs who were active in the city. Our main focus was organizing people, distributing leaflets and following enemy movements and spies. We did form a considerable number of secret cells, and as a cover, we also formed a reading club and included in it individuals who were not members of our secret cells, and we sent regular messengers to the field carrying messages and other essential supplies. Since we were handling the organizing task we established an extensive network and outreach and mobilized many young Eritreans to the cause. Within a short span of time we managed to send many people to the field. Eventually though, the flow of youth to the field attracted the attention of the enemy and they started to follow us closely and diligently. We then had come to the conclusion that the risk in operating in the city for some of us was extremely high. The movements to and from Derfo had also become very difficult because the enemy discovered that Acria is the gateway to Derfo through Mai Dbnet and as a connection line with the Zero 6 unit; as a result, the enemy began to surround the area with droves of militia. Though some steps were taken by the EPLF against the militia to remove the hindrance, the situation didn't change much.

One time as I was returning home from the city centre, I encountered a person whom I didn't expect to see in front of the Jalia Islamic School. I asked myself repeatedly, I couldn't doubt what I saw. Could it be he was back on a mission, it was unthinkable that he could have betrayed the EPLF and surrendered to the enemy! May it be someone who looks like him, may be his brother--I thought about all possibilities until I got closer to him and he smiled at me. I confirmed he was Mebrahtu Zewde, the man who recruited me! We hugged each other but I couldn't comprehend his presence in the city, deep down I was hoping not to hear that he surrendered to the enemy, and I opted to ask him if he is back on a mission. He immediately responded, "Yes, I came back on a mission." I was so happy to hear that. We talked about personal matters but I couldn't ask him where he was staying, and instead asked him where we could meet, and he said, "no problem, I will come to Gual Demequ's beerhouse" and we parted. I went home unsettled.

That night I couldn't sleep; so many thoughts filled my mind, "Mebrahtu Zewde, the man I know closely... it's unthinkable that a brave man would be afraid of battles. Did they not find anyone else to send Mebrahtu Wedi Zewde to the city in place of him, what do they think of us?" I couldn't grasp the situation. I was wrong when I thought I would return home and have a nice sleep. Mind you it was a house that Mebrahtu Wedi Zewde knew very well. Morning arrived and I was still in my thoughts.

My mother remarked, "Are you fine Tsegu, my son? You were tossing and turning all night with no sleep and you also denied us sleep. Is everything all right?" She then went to the kitchen to prepare breakfast and I followed her, "Mother, why don't you sleep in your room, what brings you to our room, you lost sleep and you made me lose mine," I couldn't find another excuse. She was busy making breakfast, and murmured, "The children left and the house became cold, and now I am worried it will even be colder if those of you, the only remaining light rays I am left with, would also disappear from my eyes, I couldn't resist my son, Tsegu. I just hope God will resolve it for us." She sounded desperate and helpless.

I changed my clothes and left the house before eating breakfast, my mother followed me, "are you all right, son," and she grabbed me by the hands and took me back to the kitchen. "My son, today you are not all right, you see breakfast is ready! Where are you hurrying to, the devil is playing with your mind..." I sat down. I was restless and took quick bites and told her, "mother, I have to go to some place, I will come back soon." I had to go fast to find a resolution for my worries and suspicions.

At Cathedral, I boarded the city bus and stepped out at the last stop at Acria, and as if I had some business, I went to Barba's brick factory. I inspected the area and didn't see any movement of soldiers; I swerved towards Adi Nefas and took the road to Mai Dbnet, increased my pace and walked straight down to the valley until I reached the house of my maternal relative Aboy Abraham Tsadiq in Derfo. There was no one home and I waited at the doorsteps until he returned.

A person who has been following me from a distance came from behind the house and approached me and said, "how are you, is everything fine?" I said, "I came from Asmara and I have a message for my uncle, I am relaxing until he returns." I lighted a cigarette and asked him, "Do you smoke?" Without waiting for an answer I gave him one. The man grabbed it; he took matches out of his pocket and lighted the cigarette. He told me, "Aboy Abraham left with his cattle to Metkel Abet, you will not find him."

I knew then he was a fighter. I adjusted the pistol that I had hidden in the back of my belt--anything could happen. I asked him, "how about Tekle Wedi Lbbey, do you think he is close by?" He replied, "Tekle Wedi Lbbey is also not close by," he went on to ask, "Do you have an urgent task?" I said, "Before we used to visit after setting an appointment but now an urgent matter has arisen and I just hurriedly came here." I responded with confidence. He said, "I can help you meet Rezene Wedi Embaye, he is here." I agreed and followed him to lower Derfo and I met Rezene Wedi Embaye.

Rezene was surprised to see me, "is everything okay, and why are you here without an appointment so early in the day." I replied, "I hope it is all right, we can't understand how you operate, and I came to verify a situation." He was surprised even more, and asked me again, "What happened?" I could see he was worried, I talked to him straight, "I met Mebrahtu Wedi Zewde, he said he was back in Asmara on a mission, is there a shortage of people willing to work that you had to send a field fighter to the city? I don't understand how you operate..." I didn't finish what I wanted to say and he said, "he is not on a mission, don't let him deceive you though I don't think that he would pose any danger, but follow him and monitor his movements from far and we will handle the case based on what eventually follows, we will be together, act slowly." He calmed me and said, "Goodbye" and left.

In the EPLF practice, after "goodbye" there is no exchange of words. The military law had sipped in the secret cells, anyone exposing any secret is killed, rape is punished by death... the motto is don't try to know what doesn't concern you, etc. Such severe laws were observed and I didn't ask why Mebrahtu Wedi Zewde surrendered, even if I ask, I knew I wouldn't get an answer. I received the directive,

23

I reported on some activities and got an appointment for the future and returned back to my colleagues in the city. This was because I had so much confidence in the youth who left to the field and who were willing to sacrifice their lives; regarding the reason for Mebrahtu Wedi Zewde's surrender, I only can ponder about it within myself. And even when reflecting about the possible existence of a rift or division within the EPLF, I couldn't find the reasons and could not find clarification for it. I felt the weight of Mebrahtu Wedi Zewde surrender was comparable to the collapse of a big mountain.

After Mebrahtu Wedi Zewde went to the field, almost all who were working with him in the cells either joined the field or went into exile, and only very few of us remained behind. However, since his return to Asmara I believed my activities could expose the new recruits and in order to find a solution, we met with the cell leaders and evaluated the situation; we passed two important decisions: First, I was to meet Mebrahtu Wedi Zewde soon and ask him why he deceived me by saying he was on a mission; Second, until the issue of Wedi Zewde is cleared and resolved, I was to stay away from the mass organizations.

Since he told me he will come to Gual Demequ's beer house, I frequented the place hoping to find him. On the third day of my visit, I found him there drinking siwa with another person. I sat a bit far from him and after about 15 minutes, I followed him when he went out to pee and asked concerning the circumstances of his coming back to Asmara. Immediately he said, "I told you I came on a mission so that the story will not be spoiled, but because I couldn't agree with the EPLF I had to leave it. If you ask me how and what, I will not answer you, but you should not be hindered in your work, you will have nothing to be concerned about from me. I hold no different views regarding the cause for the liberation of Eritrea." He gave me a convincing explanation and went back in and we continued drinking our beer.

The next day, all the cell leaders met and evaluated the situation of Mebrahtu Wedi Zewde and agreed to keep him under surveillance for a limited period, and to continue our activities with caution. After a while, since we didn't find anything of concern about him, we resolved to continue our activities as before.

But since the case was not clear to me, I couldn't forget the cause of why Mebrahtu Wedi Zewde's returned from the front and it posed a big question mark in my mind. There was also a question that my grandfather had not answered when I stayed with him in Geremi, our village before descending to Derfo and joined the revolution. What my grandfather said and its meaning still bothered me. In due course of time minor unanswered questions began to accumulate in my mind. Even when I descended to Derfo to join the revolution, and even after I was trained and graduated as a combatant, I still didn't find answers for many of the unanswered questions. Gradually I started to develop critical reflections about the nature of the EPLF, an organization whose words I used to believe like the Holy Bible.

When Tekle Wedi Libbey gave me the book, I spread my blanket under a gaba tree and started to read. It was already five in the afternoon when I paid attention to the time, and the day's cook came to tell me that I was assigned to be the cook for the next day. He advised me to prepare the dough that night so that it will be ready for the next day. That is when I remembered I was in Derfo.

The book I was reading, "Anna Karenina", is a great novel that describes love of a family and society in 19th century Russia, and it is popular all over the world and was translated into many languages. I learned that after "War and Peace", it is the second book that propelled Leo Tolstoy in the roster of great writers. Before I heard the voice of the cook, I felt like I was just roaming around Russian cities and villages, but the cook's voice brought me back to Derfo, to make dough! I was going to do that for the first time in my life.

Just like Tolstoy told his wife, that for work to be done nicely, a person must like the job and have passion for it. I understood that in "Anna Karenina", he liked the idea of a family, and that in "War and Peace", he liked the idea of patriotism. Similarly, the main reason that made me sneak to Derfo was patriotism, and I believed in that. I was ready and wanted to face new challenges, I said, "Okay," to the cook, lighted a cigarette, and gave the cook one. After we smoked, I followed him to the cooking place and with his help, I prepared the dough. It was ready for cooking, ready for the next day.

When we were having lunch, the cook observed that I didn't eat well. Before the messenger boy arrived, he scooped lentils from the dish and gave it to me. I took a small bite, the cook finished the rest. He sarcastically remarked, "Comrade, are you okay? You haven't eaten enough... still, you haven't tasted real hunger, because then, let alone lentils, you will chew wood. Tsegu buddy, here we don't have a servant or Mama to cook for us, you have to be self-reliant, just like the EPLF says, get up comrade!" He added, "Here everyone bakes his bread, it is easy to do, who do you then think knows how to cook a chicken stew... I will show you once, after that you are alone, and as for the pencils, you will teach us how to read and write." He wanted to encourage me, I liked the chat with the cook and I listened to him attentively and assured him, "You can depend on me for the pencil work."

He asked me, "How far have you gone in school? Telling by the book you were reading, it seems you went as far as a thousand grades..." At that moment, the messenger boy and others came carrying a boar they just hunted. The cook approached to help them; I watched them silently. The messenger boy shouted at me, "Mama's boy! Come here and help, remember, we will eat the boar together." I was mad and I wanted to call him food monster, but I remembered the advice of Tekle Wedi Lbbey and Aboy Abraham and suppressed my anger and walked to help them.

As if that was not enough the Tof guy loudly inquired, "Who is the cook tomorrow, don't tell me it is Tsegu, it will be a bad day." He said that because he saw my hands covered in dough. The nicer cook interjected, "why don't you be a cook tomorrow and he can start to teach us the pencil," knowing the Messenger Boy doesn't like education. But the words were bitter and heavy on him. He reluctantly agreed, "All right, I will be the cook tomorrow. When it's his turn I will prepare the dough for him, he is new... but I don't want him to cook the boar into something like what he says, "Atherzerwaise." I could tell he was trying to avoid learning to read and write. The cook asked him, "Where did you buy the freezer?" the cook had heard that when we were talking with Tekle Wedi Lbbey. The messenger boy didn't understand the question and he told him that "Tsegu needs a small freezer to cool the bites," thinking that a selfish person should keep away from a breast-feeding woman."

The next day, in the morning we descended from our positions and walked straight to the cooking area. I observed what the messenger boy was doing following everything he did in order to learn how to cook. When it came to my turn to cook, in spite of the fact that it was my first time the outcome was not bad at all. With the help of both cooks, I managed to serve acceptable food for the day. That became the first step in the change process in my life, and just like the nice comrade cook remarked, no one has cooked chicken in that place, and it finally was time to sit and chat with the Tof guy. We were metaphorically all inside the big shopping basket, as Tekle Wedi Lbbey has said.

1.2 Journey to the Rear Base Area

The number of recruits who were temporarily stationed in Zager to be sent to the training camp in Sahel was complete and the time to begin my journey towards the lowland had finally arrived. After staying in Derfo for two-weeks, I bid farewell to the colleagues and left. I left the book with the cook to be delivered to Tekle Wedi Lbbey. I was sure Wedi Libbey knew I was preparing to leave. Along with a girl named Freweini, member of the mass organization who just arrived from Asmara, we began climbing the steep slopes of the Wa'aga Mountain early morning before the rooster starts crowing and headed towards Weki-Zager. After an hour of an arduous journey, we were exhausted and thirsty and were forced to stop to rest. We chewed some Argoba weeds to wet our throats, and by sunrise we reached Kwazen in the district of Karneshim. We ate breakfast of tea and bread prepared by the EPLF units there, and after a modest lunch consisting of a cup of roasted corn beans we proceeded to Zager.

As we chewed on the corn beans with the unit members, one of them, Abraham Gures, was throwing the beans in the air to be picked by a rooster as they came down. Seeing that, Freweini reprimanded him, "Here we have people who could not find enough to eat and you have the temerity to use the corn to play with a rooster!" He ignored her; he was from the region and he had no problem walking to the villagers to eat as much as he wanted. As it cooled down and we bid all goodbyes, Abraham Gures saw us off saying, "may we meet at victory day." I didn't swallow his wishes. I thought he was not prepared for the sacrifices.

We found Tekle Wedi Lbbey on our way and he asked, "Who is accompanying you?" Freweini told him we were on our own. He commented, "Don't tell me, it means you already know your way around Bahri!" I told him that I left the book with the cook. He bid us farewell and returned to Derfo.

Early morning on the next day, we continued our way towards Sahel. Some of the recruits were just like me, they could not stay in the city anymore, and others were recruited from the countryside. Though Freweini gave me limited news about Asmara, for almost four-months I didn't get any information about the friends I left behind. Incidentally, a person named Geza'e brought me news about my close friend, Michael Barba. He told me, after you left, he was rarely seen in the city and he was murmuring, "all of them left us behind and here I am left alone with the Cathedral building; it's better to be there with the combatants. I should have left." He added, "Asmara doesn't belong to its children anymore, no one is happy, everyone is forced to leave it, the situation has changed. I couldn't continue my activities, the Ethiopian soldiers suffer when the fighters beat them in the field, and they return to avenge themselves on the innocent civilians in the city. Let alone being a member of the mass organization, being an Eritrean has become a crime. They kill indiscriminately to avenge themselves on their losses."

After two-hour journey we reached Mrara. Following breakfast, we walked for four-hours. We descended the slopes of the valley and joined the Menteble River, which is located on the side of the northern Bahri Mountains which are covered by acacia trees and is a distance of two hours walk from Ella-Ero. It used to be an EPLF camp where the cadre school was located. In Menteble, some of us suffered from blisters on our feet and we were so tired we spread ourselves in the shaded area. At about sunset, we were told to get ready and we faced the challenge of the eastern central plains. Most of us still suffering from blistered feet, we arrived at She'eb with great difficulty and we couldn't continue any further.

Freweini, who was fine when we passed through the gorges of the highlands, was challenged in the mid eastern part of Eritrea. Her feet were blistered and she couldn't walk anymore and we had to leave her behind. Later on when I returned back to accompany her, lady luck struck because we found a tractor that was snatched from Massawa heading towards She'eb where we were heading. We boarded it and continued our journey; Freweini said to me, "I think your mother has prayed for you," no one expected to find a tractor on the way. I said, "Maybe it is your mother who prayed!" The driver interjected, "I think all your mothers prayed for you," and he remembered those who were martyred on the same plains at one incident in the past. He continued,

I haven't seen a journey like that, so many people were broken, we lost camels and we were so thirsty... so many died. Once we walked for a whole night and in the morning we returned to the same place we left on the previous night. Dust storms were so severe that we couldn't tell our direction--even the veteran fighters who claim to know directions by looking at the stars and were leading the way were confused. Some lagged behind as units advanced, and when we searched for them they were nowhere to be found--it was tough, but you are lucky, God sent me to you.

Freweini asked the driver, "listen brother, where is Sahel, isn't it in Eritrea?" He explained that the situation was bad--on one side were the Ethiopian army and on the other the freedom fighters of Jebha (ELF), and the road he was taking was the only safe one. He changed the topic and asked if I have cigarettes or he should chew his tobacco. I gave him a packet of cigarettes and he was very happy and told me that there are no cigarettes in Sahel. I thought the world would be so dark without cigarettes, and in order to have an alternative, I asked if I could have some of his tobacco to chew, he said his tobacco was 'Wed Ammar' and it was very strong that I wouldn't be able to handle it. But he moved the tractor under a shade of a tree and stopped it to smoke and rest; I was determined to try chewing tobacco. The minute I put the tobacco under my lips, I had nausea and threw up everything I ate in Menteble. He said, "I told you this is first class tobacco, too strong for you", he went to the tractor, brought water and poured it over my head; I felt better and we continued our journey. After three-days of bumpy travel on the tractor, our journey ended in Bleqat. Freweini was sent to Faah-Bleqat where the women's training camp was; I was sent farther up to Mahmimet where I started training in November 1975.

Upon my arrival I found five regiments being trained at Mahmimet. I was assigned to the third regiment, third platoon and third squad where I found three people from Asmara: the martyr Berhane Gebreab and two others both named Michael, who became colonels after independence. Together with them I made a small space the size of a dog house and covered it with a blanket and leaves from Adday bushes. I laid myself there.

Berhane asked me, "how is Asmara?" I said, "You tell me buddies because it has been four months since I left it." He jokingly remarked, "If you start to say buddy, why don't you substitute it with comrade... did you come through the Sudan to say buddies?" I said, "No. the communication unit kept me in the villages of Karneshim and Bahri... to me the Btsay, (a Tigrigna version of the term comrade) sounds like a name of a dog... by the way are you getting used to the training?" I wanted to chat. "There is nothing one cannot get used to, under the likes of Mohammed, the squad leader... if you can't handle training, they make you dance, they beat you up until you get used to it." The punishment that he went through was evident on his face. I was bewildered, "what are you saying?" Tekle Wedi Lbbey had told me about the grinning mountains; it appeared the people also grin with it.

"Would you give us cigarettes, if you have any?" I gave them a stick of cigarette each, they were astonished, and they divided the sticks into two, "we will smoke half of it in rolls now and the other two before we climb to our position at night, and the rest tomorrow morning before training time." Michael fished a rolling paper from his pocket. Berhane and I smoked one roll while the two Michaels smoked the other. They didn't say a word until they finished smoking; after puffing one last time, Berhane broke the silence, "for the first time we are not smoking Kerfo."

Michael the shorter of the two Michaels replied, "It has been a while since we stopped being humans, Kerfo has made me burp blood." I asked what Kerfo was and they told me it was the stems of tobacco leaves that they don't chew because they cannot be grounded. Instead they roll and smoke those stems. I thought it might be better than tobacco and told them that a driver of a tractor gave me tobacco called Wed Ammar that made me throw up. They assured me I will get used to it, and gave me advice as follows, "When they ask you to choose your preference, tell them you prefer chewing, we chose cigarette because we thought it was available, but you know... there is none here." I asked where they get the Kerfo from, and they said, "we are tired of begging it from passersby and if you are found doing that, they make you crawl and swim in the hot desert sand" Michael the taller added, "in order not to forget the Asmara swimming pool "

I discovered there was no one from Asmara in my squad; they were all country boys, "when it comes to cutting wood, baking bread they will beat you, and maybe a city boy can beat the country boys in dismantling and assembling the rifles as well as in the sphere of political education. At times when you are left behind in running with a rifle held up over your head during training, that swimming on desert sand awaits you. Sometimes they think you miss dancing at the Copacabana and they make you do the Russian dance, a terrible physical punishment, it is akin to Tigrigna traditional dance and they put you under the sun and you almost loose breath, you hate yourself. At any rate, slowly you will get used to it. It took us time to get used to it." I thought the two Michaels exaggerated everything to help me lower my expectations and be better prepared for the worst.

The next morning after we finished training, Weldenkiel Hakhli, a member of the Halewa Sewra (the Vigilance Department) called me and started to record details of my life history and the activities that I carried out as a clandestine member of the revolution. When he finished he asked me if I have a question. I said that there were a few things that I observed and needed clarification for them. He told me he will send a teacher of the trainees. He noted his views on the paper under my life history and left.

When I returned, my colleagues had already left for political education, and I went to the cooks and chatted a little before returning to my shade to take a rest. I lighted a cigarette and I felt dizzy, a few minutes later my colleagues returned from the political education. I asked how the day's political education was. They told me, "today it was Mahmoud Sheriffo's day; it was the history of Jebha (ELF) which they said has killed many people. They say it completely eliminated members of Seriyet Addis, only a few escaped...." I interjected, "what is Seriyet Addis?" They explained, "They were Highlanders who joined from Addis Ababa and Jebha (ELF) thought of eliminating them before they overwhelm it with their big numbers... they took them to a gorge and shot them down..." that is how they explained it to us. Berhane added, "We escaped from those who strangulate with steel wires and now in the field there are other stranglers! As the saying in Tigrigna goes, 'that an adult girl attracts many men whose only intention is to have sex with her'". Thus he summarized the situation. Our stomachs were rumbling; we went to have lunch and continue our conversation the next day.

After lunch we returned to our shaded area and Michael the shorter one said to me, "brother, earlier you overwhelmed the valley with the smell of cigarettes, we couldn't concentrate on the political education... didn't Mohammed come to you?" I replied, "I don't want others to smell it, but here, have some", I gave them two sticks of cigarettes to be rolled. He replied, "Don't worry about those who are here, they are all country boys and they don't smoke, unless some city guys from the other squad come." Before we lighted the cigarettes, the martyr Mehari 'Wedi' Girmatsion, who was a political education teacher, came and took me aside.

We sat under the shade of Adday bushes and after he introduced himself to me we started to talk. He asked me if I had any questions. I said, "I know that relations between the opposite sexes and marriages are not permitted in the EPLF..." He interrupted me before I could finish, "Yes. What is that you want to know?" I continued, "When I was in the highlands with the communication unit, I knew that a combatant named Berhe was in honeymoon, and I was wondering how that was possible." He blurted and stopped my question and shouted, "Menka'a! You don't have any worthy question?" I didn't want to ask anymore and I told him I had no more questions. However, I didn't understand what the term "Menka'a" meant at that time. Mehari Wedi Girmatsion was one of those who were later branded "Yemeen", right wing, and eliminated. As concerns the case of Berhe he was allowed to marry as a special case because his family has appealed to have their only son marry in order, as per tradition, to be able to have a male child to continue the family bloodline. The case was treated as an exception and not the rule. I asked the question because I wanted to challenge any favoritism if it existed within the EPLF. I didn't get an answer.

When I returned to my platoon, my colleagues asked me how my meeting with Mehari 'Wedi'Girmatsion went, but I didn't want to talk about it. Berhane handed me the fag of my cigarette; they slept and I continued thinking: "Do you have a question? Yes I do. Menka'a, you don't have a worthy question! Indeed, a shopping basket! And unlike the messenger boy he is a political commissar!" I did not expect such an attitude from someone who is educated and with the title of political commissar. Such attitude could be expected from someone like the messenger boy with less educational background and lower rank. I couldn't comprehend anything at all. Though I tried to convince myself to let go of the incidence, the thought stayed in my mind, always disturbing me. But expecting to face many similar incidences during the course of the struggle I decided to suppress the issue and move on.

The political education continued the next day and the topic was Jebha ELF) and the instructor went on and said: "Jebha (ELF) has a sectarian ailments; highlanders and lowlanders; it immersed itself in dirty politics that divide the West and East, and made the revolution miss its path and engage in internal conflicts and to many fighters it became unbearable; attempts to rectify the path were all frustrated; many from the highlands and eastern plains of Eritrea left the revolution, some went to Sudan and others surrendered to Ethiopia, and a few others split inside the field and the Eritrean Liberation Front ELF was fragmented into many groups and new entities emerged". Mahmoud Sheriffo concluded his lecture by stating, "These were the reasons for the birth of our organization."

During the time of training that lasted five-months, we would wake up at 4 AM in the morning, spend two hours running, followed by a left-right march, we eat breakfast and we start dismantling and reassembling and greasing our respective rifles, then we go for political education after which we eat lunch, and without moving from our place, without talking to any other fighter or a citizen who is not a trainee, we eat dinner and move to our night positions--it seems exactly like the traditional highland Tigrigna dance, going in circles. However, like my martyred brother Amanuel said, "A person who is prepared to sacrifice his life should also be prepared to overcome even tougher and unpleasant repetitious situations". I was prepared for any eventuality.

The food at the training camp was bread made of 'Wed Aker' or poor quality sorghum grain, and it was served with water in lieu of sauce. I thought I had learned to make bread in a pan while in Derfo, and I would have no problems to cook. But this time I had to use heated slabs of stone instead of a pan, I didn't know how long the bread had to stay on the stone before it is ready. Two breads were thrown because they were overcooked; I learned a lesson, and realized the difference between cooking in pans and on stone slabs. But then it was the various instructions of fighters who confused me: add more fire, lower the heat, etc! But finally I learned how to cook on stone. But then, I decided it was easier to cook porridge instead of baking bread, I did just that. I didn't know what to use as sauce in lieu of butter and yogurt until Berhane came to my rescue. He told me to make the sauce from what they called "How are you?" I didn't understand what he meant. He explained to me to make a sauce out of the same flour. I stirred flour on hot water and presented it with the porridge in lieu of sauce. My first experience in preparing food alone was over.

At night we ascended the Nyala Hill and held our positions; we used half the blanket as a spread and the other half as a cover. If the ground is not too rocky, one sleeps well, otherwise, you count the stars and start to talk to yourself all night. I saw the stars in Derfo, but since I was preoccupied with either smoking or reading, I didn't pay much attention to them. But after I surrendered everything I own like the rest of the recruits, such as watches and other small personal items, and anything that connects one with his individual life, including wedding rings, were taken away. It makes you feel so empty. I had to hide the cigarettes lest they confiscate them. After everything was taken away, including flashlights, there is nothing to be read or written on, one is only left with stars to gaze at and wonder.

Astrologists study the stars that we assume are hanging in space. The invention of telescope enabled humanity to go beyond the assumptions and see the real and large stars much closer, and discern the different reflections of their colors. However, at the Nyala Hill, where you can only study the stars with the naked eye, there was nothing that I can do beyond the immediate observation of the natural characteristics of our world and admire it. True, at night, the colleagues who used to lead us in the eastern coastal lowlands on the way to Sahel were following the Northern Star as their guide. I knew that stars are important to identify a northern star and stars that direct towards it, constellation that are shaped like the tip of a spear. Similarly, step by step, I started to study the true nature of the EPLF that I from a distance used to believe was a pious and saintly organization.

During my first week of training I was given a harsh lecture as regards the military rules of the EPLF for arriving late on a training session. And pursuant to the policy of the training camp combatants get rations of cigarettes or tobacco based on the choices each make at the beginning of their training and cannot change that. But since availability of cigarettes in Sahel was highly limited those who chose cigarettes were unlucky and were not allowed to obtain tobacco. Following the advice of colleagues, I chose tobacco as my ration of choice. And one day when Mohammed came to us, I was not smoking. He asked the others were they got the cigarettes from. He left after they told him they found some forgotten sticks of cigarette in their bags.

Cursing the man, they said he was looking for an excuse to punish someone; they showed me bruises on their bodies and warned me that it was me he was after. I could not fathom, why one would look for an excuse in order to punish someone! Things were different there, if you see someone doing something wrong, aren't you expected to correct them! This man is addicted to punishing people. I gave my tobacco to Berhane to prepare it for me, at the same time warning him ofMohammed who might come back. Berhane was scolding me, telling me that tobacco is put under the lips, not on the hands and Mohammed returned before he finished what he was saying and asked Berhane where he got the tobacco from. Berhane told him it was mine. He asked me and I confirmed that. He ordered us to follow him to be punished. The time was noon and the sun was scorching hot; he made us crawl for fifteen-minutes and made us do other fifteen-minutes of Russian dance before he let us go. I felt dizzy and fell down. They picked me and let me rest a while under the shade of the Adday bushes. We returned to our place after I started to feel better. After that, I was determined to be strengthened by his deeds and wanted to show him how resilient I can be and became antagonists thereafter.

Towards the end of the training period, we were told there was a seminar to be delivered by Isaias Afewerki and all the trainees were assembled to attend. The title of the seminar was, "Menka'a the Destructive Movement of 1973." The content of the seminar which was prepared by the EPLF leadership, stated, "On June 30, 1974, a judicial committee was formed to look at the cases of the imprisoned and main leaders of the destructive movement; after it took a decision it passed the case to the leadership for action; and the leadership evaluated the internal and external situations and approved the judicial committee's decision, and subsequently on August 11, 1975 the leadership convened a general meeting, studied the case and implemented the decision, and decided that the final decision of the leadership will be explained by a combatant at future date in a written form or verbally." But regardless of that, at that time the combatant who was making the explanation was Isaias Afewerki, and that is why he came in front of the trainees and explained that the death penalty was taken on the prisoners. At the conclusion of the seminar Isaias asked if there were opinions or questions, but since the trainees knew nothing about the subject matter, the seminar was concluded without anyone expressing any opinion or asking questions.

The seminar reminded me of the time I was labeled as, "Menka'a! You don't have any other worthy question?" The remark of Mehari 'Wedi' Girmatsion popped up in my mind during the seminar. I didn't understand however why he called me Menka'a. In short, according to Isaias' explanation, "the members of Menka'a were driven by their class, they embraced risky petty bourgeois tendencies and were vacillating in the middle--kicking the bottom class of workers and peasants downwards while stretching their hand upwards to join the bourgeois class, and beginning from their unstable economic position, they developed bad and cheap behaviors of selfishness, arrogance, indecisiveness, betrayal, uneasiness, deceptiveness, etc." That was the way Isaias described them. Particularly the main leaders of the so called destructive movement he describes them as "individuals who were intoxicated by grandiosity, and as opportunism, and labeled them as instigators who had individual selfish aspirations and dreams to seize political power." That was how Isaias accused the leaders of the 1973 movement, the very people who attended the same university with him, thus exempting himself from the petty bourgeois oriented crimes he accused them of.

Looking at it from the perspective of a conscious neutral observer, the death sentence taken against the leaders of the Menka'a movement was not at all justifiable. One wonders if there were no other alternatives to capital punishment. Even if we assume they have committed what they are accused of, no one with conscience would pass death penalty on them. One cannot find justification for the decision taken against the leaders of the so-called Menka'a movement.

Once the training was completed the third regiment was sent to A'aget to help with harvesting. The road to A'aget was full of boulders and it was considered important in shortening the road distance within the transportation network of Sahel. It should have been cleared, be it by building it on the edges of the mountain or by crossing the river. There was no trainee who didn't complain about the A'aget road. It was a road that the martyr Michael Fesssahaie immortalized with his saying, "Poor Michael, you used the spade to clear goldmines, now you are clearing dirt with it." Michael was known throughout the EPLF for his technical skills. Later he became one of the leaders of the economic commission. One time a blast of a bomb was heard in the distance, and through whispering we knew that a fighter has committed suicide. "Don't attempt to know secrets that do not concern you", was the cardinal military law, and that was ringing on the ears of all the trainees when we heard about the bomb incidence. Thus, no one dared to ask the how and whys to ascertain if the death of the fighter was an accident, suicide or even murder.

While the construction of the A'aget road was in progress, they began to assign trainees to various departments. From our squad, Berhane was sent to the health department. He picked his bag and left for the central hospital at Seberqete and bid us goodbye lamenting, "I don't think we will meet again, but at least I will be out of reach of Mohammed."

A few days later I was assigned to Halewa Sewra and I was put in a group where I found a few people I knew who were in the other squads during training. I also saw some faces I didn't like while I was in the city; some of them were suspected of being enemy spies. Again, the term "Menka'a" rang in my ears. I bid farewell to the two Michaels and headed towards the central head quarters of Halewa Sewra in Faah. Later on the two Michaels were assigned to the artillery units.

When we reached at Faah, in what is also known as Sahtewil or

The Salty, the Halewa Sewra headquarters, we were divided into two groups. Those who were suspected of being enemy operatives during training and were under surveillance for months were sent for interrogation and were handed to the first squad of the interrogation department. The second group including myself were assigned to different branches of Halewa Sewra. I was relieved when the group was further divided into two. In such a secretive and closed organization where you are frequently reminded to desist making attempts to know secrets, and when you believe you are given a chance to ask a question and labeled as "Menka'a", and where strugglers and spies are gathered and assigned to Halewa Sewra units together, and where the reasons for the surrender of an individual is not explained by the organization or by those who surrender, where people who joined to struggle are branded destructive and executed: these and other observations I made in the process disturbed me a great deal.

I had surmised that I have been assigned to the security department in a unit where everything is explained. It was a security system protecting the organization that struggles to bring about "national liberation", the security of the revolution that struggles to bring about fundamental social change, the security of the group that accused the Eritrean Liberation Front of being sectarian with reactionary tendencies, the security of those who pass death sentences on enemy spies and equally on reform-minded fighters whose only crime is they campaigned for change.

In life, it is possible for one to arrange things according to one's wishes; however, things do not always follow specific plans. But in a struggle to accomplish one's goals, without reluctance, is the only way that has no alternative. Those who dream and implement objectives collectively are very few. Liberating a country is a plan, but accomplishing the freedom of human beings is a far reaching objective and is much broader than territorial liberation. It is a struggle to achieve fundamental social change.

Within the EPLF, every fighter abides by the directives of the organization. If anyone doesn't abide by and follow strictly organizational directives, will be considered unruly and an anarchist. In addition, one could be accused of being ultra-leftist or ultra-right and may even end up facing the death sentence. Such situation compels one to be curious and ask: "What kind of 'organization' gives directives to people and at the same time limits their freedom to be inquisitive, drives and steers them to wherever direction it chooses? Does such an organization have 'divine power' whose existence is not known?" In hindsight it is the secret party whose leadership appears to be omnipotent and untouchable.

1.3 From the Rear Base to Behind the Enemy Frontlines

In Sahtewil, I was assigned to a squad in the interrogation unit. I found out that my childhood friend Isaac Rezene was the medic of the squad; I found a shade to share with him without going through the trouble of making my own. Isaac Rezene joined the front in 1974, initially he served in the military units and then he was transferred to the mass mobilization department in Sahel. He was later imprisoned. After his release he was assigned to Halewa Sewra. He was such a loyal friend that he gave me invaluable advice of how to avoid being in trouble within the department. He even showed me bruises on his back inflicted on him during torturous interrogations. Isaac was so concerned about me that he gave me essential information that would help me avoid the torturous experience he went through. He told me that he was imprisoned for being a member of a secret party that was founded by 'Btsay' (comrade) Goitom Berhe.

'Btsay' Goitom Berhe was a student of the Addis Ababa University who studied law at the Faculty of Law in the Haile Selassie I University (HSIU). He was veteran combatant and one of the Addis Ababa university students who joined the EPLF in the early 1970s. Since he was serving in Sahel as head of the public affairs department in the area, Isaac Rezene worked under him. And one time during a private chat 'Btsay' Goitom Berhe confided in him about the existence of a secret party within the EPLF. Isaac couldn't comprehend what 'Btsay' Goitom was telling him and he repeatedly asked him, "do you mean within the EPLF?" 'Btsay' Goitom Berhe didn't want to talk more and warned him, "This is a matter that should remain between you and me, and I will tell you more in due course of time."

Isaac was bewildered and started to recall things he didn't observe clearly before that day. He recalled seeing some people seclude themselves for an entire day and then return from the meetings holding identical views. He was surprised how individuals from different classes, some peasants and others students, could have identical views. It was surprising to him how they could form similar opinions on given issues. He could not understand why all the people who joined to pursue a united struggle to liberate Eritrea would be divided into a group who struggle in the open and a group that struggles secretly.

A week later, when he noticed some fighters leaving to attend secret meeting that they were holding without getting permission from their squad leaders, 'Btsay' Goitom Berhe took Isaac to a secluded place and explained to him stating, "In our organization within the EPLF, there is a secret party by the name Eritrean People's Revolutionary Party (EPRP) that claims to be a Marxist-Leninist group, and there was no need for it to operate secretly but since it is a reality, one can struggle against secrets by utilizing secretive methods." He waited to listen to Isaac's view. Isaac himself couldn't understand why he was not made a member of the secret party while other fighters like him were members. He told him, "Listen 'Btsay' Goitom Berhe, in this organization, I do not understand who sacrifices red blood and who doesn't have blood to shed.""Btsay' Goitom Berhe replied, "But if they ignite fire on the haystack of the revolution, we have to pour water on it." He then hinted that he wanted him to join his party. And "sure" they agreed to work together.

'Btsay' Goitom Berhe's party started to write in Tigrigna different Marxist writings and to distribute them, but unknowingly they recruited a member of Isaias Afewerki's party who discovered all their secrets and exposed them. Isaac told me that he believed the existence of a Marxist party in a democratic revolution is essential and that he joined 'Btsay' Goitom Berhe's party because of that conviction and it was for the very reason why he was jailed and tortured.

As a new member of a squad, I was assigned to guard the prisoners and prevent them from escaping. The guarding place was in a gorge and the prisoners stayed in separate shades under the caves and to avoid exchange of information during interrogation, they were not allowed to talk to one another. To prevent the prisoners from escaping, the shades were put on the slopes, on the side of the gorge, while the guard posts were a little further, except for one fighter who was assigned to monitor the prisoners from close by and control their activities and prevent them from talking to one another and share information. The rest of the guards were positioned in high strategic positions to have a bird's eye view of the entire valley so as to ensure no prisoner escapes.

The affairs of the prisoners concerned only to the interrogators; the guards had no responsibility. Apart from the fact that we were guarding them, we were not told the reason why they were imprisoned, though we found out the reasons through our own devices.

What I learned during the almost three-month time that I stayed in that place is that the type of prisoners and the nature of their cases were varied. Some were suspected of being spies for Ethiopia or the ELF, while others were accused of killing people, embezzling the organization's properties, abandoning their positions; homosexuality, political deviation, and prisoners accused of being members of Menka'a (except those who were sentenced to death), etc. Incidentally, one of those who were imprisoned for abandoning position was Abraham 'Wedi' Gures whom I met in Kwazen on my way to the training camp and who left after wishing us, "May we meet in victory." Abraham 'Wedi' Gures was wounded in his palm in a battle with the Ethiopian forces at Karneshim; he was suspected and sent to Halewa Sewra. At the end, it was confirmed that he retreated from the battleground and inflicted the wound on himself in order to be relieved from the battle. He was punished and rehabilitated, encouraged and sent to the military units to struggle, but then he escaped and went off to the ELF. He eventually left the ELF and went to the Arab countries.

At that time, though Solomon Weldemariam was in charge of Halewa Sewra, due to the then prevailing power struggle within the EPLF leadership he was temporarily assigned a foreign relations task so as to remove him from the field. He was often outside the country and was seldom present. At the time I joined the department, Haile Jebha, Dawit Habtu and Gebrihiwet were senior interrogators, and Frawla and Manjus were squad leaders. The leaders, though they had similar views on the Menka'a prisoners, they were not in agreement with each other. Haile Jebha and his clique were openly recruiting from the squads, but the activities of the other clique were secretive and couldn't be observed. Dawit Habtu was a member of the party that was led by the Isaias clique and he was not among the so-called 'right wing' group of Haile Jebha and Gebrihiwet. At that time, following Isaac Rezene's advice to keep away from taking sides, I kept myself at a distance and continued to observe the activities of all sides as a neutral person.

Soon, Haile Jebha brought a prisoner who was said to be 'misguided' and wanted us to listen to his repentance testimony; we went to a meeting. What was considered education at that time was about 'Btsay' Goitom Berhe. The 'misguided' explained that an Eritrean Revolutionary secret party was established in the organization, and its motive was to satiate its members hunger for power. As an imprisoned person and facing the barrel of a gun, it was expected that he will not say anything else. 'Btsay' Goitom Berhe was not bold enough to explain the secret party of Isaias and his clique in the meeting.

After the 'misguided' delivered his 'educational' explanation, the people who brought him to us took him on a tour to give similar explanations. At Independence Day, 'Btsay' Goitom Berhe, just like those who were martyred with him in the institutional power struggle within the EPLF, including Teklay Gebrekristos and Michael Bereketab, and others, didn't return, and his name is not even recorded in the martyrs' register.

After three months at Sahtewil, I was assigned to the prison of the Ethiopian POWs at Gergret, an hour's walk away. One time our squad slaughtered a camel and the meat went bad and almost all of us got sick. Accidentally I was all right; I accompanied Frawla, the leader of the guard squads, to request medical help from Seberqete. This was the first time I went on a Tof mission as a messenger. We met Dr. Nerayo at Seberqete and we all returned together to Gergeret where all the sick was given medical attention and were treated in a short time.

As the Tigrigna saying goes,"one who roams around to get something that does not belong to him either gets lucky and gets what he wants or gets caught and beaten." When I reached Seberqete, I went to the valley to ask about martyr Berhane; I couldn't find anyone who would tell me his whereabouts. I found Michael 'Awer', the lab technician who was my schoolmate. He asked me, "Where do you know Berhane?" I said, "In training." He said, "Berhane did it." I didn't understand, "Did what?" I asked and he explained, "Berhane sat on a hand grenade and exploded it on himself."

On way back to Gergeret we stopped at the pharmacy camp which was halfway on the road. Dr. Nerayo said, "Let's pass by the pharmacy, we can rest a little bit and drink some water... and you can also see your brother..." We found them eating lamb meat and we ate lunch and got introduced with Hajji Mudi before returning to Gergeret.

The Eritrean Peoples' Liberation Front was busy preparing for its first organizational congress. It was a time when the preparatory committee was touring, explaining the electoral process and was also charged with organizing the elections. It was the time that many from Halewa Sewra had left to attend in the fifth round of the cadre school at Baqos, and that is why I returned to Sahtewil to fill some vacant posts in the department. By then the Menka'a members were done with the interrogations and they were placed in a separate place between Gergeret and Sahtewil--the place later to be known as Enda Menka'a. The guard squad leader at Enda Menka'a was the late Goitom 'Qeshi' Mussie.

Mohammed who was my squad leader during training came as a regular student in the place where I was assigned as a political education instructor. He was surprised and also scared when he saw me teaching. I called and assured him not to worry about the past and that he should focus on his education, grow, and continue to struggle. He didn't last long; when the enemy dropped paratroopers by helicopters in Naro, behind our defensive lines, a support force was assembled from the Sahel positions and Mohammed was one of those who went there and never returned; he was martyred along with his comrades.

After giving political education in Sahtewil to the members of Halewa Sewra for a short time, I was transferred to a place known as "Tof Aden" which was also known as Camp Nevada by the surviving members of the 1973 movement who were being rehabilitated there.

The ELF was at that time experiencing internal conflict and was in chaos and some of its members were escaping and coming to the EPLF. I was sent to Sahtewil to collect the escaped members of the group known as Falul. The founders of the Eritrean Relief Association (ERA), Dr. Bereket Habte Selassie and Redaezghi Gebremedhin had left the place a short while earlier in July 1976. I didn't know their whereabouts when I was in Sahtewil or Gergeret. Dr. Bereket is a close relative, he's my uncle. In his nature, Isaias doesn't like any organized movement or party or association, it was natural that he would antagonize them as leaders of a relief association. To gain control over the ERA, he had frozen its managers even when it was a non-political and non-partisan non-governmental organization (NGO) or charity, just a relief association founded to help Eritreans in distress.

The First Organizational Congress of EPLF was held in Faah at the beginning of 1977. Members who participated in the Congress were elected and selected from among the ranks of the military units, the departments, and top frontline commanders. Included in the list of participants were also representatives of mass organizations from abroad as well as representatives of cell organizations from inside the enemy occupied territory. Whereas the number of attendees was limited, the top leaders of the organization being members of the secret party found free tickets to participate in the Congress. On top of that, elements from the Solomon Weldemariam group that was labeled as the 'right wingers' and their sympathizers were deliberately sent to the cadre school just before the Congress in order to minimize their chances of being elected. The conspiratorial scheme had already been accomplished, and the drama and theatrics of the congress was cast as per the wishes of the secret party leadership. It is recalled by many who were at the Congress that upon observing the deceitful drama, Adhanom Gebremariam commented, "This was finalized ahead of time, and they only called us just to bless it for them." Though Adhanom was a senior military commander, he was not, however, a member of the secret party.

Habtemariam Ghebremeskel (nicknamedChipola) was one of the participants who were handpicked to represent the mass organizations in North America. We met unexpectedly in Camp Nevada as I was giving political education tothe Falul group in Faah. Chipola has gained some weight and his face was brighter than what I remember when we were frequenting the local beer house of Gual Demequ. I was not sure if it was him when he approached me with open arms. We hugged and embraced each other as old friends. After a short conversation updating about each other's situation and about old friends like Abraham, he told me that he came to attend the Congress. Chipola was one of the leaders of the Washington branch of Eritreans for Liberation in North America (EFLNA). Though I wanted to know more from him on how EFLNA conducted the election to send representatives to participate in the EPLF Congress, the situation was not favorable and we had to part and I didn't have the chance to ask him.

The political education I gave to the Falul was basic politics and I had no problem. But the ELF fighters repeatedly raised the issue of 'Jebha will melt down' which was part of the general political education and which is commonly known as the prophecy of Isaias, as presented in a document issued in the early 1970s entitled **"Nehan Elamanan" (we and our objectives).** It made them uneasy. Similarly, the 'counter revolutionary' branding of the EPLF by the ELF was a subject for debates. Since it was not appropriate for me to teach the history of the armed struggle to those who read enough to know about it as much as I did, and on top of that were part of it, I consulted with my leaders who decided to assign Mahmoud Sheriffo to teach that class. The main thing that I observed was that no fighter accepted the fact that Eritreans should kill each other. Nevertheless, the recklessness was like the elephants squashing the grass, involving mutual annihilation. It is argued in some circles that as a result of the internecine fighting between the two fronts, Isaias' dream was realized and finally after the battles of 1981, the ELF was pushed out of the Eritrean field and it splintered into several splinter groups when it entered the Sudan; subsequently the EPLF as the sole front monopolized the Eritrean field.

The first organizational congress was conducted in 1977 as I was teaching the Falul. That congress had decided well before hand about the situation that the Eritrean people find themselves today. At the congress, Ramadan Mohammed Nur became Secretary General with Isaias Afwerki as his Deputy, Ibrahim Afa, Senior Military Commander, Haile Derou, Head of Political Education, Alamin Mohammed Saed, Head of Information Department, Ali Saed Abdella, Head of Halewa Sewra, Petros Solomon, Chief of Military Intelligence, Sebhat Ephrem, Head of the Public Administration Department, Uqbe Abraha, Chief of Logistics, Berhane Gerezgher, Head of the Medical Department, Mohammed Saed Barih, Chief of Foreign Relations. It was evident that they were all members of the secret party. However, even if Ramadan was elected as Secretary General, the real authority remained with Isaias Afwerki as head of the secret party. At that congress, as has been already crafted and expected, Solomon Weldemariam was clearly defeated and was replaced by Ali Saed Abdella as the Head of Halewa Sewra. Solomon was stripped of his authority as head of the Halewa Sewra Department and was now placed under the mercy of Isaias.

As the congress was underway, Isaac who was Halewa Sewra leader behind the enemy defense line, abandoned the organization and surrendered to the rival ELF. There was rumor that he was a sympathizer of the Solomon Wedemariam's group. At the same time, his deputy Weldenkiel Hakhli was accused of sexual crime and was imprisoned and sent to Sahel. Ali Saed summoned Mussa Naib and me and informed us that Musa Naib was appointed as the head or commander of the behind enemy-line Halewa Sewra and that I was assigned as commissioner of the guards' squads. We were sent to Adi Rosso inthe surroundings of A'ala. Weldenkiel Hakhli was the one who recorded my life history and recommended that I be assigned to the Halewa Sewra.

After they eliminated and controlled the Menka'a movement as well as Btsay Goitom Berhe and his group, what was to follow was the suppressing of any opposition by employing pretexts of eliminating "anti-revolution" elements like the so-called 'right wingers'. It is claimed that at the time of the 1973 movement, backward and sectarian sentiments were used to agitate support, such as using soccer teams slogans like: "The Hamassen team came out victorious; the Akele Guzai team was vanquished; The Semhar team came out victorious, the Denkalia team is defeated..."Isaias found an excuse to use against those agitating for change and used the regional sentiments expressed by a few of those advocating for change to label them as regionalists.It was by using such divisive tactics that Isaias and his inner circle of party adherents were able to hit two birds with one stone; on one hand to eliminate their so-called ultra-left rivals, and on the other hand, since they wanted to paint a picture of themselves as progressives, they accused the other group as narrow-minded right-wing regionalists. They wanted the group they labeled as right-wing to bear the responsibility for the elimination of the so called left-wing Menka'a. They published on the front's magazine called Mahta, under the title of **'Another Menka'a that uses the name of Menka'a'**, and their main goal was to wash their hands clean like Pilate did in the case of Jesus. They used the media that was under their full control to portray the so-called 'right wingers' as reactionary, backward, sectarian, and a movement of the power hungry individuals.

The issue was not whether one party was right or wrong, it was a conviction that no other party should exist, other than that controlled by Isaias and his clique. It was aiming to advance the supremacy of the left-leaning party of Isaias by spilling the blood of innocent patriotic Eritreans. All initiatives were at one time branded sectarian and on other times adventurist, etc. with severe consequences to its leaders and members. The backbone of any future movement was broken, the only secret party the EPRP which was later named the Eritrean Socialist Party (ESP), led the struggle all the way up to Independence.

Isaias has wrapped himself in so many philosophical cloaks; sometime he is a follower of Mao, or a Marxist, and other times a disciple of Adam Smith. He didn't leave anything unused. And as Machiavelli's political philosophy indicates Isaias believes in the motto of **'the end justifies the means'.** He exploits everyone by being a monster camouflaged as a human person; even his comrades and colleagues are not spared from his devilish nature. He never trusted

45

anyone or any association, but always managed to use the work of others to his benefit and often shines with the sweat and efforts of others. He was and still is a skilled wolf that uses any means to protect his power and interests.

The EPLF, according to the declarations of its First Organizational Congress, pledged to be "an organization that struggles to establish a popular and participatory system of governance in which the masses were to play active role in running it; that it believes the system it aspires to establish is from the people and for the people; and that strongly struggles to ensure that all Eritreans will freely enjoy the fruits of their struggle for independence. However, Isaias and his clique had previous to the congress established a secret party while condemning others to death whose only crime was attempting to establish parties that will enable them to compete for the seizure of political power within the EPLF, and many more disappeared without trace. So, how was the secret party of the Isaias clique formed? Was its objective to rid the Front from opportunists seeking power or was it formed to protect the power base of Isaias and his cohorts that he manipulates.

Two weeks after the first congress, Musa Naib and I headed to the Highlands. We left behind the rugged Sahel Mountains which offers only heat waves during the day and chilling weather during the night. We crossed the gardens of Filfil and Solomuna and continued breathing the cool air of the highlands until we reached the semi-arid southern section of Bahri, to the farm of Degiat Giorgo Habtit, in the surroundings of A'ala, and joined Halewa Sewra units that were stationed at Adi Rosso.

Though I passed through Derfo, in the northern section of Bahri before I went to Sahel for training, I didn't pay too much attention to the climatic conditions and food resources of the region nor did I compare it to that of Asmara. The rivers of northern Bahri and the gardens of Filfil and Solomuna, the coffee plantations of Fshey and Mrara, the temperate climate of Fagiena, are all places that are still imprinted in my mind and which I would admire forever. The area is semi-arid, with temperate mild climate and it is suitable to grow a variety of crops. The rich alluvial soil that is carried from the highlands by the runoff of the rivers is deposited on the river banks and enables growth of vegetables and fruits like oranges, mandarin, papaya, mangoes, as well as coffee beans, and food crops like maize and other cereal grains.

When I was preparing to go to the highlands, Girmay Mehari, who at that time was deputizing Ali Saed in administering the department of Halewa Sewra, teased me by saying, "You came here looking as fresh as a bride and turned into the looks of an oven, maybe your mother must have been praying for you that now, within a short time you are returning to the highlands," He added, "don't forget to send us cigarettes".

During the almost fifteen months that I stayed in Sahel, my skin was so burned one could not tell the difference between my face and the face of the Sahel mountain rocks. But when I started to feed on the mangoes and the maize of Solomuna, slowly my skin began to regain its original complexion. When I reached Filfil, I asked about Tekle Wedi Lbbey but I couldn't find him since he was in the surroundings of Asmara. I wrote him a brief letter informing him that I have been assigned in the areas behind the enemy-lines. I remember all that he told me. After fifteen months, Gou'mesh, who was in charge of the Solomuna special case unit, offered me with three sticks of cigarettes and I bid tobacco farewell, though I couldn't bring myself to throw away the ration of tobacco that I received in Sahel. Still, after smoking cigarettes, I was not satisfied and felt like putting some tobacco under my lip. Getting used to tobacco develops strong addiction! Even the three cigarette sticks didn't last for too long.

In Adi Rosso, the guarding squad welcomed us with a great spirit. After Isaac surrendered, Kaleab 'Wedi' Rebbi had replaced him and became in charge of the unit; he called a meeting and introduced us to all the members of his team. After the meeting, they slaughtered a goat in our honor and presented it with bread made from flour that was captured from the enemy supplies; thereafter, it was all eating and drinking. But honestly, there were no alcoholic drinks to go with the excellent food. The martyr 'Wedi' Teklom readied his musical instrument the Krar and started to sing a famous Tigrigna song, while martyr Kiflemariam picked a drum and begun beating it and the party started in earnest. I tought, "of course after all these food one wishes for a girl to sneak out and join him, who can blame Weldenkiel Hakhli was right!" Simultaneous with my thoughts I gazed at a girl with a braided hair who was sitting across from where I was.

To liberate their country from occupation, fighters have been transformed to non humans. They even had to stop what animals naturally do to procreate. Having sexual relation was not only a sin, it had become a crime. The fighters realized that if not treated so, children would certainly be produced, and it was evident that it would be difficult to raise children while at the same time fully engaged in the liberation war. Thus, forced by the circumstances imposed by the war, the EPLF adopted a policy of imposing the unnatural conditions of life for fighters. However, the fighters didn't attempt to find a solution beyond that--it was like wanting to become a martyr before you die! What can be done! After eating and drinking, human beings become the real human beings that they are. In our case, we tried to fight against the nature of human beings.

Tsgereda (Gual Signora) that is how they called the girl with the braided hair who hailed from Keren. She had well built body and she was very beautiful. Her eyes captivated me and I went into deep thoughts, and began to consider all possibilities. On the one hand I wanted to be a fighter, but on the other hand I wanted to be a human being with emotions, feelings and desires and I got mixed up. When I was conducting political education class in our unit, she was staring at me and when I looked back at her, she diverted her stare and pretended as if she was looking elsewhere. In the process she dwelled in my heart. After a few days in class, the braided hair girl began to come to me to ask questions that she didn't understand in the class. I started to read something else in her eyes, and I noticed the motive of her coming to me was not intended to ask class related questions but an excuse to stay behind. Occasionally our eyes started to clash, and chimes of love started to play in our hearts.

Tsgereda Gual Signora started to do me favors by taking my clothes along when she went to the river to wash her clothes. Slowly we started to pick lice from each other's hair; we agreed without words. But in spite of the fact that we knew the rules of the organization as concerns sexual offence, that is to say that acts of rape was punishable by death and other sexual offences were given lighter punishments, some of us were not hindered of having a relationship. However, being aware that Weldekiel 'Hakhli' was accused of engaging in sexual intercourse and was sent to Sahel as a prisoner, while others were sent to Hashmet on the shores of the red sea as a punishment of hard labor to collect salt which made us a bit worried. One night after dinner, we both went to my resting place; we sat and stopped conversation about political education and we started to listen to songs. We were passing the time by joking about our past city life and laughing.

Later on, in addition to the teaching job that I was doing, Mussa asked me to help him investigate a sexual offence case. I didn't feel comfortable to investigate an act I consider to be natural to any human being, but I had no choice but to accept it. I brought the file of the accused girl who was from the artillery division and called her. I asked her why she was at Halewa Sewra. She pointed with her finger at the accused who was sitting across from where she was sitting and told me that she went to him on her own and they had sex and that is why she was sent to Halewa Sewra.

She said, "even now if I was not imprisoned, I would not leave him alone, and here you are making him sit in front of me and I couldn't resist it!" After hearing her words and understanding that they were driven by love, I could do nothing except tell her, "you shouldn't have been exposed, the situation doesn't allow that," I told her to go back to her place. I reflected on my own situation and tried to see things by putting myself in her shoes, and tried to find a solution. I called her later on to sign her statement and told the guard to allow her to take her things. She asked me, "how about him?" I replied, "He will also be released after we complete his investigation." She was not happy   to   be   released   alone   leaving   him   behind.

Fighters volunteered to give their lives, and in the course of the struggle there were social hindrances that seem insignificant but leave scars on the moral and spirit of the fighters. They pull them back in their struggle to achieve major goals; we were witnessing that. The situation was difficult and required perseverance and patience. Though it is natural for men and women to fall in love, the struggle had not created favorable conditions to accommodate that. Foreign visitors could not understand it when they discover that sexual relations were not allowed in the Eritrean revolution. It is unlike anywhere in the world. There are hermits who shun the worldly life and Christians who chose to become monks, but that is based on their individual choices and they can stop it any time they wish so since it's not imposed on them. But for the freedom fighters, it was not a choice but a reality driven by the circumstances of the struggle.

In addition, the structure of the squads and platoons in the organization severely exasperated the situation. A basic squad or group of fighters was led by a squad leader and it was a miniature sample of Eritrea that contained the common characteristic features of the society. It contained peasants, workers, merchants, students, intellectuals, street boys, etc. -- in short, all ethnic groups and classes who came from all corners of Eritrea were represented--, indeed, it was like a shopping basket which contains different merchandise items inside it. To integrate into the squad of a fighting unit, and to exist in a coordinated and collaborative manner, one has to make 'class suicide' and blend into the new social reality and norm of the squad. Most of the time, the peasants, and to a lesser extent the workers, were the leaders of the squads and platoons, while students, or those who have attained some level of education, became commissioners. Owing to the composition of the squads contradictions and conflicts within the units becomes inevitable.

The EPLF convinced its members that it is an organization that adheres to the ideology of Marxism-Leninism and claims to be a national democratic front; as per the teachings of the front the organization claims to be based on the alliance formed between peasants and workers. The political indoctrination of the EPLF characterized the petty bourgeois as indecisive, vacillating, unreliable and unable to have a stand and fight with resolve. However, the organization never clearly established the criteria of how a petty bourgeoisie is to be defined. Since anyone with a certain level of education was labeled as petty bourgeoisie, the educated fighters often attempt to imitate the mannerism of peasants by wearing shorts and gaiters, and grow their hair and stick a wooden comb in it. Most of the members of Menka'a were either university or high school students and they were characterized as petty bourgeois.

Memhir Oqbay, a teacher by profession who joined the front in the mid-1970s was assigned to Halewa Sewra. Being aware of the negative way educated people were seen in the EPLF, he stated the level of his education as illiterate, and his roommate 'Sekouf' who was a participant in the illiteracy eradication campaign started to teach him basic Tigrigna alphabets. Those who knew Oqbay as a teacher changed his registration form and made him teach academic subjects. When 'Sekouf' saw Oqbay teaching and writing with a chalk on the blackboard, he could not believe his eyes and left the class and ran away. He was asked why he did that, and he said, "I was embarrassed even to see him." That is why he was given the nickname, 'Sekouf', which means timid. It went to the extent that in normal conversations names of farm tools and names of trees will be raised, and then the peasants would ask the urbanites in a belittling manner, "Do you know what Kerfes is? How about Kli'aw? You do not know that, where do you come from! 'Wedi Akheza' could not put up with that humiliation any more and he asked back, "Do you know Fiat 124?" He added, "Don't disturb us any longer, we keep our Fiat 124, and you keep your

Kerfes." Slowly the situation started to improve.

However, the city boys and the street boys were also making fun of the peasants. 'Wedi Akheza' was a street boy born and raised in Massawa. When they started to call fighters, Massawa boy, Asmara boy, etc, based on the place where the individual grew up, he asked the peasants how they knew who grew up where. They gave him different reasons. He told them, "No, you identify a city boy by his left armpit which is supposed to be hairy." They would ask him, how about us? He would say, "Since the peasants always carry a stick that they lock in their armpit, the hair of the armpit falls and your armpit is bold. And then, you threw away the stick during training and replaced it with a smaller stick that you put on your head, it makes you blubber Kliaw or other tree names and suffocate us."

Because the number of women fighters was much lower than that of the men, it was very difficult for many to find a companion with similar socio-economic class and educational background. In short, the social structuring of the basic unit, that is the squad of the fighters was very mixed but genderwise skewed. Hence, the only common factor binding all of us was nationalism. It was a new society that the organization created, and all fighters carried that burden and had to live in it in unison in order to ascertain national liberation.

As I have mentioned above, on top of the job of a commissar, I was also given an additional task of interrogation. The cases arising in the areas behind the enemy defense lines were mainly dealing with people suspected of spying for Ethiopia, abandoning their units, sexual offences, and a few cases dealing with murder, theft, and financial embezzlement. On top of that there were also cases of individuals who surrender from the ELF or Ethiopia, and POWs. Since there was no department of military training in the south we were also receiving and dispatching new recruits to the training centers in Sahel.

The head of the branch of Halewa Sewra in the areas behind the enemy defense lines had the authority to decide on jail terms ranging from six-months to one year. Only members of the political office or the central leadership of Halewa Sewra had the authority to decide jail terms above that range. The maximum sentence for capital punishment was however passed on Ethiopian spies and on those who committed homicide. However, some of them were given lenient sentences and were made to join the revolution after undergoing a rehabilitation program. As concerns the death sentence that was passed on those who were accused of political crimes and were executed, of the leaders of the Menka'a movement, the death sentences were passed by a judiciary committee selected by the EPLF leadership which composed of Ibrahim Afa, Beraki Gebreselassie, Hasen Humed Amir, Mohamed Saeed Bareh among others. The death penalty which was decided by the committee was approved by the EPLF leadership and was executed on the second half of 1975. Though the execution was already done, later on, in order to legitimize the said sentences of capital punishment, the cases were brought to the First Organizational Congress for approval, in 1977.

As for the members of the Yemeen movement who were arrested after the first organizational congress and were also executed in 1980 – including some remnants of Menaka'a - in a place called Arag, the decision of capital punishment was taken solely by Isaias Afewerki without consulting the EPLF leadership. The EPLF political bureau members were not only excluded from the decision, but also were not aware about the execution of the Yemeen until Teklay Aden (EPLF Central Committee member and the Second man in the Halewa Sewra) revealed the executions of Menka'a and the Yemeen in the Ethiopian Radio after his defection to Ethiopia.

After Teklay Aden revealed the execution of Menka'a and Yemeen, members of the Political Bureau were tasked to propagate against Teklay Aden's statement. At that time Mesfin Hagos member of the Political Bureau asked about the fate of the Yemeen and he was informed by Ali Said (Head of Halewa Sewra) that they were executed by the order of Isaias Afewerki. The Political Bureau members didn't hold Isaias accountable for what he did. At this point Isaias became omnipotent to whom nobody can ask him whatever decisions he made.

Chapter 2. **INITIATING AN OFFENSIVE**

2.1 Liberation of Cities and Strategic Retreat

Based on the First Congress' resolutions which provided for a strategy of liberating people and territories in stages, the EPLF strengthened its military capabilities in order to liberate the cities, and thus took the initiative to liberate towns. The military committee that was led by Ibrahim Afa, and whose members included Petros Solomon and Uqbe Abraha, respectively representing the military training, military intelligence, and weaponry and logistics departments, developed a strategy and planned and executed attacks to liberate a number of towns. The superiority and strength of the EPLF was mainly based on the resourcefulness and dedication of its fighters, driven by the motto, "You stay behind and I will move forward and die first." This was the principal secret of EPLF's victories. With such a dedicated force, military plans were efficiently hitting their targets.

In 1977, Karora, Afabet, Keren and Dekemhare, and also the towns on the Asmara-Massawa road, from Seidici until Edaga were captured by the EPLF. Agordat, Tesseney, Mendefera and Adi Kwala were also liberated by the ELF. The forces of the enemy were demoralized, and reached a stage that they have to run away to save their lives, while for the freedom fighters who were in high spirits, it was a time to advance. After Dekemhare was captured, in an attempt to liberate Segeneiti, there was a fierce battle at Forto against the Ethiopian Army, and many fighters were martyred. In that battle, from among the senior leaders, Weldenkiel Haile, one of the top leaders who were leading the battle was courageously martyred in Segeneiti the town of his birth. It was Weldenkiel Haile through Mebrahtu Zewde who recruited me in Asmara to send recruits to Derfo. Wedi Rebbi, a member of Halewa Sewra stationed behind the frontline area, miraculously came out of the fierce battle without a scratch, but with bullet and shrapnel holes on his jacket and pants. A few days later, following a serious confrontation with enemy, Segeneiti fell to the EPLF. The enemy forces were now restricted to Asmara, Adi Keih, and Massawa. The Ethiopian army in Eritrea brought additional reinforcement from Ethiopia and the Derg enhanced its diplomatic offensive, and appealed for help from the Soviet Union, Cuba and South Yemen, who stood by Ethiopia and supported the regime with human resources and military hardware and equipment.

In order to expand its operations, the branch of Halewa Sewra which was behind the enemy defense lines areas relocated its offices in the Central Bank of Dekemhare and the Rosati building; the branch that was at Addi Rosso became a sub-branch to hold spies and enemy operatives who were being captured, surrendering soldiers and POWs, in order to keep them in the camp until they were dispatched to Sahel. The military strategists of the EPLF were preparing additional support forces around Massawa in preparation for an attack of the port city to make apply and occupy the enemy forces from reinforcing their strong hold in the southern region, and an independent Halewa Sewra unit was also established there. Though the Massawa attack was first planned only to occupy the enemy forces in different zones it went further upto trying to liberate the port city of Massawa.

The battle of Massawa was very tough and it would be difficult to make an assessment of it based on the uneven balance of power. The Massawa offensive to liberate the port city by the EPLF was driven by victories made in liberating other towns, and was unduly influenced by the successes achieved that far. It was pushed by a blind desire to liberate Massawa at any cost, devoid of a thorough study and strategic thinking. During the course of the fierce battle one experienced war veteran and squad leader who fought and led at the battle, abandoned the battle field on his own and surrendered to Halewa Sewra at Addi Rosso. The surrender of an experienced freedom fighter is an indication of the nature and gravity of the battle waged to capture Massawa. Stuck in a salty sea, and suffering from thirst and exposed to the risk of sunstroke that causes loss of direction and disorientation, and at the same time facing heavy artillery bombardment and the smell of gunpowder, the said combatant had to leave the battle scene and report at Adi Rosso.

The battle for Massawa was the time during which one of the commanders, Gerezgiher Wuchu, said, "It seems the enemy has brought arms that scare us, so go ahead and bombard us together." It was a battle that was led by the likes of Adhanom Gebremariam. The Salina battle in Massawa was on the side of the EPLF fought with light weapons against the enemy's Stalin Organs and other heavy equipment that is to say a Kalashnikov against a tank. In short, it was an uneven battle that took the lives of so many brave fighters. It was a battle where many graduates of the eighth cadre school and members of 'Falul' (the democratic movement in ELF labeled anarchist) were martyred. Some political critics argue that the battle of Massawa was deliberately planned by the EPLF to get rid of the Falul; however, the losses were not only affecting the Falul alone but it included EPLF fighters among them cadres some of whom were candidates for membership of the secret party's leadership.

But the second, and the most difficult battle that challenged the freedom fighters was to capture a town for the first time and be able to master the skill to administer its civilian population. Leaving aside some shortcomings, the forces of the EPLF, in addition to the dedication and readiness of its members to sacrifice, was fit enough. But what is now taking the country downhill is its inability to master the skills, its inexperience or lack of expertise in administering civilians. The current sickness has its source when EPLF began to administer the liberated towns.

According to the unwritten policy of the EPLF leadership, the yardstick for appointment of personnel to administrative posts is not level of skills of an individual but one's loyalty to the organization in sort the secret party. The educated members seen as petty bourgeois were treated with suspicion, hence less educated but loyal members of the organization would be assigned to leadership positions and supervise the more educated staff as their subordinates. Most of the time, such leaders hinder the more educated and skilled members and disable them from being more productive in their specific areas of expertise. Thus, owning to such practice talented and skilled people became frustrated and their work hampered. The leadership of the EPLF interferes in everything and is unreliable as it adopted a dictatorial system of governance, and became oppressive and monopolistic. Such pattern of governance was witnessed during the early days of the administration in the liberated towns. There was a time when wounded senior leaders came to Dekemhare for treatment and one would observe them engage in drinking and prostitution with those who were administering towns the likes of Teklai 'Aden', and because of their behavior the wounded senior leaders were expelled from the town. In short, apart from lack of able leadership the military organizational structure being top down and regimented was also unsuitable to administer civilian population.

In mid 1978, I was sent from Dekemhare to the eighth round of the cadre school at Menteble. Haile Derue a member of the Politbureau, and Ahmed Al Qaisi, a member of the Central Committee were in charge of the cadre school that was known as the "Department of Awareness Raising" and were managing the political education program. As we were learning political economy and dialectical materialism, focusing on economic and political education as well as in depth coverage of the history of the Eritrean struggle, the enemy started to push heavily, a few of us were immediately sent back to our regular places of duty whereas all the rest participants at the cadre school were sent to reinforce the Massawa front. The enemy mobilized all its resources and did all it could to undo all the losses it previously suffered. Russian military advisers joined the ranks of the enemy. The gains made by our gallant forces during earlier victories began to crumble as towns were re-captured by the enemy one after the other.

Such deteriorating situation left an unbearable scar on the back and psyche of the EPLF. Mehari 'Wedi Sheka', member of the Central Committee, Administrator of the southern region, and senior commander of the Adi Keih front was martyred at the battle of Adi Keih. Like the rest of the towns, it was not possible for the EPLF to capture Adi Keih. After assessing the changes in the balance of power which was tipping in favor of the enemy, the leadership of the EPLF evaluated the military setbacks that it suffered, and decided to reposition its defense lines. The strategic retreat was caused by the change in the balance of power due to, among other reasons, the external intervention by the Soviet Union and its satellites (Cuba and Yemen in particular), who came to the rescue of Ethiopia with physical and logistical support. The strategic withdrawal which was a courageous and efficient decision was among the most significant and historic decisions taken in the history of the Eritrean armed struggle.

At the cadre school, Haile Derue started the brief, stating that some of us will see our hair raised: "we will withdraw from all the towns in stages and we will return to our defensive rear base area of Sahel. We will engage the enemy in a place and time of our choice; we will revert to our mountains until the river storm passes. Therefore, except those who are needed to return to their formal duty stations, the rest will be mobilized and sent to the Massawa front." He then saw off all the participants of the eighth round of the Cadre School to the Massawa Front save those few like me who returned to their normal duty stations.

When I returned to Dekemhare from the Cadre School, I found our members busy searching for a place to retreat to. They ultimately decided to move down to Mai Habar and were preparing for the move. Musa was transferred to Keren, and the unit led by Rezene Seyoum went down to Mai Habar. A short time later I was called by the headquarters for a meeting and I returned to Sahtewil via Keren.

I came across unusual andunique information during my brief stay in Keren. While sitting in his office looking at the desk of Musa, the chief of Halewa Sewra in Keren, I found a document entitled, 'The Berlin Manifesto' and I became curious and read it. I immediately found out that it was not the same as the copy that was read to all EPLF members. This version was only distributed to members of EPRP and it was very detailed. The purpose of the Berlin meeting to my understanding was meant to buy time so as to carry out the strategic retreat without military offensives and the document contained details of negotiations going on with the Derg through the mediation of the East German government in East Berlin. Immediately my thoughts went to Isaac Rezene and what 'Btsay' Goitom Berhe confided in him about the secret party of Isaias and his clique.

Towards the end of the seventies when I stayed in Dekemhare, the squabbles between the ELF and EPLF were reflected on the engagement with the enemy. The ability of the military was divided and was being pulled towards two directions and logistic coordination was stretched and pressured the military leadership. Sometimes the shameful confrontation was escalating to military engagement at times ending up into civil wars. For instance, in the mid eastern section of Eritrea, in a place called Tselam, some members of the EPLF mass organizations were taken prisoners by the ELF and they were being moved to Barka through Mai Ayni. A battle took place between the two fronts, and the fact that a battle ensued in Mai Ayini and the prisoners were snatched from the hands of the ELF, made the battle a special case. It was at that time that one of the rescued prisoners, Aboy Abraham Tsadeq, who was taken by the ELF in Derfo, was freed and was able to see the light of day. It was after several years since Derfo that we met in Dekemhare, and expressing his joy he said, "Well done oh son of the blessed woman, who can deny you of your courage, we saw those monkeys who were pretending to be lions and who made us suffer in holes, run away? Thank you."

It was a bad scene that one would not wish to see. Brothers and sisters, childhood friends and neighbors, hailing from the same place across from each other, close people who are only separated by a fence wall, employees and employers, children of one country, a country that both members of the two organizations martyred for their country-ending like this-killing each other! Why? On which boundary did they disagree? ELF is reactionary, EPLF is counter-revolutionary, and for such slogans one shoots at his brother and sister from a barrel of a gun. Wrong. May God the omnipotent reject the Eritrean leaders! Such were the sentiments of popular anger and disappointment.

With external intervention, the situation worsened, the balance of power was tilted in favor of the enemy and we were compelled to retreat to May Habar from Dekemhare, so that we can lean on a place that the enemy will not dare approach. The Halewa Sewra unit that was in the environs of Massawa retreated to Ginda'e and the one in Mai Habar also retreated to Ginda'e and the two were consolidated. Ali Bekhit Awelkher 'Awer' took charge of everything as the leader of the consolidated unit behind the enemy defense lines. I became a support officer and stayed there, while the other leaders of behind the enemy line area together with those Halewa Sewra members that had moved to Makalasi retreated to our base area in Sahel.

In such a difficult time of retreat, members of Zero 6 carried out an unsuccessful operation inside Asmara and Abraha "Tagliero" who was part of the operation was suspected and sent to Halewa Sewra in Ginda'e for interrogation. The operation was aimed at taking diamonds that were claimed by Abraha "Tagliero" to be in a shop owned by an enemy operative in "Campocitato," since Abraha "Tagliero" was the central person of the operation, and the said diamond was not found, he was suspected that he had hidden the diamonds and thus sent to Halewa Sewra for interrogation.

I investigated the case and found out that Abraha "Tagliero"'s tip was based on probability and not on concrete information and I believed his statement that he passed the tip based on national interest and had him released. According to his preference, he was sent to Sahel to continue to travel abroad. Since he was a famous person, and during a casual conversation I asked him why he is called Tagliero. He told me that he had once kidnapped a son of a rich Italian guy named Tagliero and took him to a famous bandit (shifta) named Tekle

Gilagabir for upkeep and demanded a ransom that was paid to him after which he released Tagliero's son. Thereafter "Tagliero" became his nickname.

Abraha "Tagliero" was so greedy about money he always tried shortcuts to get rich. He once claimed to have a map of a location where treasures were buried during the Italian era and he made many people dig in the environs of Barborella on the northern outskirts of Asmara, promising to pay the people after they find the treasure--they didn't find anything and their efforts were wasted.

The members of Zero 6 who knew about the past life and stories of thefts that are attributed to 'Tagliero' assumed their failed attempt to find the diamonds was because Abraha 'Tagliero' had taken them for himself and was the reason that he was sent to Halewa Sewra. However, following interrogation 'Tagliero' was cleared of the accusation and he was sent to Sahel with the retreating forces to proceed to Sudan. He reached Jelahanti where the war disabled camp was located, and as he was there, in his attempt to save a generator that was being carried away by flood he was swept away by the flood along with the generator he tried to save.

After evaluating the fluid situation around Ginda'e, the departmental leaders and military force commanders withdrew from the town in an orderly and organized manner. Fortuitously, I met both my immediate elder brother Amanuel and my childhood friend Bitweded Abraha in a meeting in Ginda'a. Amanuel was wounded on his back during the battles of Massawa and he was recuperating. It was during this meeting that he told me that our younger brother, Mussie, was martyred in 1976 at a place called Genfelom during the battles that were waged to liberate Keren. After the Ginda'a meetings, I left towards Filfil and Amanuel headed towards Maamide. Before we had a chance to meet again Amanuel was martyred in 1979 at Bet Humed in the environs of Nakfa.

During the difficult period of withdrawal, I stayed in northern Bahri with the EPLF units that operated behind enemy lines. The area is lush, full of trees and plantations, with rivers crisscrossing it, and surrounded by a range of mountains that the enemy could not easily penetrate. Halewa Sewra started its operation in Awhitet, an hour's walk from Filfil in a camp that was established by Ashaal 'Wedi' Zere.

Tsegereda 'Gual Signora', the girl with the braided hair, continued her march with me during the withdrawal. She was appointed as a squad nurse and took care of the EPLF members and the prisoners.

Our friendship developed into a love story and it became obvious to the squad members. However, since there was no evidence of asexual act that can be proved, there was nothing to complain about. But the love between two of us flowered and reached a level where we could not contain and hide it anymore. Neither of us felt that intense love in our lives before; maybe it is because we couldn't openly express our feelings and consummate our desires. Whenever we found privacy in seclusion, we considered it a special opportunity as if it was only given to us and not to the rest of humanity and we enjoyed it very much.

Within one month after we arrived at Awhitet, I fell ill with malaria and Tsgereda Gual Signora was never that happy. She didn't want me to suffer of illness, but she was happy she could keep me in her lap and give me warmth. When she made round to the other patients, she would be in a hurry to finish with them so that she could return fast to be with me. I was also frequently disturbing my colleagues demanding that they call her for me.

No one is able to deny you the natural things that you want and wish for as long as you are in this world. And since the Almighty God doesn't watch a human being he created in his image to suffer without helping him, soon the EPLF adopted a policy allowing relationship between a man and a woman. The act that was not a crime or a sin, and that was blessed by God, an act that used to be a punishable crime, and that touched the moral and loyalty of many freedom fighters, finally regained its legitimacy and was allowed. Such love relation was special and different within the EPLF.

It was not only the organizational activities that were centralized in the EPRP. Isaias managed to centralize and control even the individual life of ordinary fighters. Lovers were forced to notify the leadership about their private love affairs just because Isaias wanted to know private acts or movements of each individual freedom fighter. Needless to say, a private love affair should not under normal circumstances concern anyone else apart from those involved in it.

When Tsgereda Gual signora was asked to describe the new situation relative to the tight situation that prevailed before, she said, "Two things affected me in my life, the first is in dealing with what you want and wish for but it is denied to you, and the pressure it creates inside you and the satisfaction you get by overcoming the challenges one faces to realize it in your own way. The other is when they tell you that you are allowed and you do what you couldn't do until then openly, to be free and do whatever you like in this world openly, to satisfy your desires, and the satisfaction that freedom gives you is immeasurable. To stay in the gardens of Fifil, eating oranges and stay in the embrace of the man you love and be seen by others was something that doesn't cross the mind. The revolution didn't make us offer personal sacrifices only, but it also made us live, think and behave unlike human beings."

At the beginning of the strategic retreat while I was in the northern Bahri region, Estifanos Bruno, a member of the Central Committee, was administrator of behind the enemy lines under the overall authority of Sebhat Efrem, who was a member of the Political Bureau and Head of the Department of Public Administration. After a short period of time, Ali Bekhit Awelkhier 'Awer' who stayed as a commander of behind the enemy line area of Halewa Sewra in Awhitet, was transferred to the central Halewa Sewra and I replaced him as a leader there. I was appointed to be in charge and Tekhlay 'Aden' a member of the Central Committee who was directing the office under Ali Saed Abdella introduced me to the members in that area. Tekhlay 'Aden' worked hard to improve the activities of the Department by changing the image and structure of the Department, including the process of reporting of cases about people accused so as to make it accountable, and he also introduced other major improvements in the system. He would look at reports critically and make constructive comments on them and this way he made a qualitative change in the system. In short, Teklay 'Aden' was a person who contributed immensely in the operational modalities of Halewa Sewra. On top of his work in Halewa Sewra, Tekhlay 'Aden' worked directly under Isaias as a head of the committee of the party in the base area in Sahel.After I found the document of the Hidden Party, though I tried to follow the movements of the leaders more attentively, there was no particular incidence or movement that I noticed, and there was no member of the party in my squad. But in my mind, I kept the conviction of its existence.

Towards the end of 1978, Estifanos Afewerki 'Bruno' from the leadership of EPRP called me to his office in Sabur and informed me of the existence of the secret party that operated within the EPLF. He also told me that it was a Marxist-Leninist vanguard party that directs and leads the struggle. He further told me that beginning with Isaias, all members of the Political Bureau and most of the Central Committee members were also members of that party. He disclosed to me that I have been nominated to be a member and that he has been monitoring and studying me to see if I qualify for membership and that he found out that I was cleared or vetted. Therefore, after disclosing that to me, he asked me if I had suspicions about the party. Based on the document that I saw in Keren at Musa Naib's desk, after I explained to him that I knew about it, he told me that secrets have to be well kept. He then gave me the constitution of the party to read and instructed me to discuss it with other recent recruits of the party and he explained the structure and workings of the party. I was subsequently assigned to a local cell and started to carry out party activities.

After the strategic withdrawal, there appeared many new developments. The EPLF moved from its stronghold in Fah-Bleqat, and retreated towards west in a place called A'arag, in Sahel, where it established its defenses. The units that were stationed behind the enemy lines also retreated to places that the enemy could not easily penetrate with confidence. In the liberated and semi-liberated areas, the Kebele structure that was formed by the Derg was dismantled and replaced with 'Challenge Committees'in order for the people to self-administer themselves. But following the strategic withdrawal of the EPLF, the Derg replaced the EPLF committees with the former Kebele structure. The enemy utilized the Kebele system to gather intelligence information and it took action on members of the mass organizations through the Kebeles or similar other civic organizations of its own. It was during this time that the EPLF distributed leaflets in the towns and villages, as a warning to those structures that have become tools of the enemy, the leaflets read, "The Derg's Kebeles will eventually be cleaned like chaff." Based on the warning, while many abandoned the Kebeles that were formed by the enemy and went down to Bahri, the EPLF took measures against those who did not heed to the warning and remained in the service of the enemy. Those who were caught were sent to Halewa Sewra and after interrogation they were punished accordingly and were confined to the liberated areas.

In addition to the conflict that was raging against Ethiopia, the conflict between the EPLF and the ELF reached on its highest stage. The EPLF was convinced that the balance of power had shifted in its favor and prepared itself to take advantage of the situation. The EPLF directed its entire media offensive towards campaigning to discredit the ELF before the attack. It was evident that the end of the ELF was fast approaching.

In foreign affairs, the intervention of the Soviet Union was taken as a critical factor in the war between the occupying army and the army of liberation, and protest demonstrations were held against external intervention inside and outside Eritrea, and particularly in Washington, DC where a number of young Eritreans carried out a hunger strike. However, the Soviet intervention has also had negative impact on the Eritrean movement. The EPLF and the Eritreans for Liberation in North America (EFLNA) strongly differed as regards the characterization of the Soviet Union. Whereas EFLNA defined the Soviet Union as "Social Imperialist and Revisionist", the EPLF on the other hand refrained from labeling the Soviet Union at all. The USA based mass organization condemned the EPLF and labeled it as reactionary and thereby terminating the organic relationship with the front. With the exception of a few who kept their loyalty to the EPLF, the majority of the members withdrew their membership and support from the association.

The difference was based on the ideological viewpoint of the two sides. While even the fighters who were receiving the bombs and artillery, and tank fire on their backs, who were either killed or wounded didn't hastily describe the Soviet Union as revisionist, those in the mass organization who lived in the comfort of the western countries and didn't experience even a runaway shrapnel were removed from reality and engaged in theoretical and philosophical discourse. Ultimately the mass organization (EFLNA) hastily severed its relations with the EPLF, instead of patiently pursuing the dialogue option. When I explained the situation to the members of my unit, Gebrehiwet 'Wedi Belih' remarked, "We are left alone without antagonizing the Soviet Union, what will happen if we openly challenge them? It is better for them to say to the Soviets to give more bombs to our enemies so that they can do a better job in bombingus."

After the strategic withdrawal, the EPLF employed all its human and material resources as well as ingenuity in order to change the balance of power in its favor. The clandestine cells of the mass organizations in Asmara started to penetrate the Derg Government structures and were supplying the front with vital military and other intelligence related information. The clandestine cell organizations went as far as subverting the information that was being passed by enemy spies to the enemy in the torture house of Mariam Gmbi regarding the activities of EPLF clandestine mass organizations. There was also no problem for the EPLF to kidnap suspected spies of the

Derg and to smuggle them out of the towns and take them to the liberated areas under our control.

Dedicated members of the clandestine mass organizations like Afewerki Teweldemedhin (Bureacracy), Rusom Teklemariam (Tarzan) and others played a critical and invaluable role in the intelligence gathering activities. Documentary material that could be used to write the history of the heroic deeds of those martyrs who played an important and critical role in the intelligence gathering and analysis is not in short supply. On my part, though I took an initiative to write about Afewerki Teweldemedhin, his code name Bureacracy, who terrorized the enemy, I was nonetheless unable to fulfill my wish because the necessary reference information is kept secret by the PFDJ regime of Isaias Afwerki and is off limits; thus the untold stories of such unsung heroes of our revolution who contributed greatly in the Eritrean struggle remains deeply hidden in the secret archives of the ruling party. This is chiefly because Isaias Afewerki does not want the names of heroes to be known to the public. He does not want any person other than himself to be recognized as heroes in Eritrean history books, let alone to allow institutions and streets named after them.

After I was assigned to the Halewa Sewra behind the enemy-line areas, I tried to make the intelligence information gathering activities more efficient by setting up sub-branch units in A'nagule, near Weki-Zager, and another unit in Adi Rosso, in order to carry out counter-intelligence activities and to collect information from inside the enemy circles. These sub-branches faced no problem in identifying former mass organization members who became recruited as enemy spies following the strategic withdrawal and submitting their names to the front for action. After studying the situation around the A'nagule branch diligently, I made the surrounding area to be the responsibility of the central branch, and disbanded the A'nagule unit and in its place set up another sub-branch in Foro in the eastern coastal area to look after similar cases of betrayal and becoming enemy spies that occurred following our strategic withdrawal from the area around Foro. I organized the sub-branches to be responsible in their respective zones.

The cases from Asmara and its surrounding villages were directly transferred to the main branch of Halewa Sewra behind the enemy-lines in Awhitet. The case of one suspected spy who was kidnapped from Asmara confirmed that the network of EPLF intelligence was well established inside areas under the authority of the Derg regime and efficiently performed intelligence gathering activities there. In the case of the above noted accused, reports about EPLF clandestine mass organization members that he passed to the torture center of Mariam Gmbi, that is to say, headed by Ashagrie the chief of enemy interrogation unit, was presented to the accused as evidence. The fact that his handwritten reports to the enemy about the mass organization's activities would reach the hand of the EPLF fighters from the secret dossier and records of the enemy, didn't occur to him. He was bewildered realizing that no action was taken against those members of the mass organizations he accused substantiatedwith concrete incriminating reports. On the contrary, warnings were given to him by the EPLF to desist from the spying activities he was engaged in. He did not heed to the warning of the front and when complaints against him mounted, he was kidnapped and sent to Awhitet for interrogation. But it was evident that because there were no Eritreans trusted by the enemy in Mariam Gmbi the information sources from there must be an Ethiopian.

Before I travelled down to the Halewa Sewra central office to make a general evaluation of the activities, I personally observed the situation of the units in the southern and eastern regions. The southern units had no problem because they were camped in a location that the enemy cannot reach easily and were carrying out their activities with ease. But the location of the eastern unit of Halewa Sewra and units of other departments that had retreated to the area worried me because I found the area not to be suitable. The location was situated in a place in which the enemy could easily access it and attack from the port city of Massawa using the coastal sea route of the Red Sea. After I participated in the assessment meeting of Halewa Sewra, I wanted to check the situation of the units; I went to Port Sudan, and then arranged with the naval units of the EPLF and sailed with the navy and through the eastern plains of Dankalia Ireturned to the station behind the enemy-line areas.

I sailed from Swakin the ancient port south of Port Sudan. Arafat was one of the smallest boats in the fleet that transported arms and supplies to Dankalia. Whenever a ship cut the sea and passed close to it, the waves that are created almost tipped it over. When the captain of Arafat detects large ship approaching he changes the course and stayed off the reaches of the waves created by the passing ship. Arafat was a boat made for short journey and fishing. The sailors, named Ami Farah and Vasco, were highly experienced seamen and they know the depth of the water by its colors and smell, and could sail using compasses and sextants, and they pilot the boat by checking the location of islands and the coastal hills in daytime, and at nighttime they sailed by referring to stars as their guide. The sailors with whom I traveled gained their profession through experience and not through schooling but anyone travelling with them would feel very confident and secure.

The trip took seven days and Ami Farah was our captain. During the first night let alone those of us without sailing experience even people like our colleague Ibrahim Sa'id, the one in charge of the health section of behind the enemy-line areas, with his vast experience in sailing did not manage to sleep. We couldn't overcome sleep and we were just taking short naps. Since I was traveling by sea for the first time, and because I could not swim, I stayed alert for fear of rolling over to the sea. On the third day of our journey, Vasco detected a ship from a distance, and he turned the direction of the boat by 90 degrees to escape the risk of being washed by water caused by the waves that the spotted ship creates. Immediately after the ship passed he returned the boat to its original direction.

In the first three days, the sea was calm as if it was told not to move, but on the fourth day it became rough, and the waves splashed against us and water started to be accumulated in the boat. All of us carried pails and started to scoop the water out. But since the waves increased their rage, what we scooped out literally became scooping the sea with a pail and didn't remedy the situation. All of us were worried; the only ones with no signs of concern on their faces were only the children of the sea, Am Farah, Vasco and Ibrahim. Vasco assured us that there was no problem and he switched on a small generator and pumped out some of the water on the boat and that had pushed the boat down. When he stopped the generator, we picked pails to empty the water, but he told us to save our energy as he was also saving the fuel of the generator and we should wait because we couldn't do much. We were a bit comforted.

On the fifth day, the sea calmed and the journey was smoother; when we reached near the Dahlak islands, Vasco and one of the sailors went down and brought Kalashnikovs and Machine-guns and distributed it to the fighters. They assigned us positions on the boat and announced, "We are around Dahlak, the large island on the distance is Dahlak Kebir where the Russians are stationed, they do not move far from their location, but as fighters, we have to be ready just in case."

It was a new experience for me; out from the guerilla ambush tactics against 'Wedo Geba', those who surrender to the enemy and direct their guns against freedom fighters, I switched to the guerilla tactics of the sea in the boat of Am Farah and his sailors. Again the sea was calm and on the sixth day when we crossed the 'Gulf of Zula' we saw an Ethiopian Patrol ship berthed and we went far towards east and on the seventh day we reached Dankalia, at Kor Humer, and Am Farah and his sailors berthed the boat on the harbor of Gela'alo.

As we disembarked from the boat, after days on the sea we were unable to walk straight on the land, totally disoriented and took us a few minutes to adjust. In Kor Humer, we rested in a straw hut for a little while and after drinking water from a goat skin, we left Gela'alo travelling on the vehicles that were there to transport the supplies of goods and reached the area were our units were positioned.

When I reached the east, I met with the leaders in the area and evaluated the situation of the unit, and we carried out surveillance on the surrounding areas, and to avoid losses, we studied and decided on the locations to which the unit should retreat in case the enemy carries out an attack. Following that I called a general meeting of the members and after evaluating the situation, I gave the necessary directives and continued towards the south. I conducted similar meetings in Ali-Gedde and gave similar directives and in a matter of two weeks I returned to my camp in Awhitet.

As Chief of the Department of Halewa Sewra and secretary of EPRPin the Sahel defense lines, Tekhlay 'Aden' had considerable influence on the fighters of the Sahel region and became popular. At that time, he had a good physical fitness in relation to his age, and he was an avid reader. On top of being industrious he always came up with new ideas and pushed for change. He was loved by all fighters be it the members of Halewa Sewra or the other fighters in the base area. In 1981 when I and my colleagues were casually listening to Radio Ethiopia, we couldn't believe when we discovered that Teklay 'Aden' had surrendered to the enemy. It was an incident that we never expected. Though the reason for his surrender was not clearly known, those who know the character of Isaias Afewerki, suspect that the surrender was a result of Tekhlay's popularity among the fighters and his strong relations with them. They argue that Tekhlay Aden's popularity may have threatened Isaias' power base and that might have been the reason for his disagreement with Isaias and his surrender. There were talks about his difference with Isaias regarding a few issues, and Isaias's often quoted statement, "I don't understand where all this show off will lead to," was considered a threat to Tekhlay 'Aden'.

After the surrender of Tekhlay Aden, many members of our mass organizations started to escape from Asmara and go to Sabur in northern Bahri. Among those coming was an Ethiopian first sergeant who was said to have surrendered to the EPLF and was sent to Halewa Sewra. When asked the reason for his surrender, he said that the mass organizations advised him to escape before the enemy takes steps on him. The officer was working as registrar at Mariam Gmbi, and was bribed by the mass organizations and was feeding them information from inside Mariam Gmbi. He was the Ethiopian who passed the report that the Eritrean spy submitted to the Derg against the mass organization members to the front resulting the kidnapping of that particular spy.

Afewerki 'Bureaucracy' was one of the mass organization members who escaped and went down to northern Bahri after they were exposed. Bureaucracy's activities were exposed by the enemy and he reached a level where he couldn't operate anymore. At that time, based on the promise given to him to be escorted overseas the Ethiopian sergeant who was a registrar at Mariam Gmbi was sent to the headquarters of Halewa Sewra in Sahel and then left for Sudan to travel further abroad as a refugee. A few members of the mass organizations who were either advanced in age or couldn't become combatants for different reasons were sent overseas by the foreign office of the EPLF. At that time a football player of the Hamasien team Bokretsion and Bureaucracy were sent overseas.

The relations between the EPLF and the ELF deteriorated further, reaching by 1981 into military confrontation igniting the battles in Semhar and Dankalia in the south eastern plains of Eritrea. The combatants of the ELF abandoned their positions at first heading to the surroundings of Embasoira Mountain, but later retreated to western Eritrea. The participation of theTigray People's Liberation Front (TPLF) in the battles against the ELF made the balance of power to tilt in favor of the EPLF. The fierce battles continued causing the combatants of the ELF to retreat from east to west, and ultimately entered Sudanese territories. They left Eritrean territories and camped in Karakon and Tahday inside the Sudan. The founder of the liberation war of Eritrea Jebha (ELF) was thus pushed out of Eritrean territories leading people to say that the prophecy of Isaias which stated that, 'Jebha will wither away' was fulfilled, leaving thereafter only one front in   Eritrea.

When I was in northern Bahri, the cases that were attended by Halewa Sewra in the areas behind the enemy defense lines mostly involved enemy spies who were organized by the Derg under the mass associations, be it Kebele or other youth and women associations, etc, who were paid money for their services of providing information on the activities of the EPLF clandestine activities. There were also cases of those who either surrendered or were captured, from Ethiopian enemy soldiers or ELF combatants, and other prisoners whose cases included murder, theft, etc.

There were also cases concerning EPLF instigated land reform and adjudication over property. Based on its socialist orientation regarding land policies, and its conviction that the poor peasants should end up being major beneficiaries, the EPLF implemented land reform in the villages under its control thereby causing resentment by those who posses big farming lands. The affected sectors of the society began to sabotage the reform by creating obstacles in its implementation. These people were also put in detention by our Department. When the EPLF withdrew from previously liberated villages, those people who felt aggrieved by EPLF land reform raised Ethiopian flags and enthusiastically received the Derg, and became ready tools of intelligence for the Ethiopians. The enemy was able to use them as tools by putting them in the Kebeles and other mass organizations that it formed.

In such a situation the fighters tried to fight it with whatever means at their disposal in order to protect the EPLF from enemy intelligence activities. And to cultivate a healthy relation between the fighters and the people initiatives were taken to educate the leaders and the fighters through seminars and the Halewa Magazine the Department published. However, some leaders crossed the boundaries of authority they were given and by going over surveillance, were obtaining false testimonies through coercion and force on the suspected persons sending them to Halewa Sewra. Such cases were re-investigated and those who were found to have been forced to give false testimonies but were innocent were released and a special circular was sent to all leaders instructing them not to use force and coercion while interrogating an accused person. But since there were losses inflicted on the fighters by the enemy and that putting pressure on them, there were times when leaders reached a point where they violated guidelines and took individual decision.

Tekie Zewengel, one of the public administrators in the surrounding of She'eb Gedged who suspected a woman of being an enemy tool and he established a case against her through coercion and sent her to Halewa Sewra. Since he violated the standard guidelines concerning interrogations, that were spelt out in a circular, and since that resulted in consequences, that were unjust he was brought to Halewa Sewra. His shortcomings were a result of his concern for national interest and he had no personal interest in what he did. Therefore he was made to stay with the members of the unit until his case was investigated, and a decision was made to punish him with watering and cultivating the garden for two months. The case was explained to the woman and she was asked to forgive the wrong done to her, and she parted saying, "My sons, you are going through hardships for all of us, dry wood cause live wood to burn, I have forgiven you." Tekie Zewengel didn't delay in escaping in the middle of his punishment and was on his way to surrender to Ethiopia in Asmara when he was caught in A'rgolo in the environs of Asmara.

Later on, it was confirmed, the reason for his attempt to surrender was not the punishment that was decided on him. When moving to educate and agitate the people, the members of the mass department, as needed, they moved individually or as a team, in two or three people. Tekie Zewengel was in charge of the unit in the capacity of a commissar. Most of the members of the unit knew the language and culture of the surroundings and Tekie Zewengel, before becoming a fighter, was a teacher in Ginda'a and he knew the language and culture of the surroundings very well, he was a cadre who has nurtured acceptance.

When he was educating the people, many times he was accompanied by a girl from Keren named Haregu. Once Haregu told Tekie Zewengel that she was pregnant, and he was scared, but being an Asmara boy, he tried to find a way out. Heregu's belly was growing larger by the day and to avoid detection by the unit members, he started to send her alone or take her along with him. One day, Ahmed Sheker a dedicated member of the mass organization who used to sneak out of Ginda'a and meet with him, went to Asmara and brought him a stretch cloth to hold a belly. Haregu put on the stretch cloth and she felt good. But until when can such a trick serve? Whenever Tekie Zewengel looked at Haregu's belly, he must have been seeing the baby inside. Eight months passed without the members of the unit noticing the pregnancy and Haregu asked for permission to see her parents and went to Keren.

Haregu reached home and took off her gears, changed her clothes to blend with the civilian population, braided her hair and looked like a beautiful bride. Soon the stretch was thrown away. The care of her parents was so good she resembled her younger sister. After a month, she went to the maternity hospital in Keren as a civilian and delivered her baby. The little baby girl that resembled Wedi Zewengel was born. Haregu, returned to the plains of She'eb to resume her struggle before she recuperated enough. Her mother didn't wait long, she took the baby that her father hasn't seen yet, through Sudan and sent her to her aunties overseas.

Tekie Zewengel was restless when he stayed with Halewa Sewra. It is difficult for someone who is used to work to stay in one place without work. Because of that, though he was passing his time reading books that were given to him, it was evident that there was something bothering him though it was not possible to say exactly what. The natural sexual urge that caused the accidental pregnancy, in a place where it is not only impossible to have seclusion, but difficult to admit that someone had sexual intercourse, had created pressure on him. After he was caught in A'rgolo around Asmara when he attempted to surrender to the enemy and he was brought back to Halewa Sewra, he disclosed that his frustration was because of the baby who was sent overseas before he could see her and that was the undisclosed reason that remained unexposed until his capture.

Coercion to force a testimony under duress during interrogation was not applied on civilians alone; it was also often practiced on fighters. Before we left for the training camp from Zager, Geza'e the one who brought me news about my friend Michael Barba, and also was part of the group going to the training camp who went as far as She'ab Gedged with me, I never met him again until he was accused of spying and brought to Awhitet with three others. I found the case absurd. Geza'e whom the Derg members gave trouble to, and was not able to work in the city and had to escape to avoid them and join the struggle, after years of struggle alongside those who didn't know each other in the city, testified that the enemy sent them to carry out intelligence activities against the EPLF and were brought to Awhitet. I couldn't understand the case at all.

After reading their accusation documents, I was astounded when I went to the place where they were kept to meet them in person and found their legs and hands swollen and wrapped in gauze. I called Tsgereda Gual Signora and asked her to give them medical attention and to be kept under guard. I asked about Michael 'Forma' who was accused with them and they told me he escaped and went to the Sudan. I carried the files and went to Estifanos Bruno, the administrator of the area, and explained the matter to him. We agreed that I should handle the case myself because it was serious and that the people who interrogated them violently should be punished. The case was investigated, and found that the accused had no relation at all with the enemy. The issue was a misunderstanding between city boys and country boys where the leaders of the regiment claimed that the city boys look down on them and are not obedient. They falsely accused the city boys, claiming that their aim of joining the revolution was in order to sabotage it from within, and therefore severely beat them and only stopped beating them after the accused were forced to admit of being enemy spies when they in reality were not. Since the allegation was very serious, the accused were sent to a central location where they were encouraged and rehabilitated and released.

I asked Geza'e about the case and he said, "The case was physics." I interrupted him "what?" He said, "Artillery works based on numbers and physics, but those people count based on hills and trees, and we couldn't understand each other, which is the cause of the conflict. And that Michael 'Forma' guy was crazy, he used to tell them that he will insert the artillery bombs in their mouth, or their bottom, he used to say things beyond their comprehension, it is good he was out quick enough, they would have reached a level of killing each other." He was silent. I asked again, "I don't understand what you said about physics?" He said, "Oh Tsegu, you have become like them! Physics is... Forma and Wedi Halima..." He laughed hysterically, "by the way, I confused you, and I meant to say Chemistry." He laughed again.

"We trusteded in those people as our national leaders and we did everything they asked us to do but they never accepted us as national fighters. They didn't give us a chance to improve on their directives by adding the little that we know; it was just Do as We Say. And Forma would tell them, this is not like milking a cow, an RPG bomb unlike the bullet, is light on its tail and heavy on the head, and when it is forced the wind will push the tail and pull it backwards... and it sways a little against the direction of the wind, when the wind blows towards the right, the bomb will pull backwards and your target sways to the left and the opposite if the wind is blowing to the left. But a bullet is light and wind sways it fully and it follows the path of the wind--he tells them that but they could not understand him. That is physics. As for Chemistry, you know the difference of views was between Forma and Wedi Halima that is the case." Engliz who was a football player withthe Hamassien team, who was with the accused, explains it in the following words, "We admitted we were spies in order to relieve ourselves from the continuous beating and torture otherwise we would have ended up dead."

'Wedi Halima' and the others were brought to Halewa Sewra and were given the necessary punishment. I gathered the battalion that was stationed in the surroundings of Solomuna and explained the situation in detail, and told them to learn from the mistakes of the regiment leaders. I calmed the situation by explaining that there was no enemy infiltration at all and that they should continue their struggle with confidence.

2.2 Covert Operations in the Belly of the Enemy

I was among the first members of Halewa Sewra who entered Asmara on the day of liberation of the city. Based on the directives we received, we went straight to the interrogation centre to Marian Gmbi to carry out our activities. On the corridor walls of Mariam Gmbi, I recognized the picture of a person whom I knew and who was executed by the Derg. The caption read, **'An important traitor and criminal'**. The picture was lined along with similar pictures of mass organization members on whom similar actions of execution were taken; my body became numb when I saw the pictures. We picked the picture from the wall and took it to the car which brought us there. We took full control of the documents that we found at Mariam Gmbi and left security guards to secure the place after we took two large files along with us and went to our place of work.

The dedicated clandestine city fighter was suspected by the enemy and was under strict surveillance. The enemy wanted to apprehend him with concrete evidence and he was caught in Dire Dawa while he was at a reception planning to talk to an enemy recruited double agent of both the EPLF and the enemy. Present in the lobby of the hotel were people whom he had already placed on his radar suspecting them of being security personnel of the Derg. He suspected their movements and he retreated back exited and started to run away from the hotel, but they run after him and shot him in the hand and he fell down about hundred meters away from the hotel.

This dedicated member of the clandestine mass organizationwas a handsome guy who grew up in Addis Ababa, well known for his elegance, and he possessed mastery of the Amharic language and excellent knowledge about the history and culture of the society. He had many friends from among members of the Ethiopian navy and air force. He had no problem moving around Ethiopian provinces and Eritrea, and he was an adventurous but secretive person. He was operating from a house camouflaged within a laundry business. He would spend nights in different places and even when people escorted him he would not show them where he lived and he often kept his whereabouts unknown.

He was able to transport the radio communication and other equipments from Asmara to Addis Ababa through the Ethiopian air force planes. An Oromo Officer with the rank of a major who worked as chief of logistics at the air force base in Asmara used to transport the communication and other equipment pretending they belonged to the Ethiopian military, and he was rewarded with considerable amount of money for his efforts. Thus no problem was encountered in moving equipment between Asmara and Addis Ababa. In addition, this dedicated patriot used to transmit important intelligence information he obtained through his friends in the navy and air force and information he received from other members of the mass organization to the front. He was sending timely information concerning the troop and weaponry movements of the enemy to Eritrea directly from Addis Ababa through clandestine radio messages.

Towards the end of the seventies when I was at Awhitet, it was decided that the intelligence gathering activities in Asmara should be revived. Mebrahtu Tekleab, nicknamed Vinak who was wounded while in the army and was assigned to Halewa Sewra in Sahel which he refused and instead returned to work behind the enemy defense line areas, was assigned with me to do the surveillance part of the branch.During the time when he operated in Asmara as a member of the Fedaeyeen squad, he worked closely with the members of the clandestine cell units that were carrying out high level operations, and particularly with Russom Teklemariam (Tarzan) who was the leader of the mass organization in Asmara. Russom 'Tarzan' lived in an apartment building above Bar Tunnel, across from the Asmara municipality building. One day, instigated by the local Kebele office, the apartment where he lived was thoroughly searched and security officers were stationed there to guard it.

Afewerki Teweldemedhin 'Bureaucracy' was approaching Tarzan's house when he observed the building was surrounded by Derg soldiers and it was being searched. He leaned on the fence of the municipality building and observed the search activities from a distance. That night he had met Russom 'Tarzan' and then left him in the apartment and went away for an errand and when he returned he realized the apartment of where Russom Tarzan lived was encircled. If a small tape recorder that Afewerki Bureaucracy left under Russom Tarzan's mattress is found, it was not difficult to conclude that it would be the end of Russom 'Tarzan'. Soon he witnessed Russom Tarzan in handcuffs being taken away on a car by the soldiers. The minor incident of a tape left under a mattress resulted in a colossal damage.

The biggest worry was not the incarceration of Russom Tarzan or his martyrdom, but what could follow if Russom 'Tarzan' spills information under torture. He was in charge of all the clandestine activities in Asmara, thus it would result in exposing operation of all the secret cells in Asmara and the capture and eventual execution of many dedicated members. Afewerki 'Bureaucracy' immediately realized the capture of 'Tarzan' will result in hampering the activities of the EPLF in Asmara. Immediately he acted by contacting the communication department of the EPLF seeking to find a quick remedy to the tragedy.

The officeers of Mariam Gmbi considered the arrest of Russom 'Tarzan' as a major breakthrough and turning point in uncovering the clandestine activities of the EPLF. At first, selected interrogators tried to get what they want from 'Tarzan' by treating him well and offering him many things. However, after the initial non-violent method failed to deliver required result the interrogators reverted to beating and coercion in an attempt to obtain confession from him. As a standard and proven practice, if an interrogator handles a case scientifically, the interrogation will be successful. An able investigator follows a suspect thoroughly and collects enough evidence that a suspect cannot evade or deny. But when one embarks on interrogation with inadequate evidence it enables the suspect to control and manipulate the interrogator as he wishes and succeeds to escape his predicament. Employing force and coercion would not enable one to defeat a suspect spiritually but many use force and torture to obtain information from a suspect. But because all Eritreans were suspected by the Derg of harboring sympathy to the liberation fronts, they were indiscriminately tortured irrespective of the value of the information they may divulge.

In the experience of the EPLF, there were combatants who under torture admitted they were spies, but after taking their ages into consideration they were rehabilitated after serving their punishment and were educated and were made to continue to struggle and serve the cause. After many years, their consciousness level increased, and they asked for a review of the false confession they made under duress and demanded the records be expunged from their dossier so that their historical record would be straight. There were fine combatants whose cases I personally reinvestigated and corrected. Such incidents are not limited to underdeveloped countries, it also happens in developed countries like the USA. According to the Chemistry book of Campbell Bio, in 1984 Earl Washington, an African American, was accused of raping and killing Rebecca Williams and was sentenced to death. In 1993, there appeared suspicion on the proceedings, and the decision was revised. In 2000, Washington was released after DNA investigation showed that the culprit was Kenneth Tinsel and not Washington who was wrongly jailed for 17 years.

Before they started to beat Russom 'Tarzan', they put him together with others who were interrogated and tortured and were hardly able to walk due to beating; their legs and other part of their bodies were wrapped in gauze. Followingthat, they tortured him using the torture method known as Number 8, a method where the person is tied up and hung upside down, and his feet are beaten with a stick; stuff his mouth with dirt and smelly rugs and then the person is made to roll in a pond of dirty water; then put one under electric heat and whip the person under interrogation. The interrogators employed on him every method and tool they had in order to break him down.

After he joined the prisoners who were unrecognizable due to the beating they suffered from, he saw some of the members of the mass organization that he knew though they didn't know him. He whispered to one of them, "Are you fine with the pain?" The man replied, "It is better if they finish us off than this; they have beaten us till we were almost losing our breath, but there is nothing that can't be resisted, we are used to it." It was in this situation that a new development unfolded in Mariam Gmbi. One day in the morning around 8 AM, when the investigators called him for interrogation they found him dead in the corner of the cell wrapped in his blanket. Rusom 'Tarzan' was thus martyred. Until Independence Day when his colleagues in the struggle disclosed the heroism of Tarzan, the officers of Mariam Gmbi didn't find a clue as to how his life ended.

The activities of the mass organization in Asmara continued as usual and the senior officers of the Derg were frustrated. Though they found a few leads based on the searches they conducted, they didn't achieve much. They realized they had internal problems and they started to monitor and investigate their own members. They made sure that secrets are handled by the well trusted personnel and decreased the trust they had on certain individuals and limited the activities undertaken by some individuals. Following such measures of the Derg Tekhlay 'Aden' surrendered and as a consequence the Ethiopian sergeant who was the registrar at Mariam Gmbi surrendered to the EPLF. Soon, Aferewrki 'Bureaucracy' and his colleagues reached a point where they could not operate freely and left Asmara and reported to EPLF units in Bahri.

This was the first time that I together with Vinak met Afewerki 'Bureaucracy' in Sabur, northern section of Bahri, and I was introduced to him. That was the first and last meeting I had with him. Before we parted, he had told me that he had plans to go overseas. After he was wounded in his leg, it was not possible for Vinak to continue with the Fedaeyeen unit and instead he was assigned as a follow up director to look after the clandestine activities in Asmara. Since he was not willing to work in the departments, he prepared all the requirements for the work to continue and requested the leadership of the EPLF to assign him in the military forces and his request was accepted. The time when he was assigned to the military coincided with the civil war and he was active in the battles that resulted in the ELF being pushed out to the Sudan.

After the Dire Dawa incident Afewerki 'Bureaucracy'the dedicated clandestine combatant was arrested and was interrogated in Addis Ababa, and all the equipment including the cars the secret cells used were caught, some of the members escaped and the cell stopped its activities because it couldn't operate anymore. In order to get more intelligence the Derg sent him to Asmara to the investigators at Mariam Gmbi who were believed to have a good knowledge about the Eritrean revolution. But since they couldn't get more information than what they got in Addis Ababa his case was passed to the decision makers and they sentenced him to death. He was sent to the Sembel prison and joined the rest who were awaiting the implementation of their sentence.

In Sembel prison, he organized some prisoners and contacted the communication unit and said that he had money that he needs to withdraw from the bank and attempted to be freed from prison by the EPLF Fedaeyeen operation. Unfortunately, he didn't succeed in his plans until the last day when Derg soldiers took him out at night and shot him in the village of Qushet. It wasAfwerki TeweldemedhinBureaucracy's picture we found hanging on the wall of the corridor of Mariam Gmbi with a caption that read, he was one of the main spies of the EPLF.

After Afewerki 'Bureaucracy' told me he was planning to go overseas, he travelled to Sudan and then to Somalia through which he re-entered Ethiopia. When Russom 'Tarzan' was arrested by the enemy, members of whom Vinak trained and known as Deqi arawit, 'children of monsters' were sneaking in to Asmara on special missions. The main concern was the arrest of Russom 'Tarzan', it was one of the main issues that had to be resolved and frantic movements were going in Asmara at the very moment in order to find a solution to Russom Tarzan's arrest. The main and special mission was to find a way to free the dedicated struggler from behind jail bars of the enemy; the second plan was to confuse the enemy with misinformation, or dry out the information sources and channels of the enemy.

It was not new to free prisoners from enemy jails by using special skills and employing force. In 1975 the ELF had recruited the police force, known as Dugana, at Sembel prison and freed all prisoners there and took them to the liberated areas. They asked all the prisoners, apart from their own fighters and mass organization members and civilians, about their preferences and choices and they escorted all of them to wherever they wanted to go. Among the prisoners freed at the time were people like Haile Weldetnsae 'Derue' who were members of the EPLF and after ascertaining their choices they were sent to the EPLF. Others like Bereket Fesseha 'Ghandi' who killed Azieb Nega and was imprisoned in Sembel and others decided to go overseas and they were sent away.

Similarly, the EPLF freed prisoners from the Sembel Prison in 1977. In that operation, which was executed after a thorough study by the EPLF units that operated in the surroundings of Asmara under the leadership of Vinak and others in collaboration with the Dugana police who worked in the prison, the prisoners were freed and taken to the liberated areas. They were allowed to go to places of their choice.

The studies that were conducted to free Russom 'Tarzan' and other patriots from Mariam Gmbi prison were more complex than usual because it required sneaking inside and recruiting officers most of whom were Ethiopians, through bribing or by other means, utilizing the already recruited Ethiopian sergeant registrar as a communications channel with our imprisoned comrades, and obtaining essential information through him and through prisoners who were transferred to Sembel from Mariam Gmbi. However, Russom Tarzan could only go out of Mariam Gmbi, either for health reasons or excuses related to money, that is either to go to a hospital or to the bank, however all plans to kidnap him that way failed.

The final and only choice left and also proposed by Russom Tarzan, considering the fact that the enemy would use excessive force and torture to extract secrets from him and imagining that he may not last long withholding secrets, was to bring him some means to avoid the leakage.

The requested solution was tough and hard to accept. It is very difficult to assist your own comrade and brother in arms, who struggled with you in the good and the bad times, one who knows your shortcoming and strived to correct you, to assist such a gallant comrade to commit suicide is very difficult to swallow. Even professional doctors would find it difficult to help someone desperately ill end his life instead of struggling to save it. But our case was an extraordinary situation--your brother and colleague who was being tortured and suffering at the hands of Mariam Gmbi interrogators, with no assurance that he would resist that and the possibility that he might succumb and reveal vital, secret information to the enemy, and at the end he asks for your cooperation knowing that the gorges of Qushet were waiting for him, a request from a person who thinks far ahead and always willing to sacrifice himself on behalf of his people, was a request knowingly and consciously made by Russom Tarzan that no matter how hard had to be accepted. And the case reached its conclusion. The far-sighted and very intelligent Russom Tarzan wanted to be loyal till the end protecting the comrades who following his example were martyred after him. Russom Tarzan left us an everlasting memory of martyrdom by sacrificing himself for the sake of his people and may God receive him in heaven. The secret which puzzled the Ethiopian security personnel was a small cyanide pill that was sneaked in.

The two files that we took from Mariam Gmbi when we liberated Asmara contained documents concerning the case of the two giant martyrs, Russom Tarzan and Afwerki Bureaucracy. At that time, since we didn't know Russom Tarzan in person we did not take his photo along with that of Afewerki Bureaucracy from among the pictures of the victims who were executed by the Derg. These files, until the day I abandoned the Isaias regime and left, were kept sealed in the secret archives of the Ministry of Interior, which was later called Department of National Security. When the Isaias regime was asked for permission to access the files so that the history of those courageous martyrs can be written as a book it was not willing to grant permission. Therefore, the attempt to write the history of fallen fighters was and is still sabotaged. However, in order to document history, I managed to obtain copies of some parts from the files, particularly documents pertaining to the case of Afewrki Bureaucracy, including the death sentence that was passed on him, the signatures of the persons who took the death decision, and the date and the reason for the sentence. Also I had interviewed the air force major who was in charge of logistics, which after the downfall of the Derg remained in Eritrea and was working with the Catholic Relief Service (CRS) of the Catholic Church Secretariat in Asmara. We met several times during the time that I was for a limited time, the Director of the Religious Affairs unit of the Ministry of Interior/Local Government. When I left Eritrea, I handed the documents that were in my possession to people I considered close to Afwerki Bureaucracy.

In the interview I had with the Major, when he was asked why he cooperated with us, he explained the reason why he cooperated with the EPLF was because he being an ethnic Oromo comes from an ethnic group that was marginalized and oppressed in Ethiopia and therefore he sympathized with the Eritrean cause. But it was not difficult to guess that he betrayed the system that he served because of financial benefits he was receiving from dedicated members of the clandestine mass organizations with whom he was cooperating. After the fall of the Derg in 1991, he was not willing to return to Ethiopia.

Chapter 3. THE RED STAR CAMPAIGN AND ITS REPERCUSSIONS

3.1 Alpha Project: Retreat to the Western Lowland Plains

Alpha project was the Red Star campaign's operation behind the enemy-lines that was initiated towards the end of 1981 by senior Derg leaders with the help of senior Soviet advisers. The entire military campaign was undertaken with the Ethiopians armed to the teeth by Eastern Bloc countries, mobilizing all the tanks and other powerful heavy equipment. Its primary aim was to squash the semi-guerrilla units and departments that were stationed in southern and northern Bahri, and its main objective was to encircle and control the EPLF base area and stronghold in Sahel and to extinguish the Eritrean revolution for good. The EPLF forces that were at Fifil and its environs crossed the Asmara-Keren highway, and through Leito river, they headed towards the Gash and Mereb river basins, while the forces that were in the environs of Addi Rosso crossed both the Asmara-Adi Keih, and Asmara-Adi Khwala highways and ascended towards the west and connected with the other units of northern Bahri. The units that were positioned in the east around Foro turned back and leaning towards the cliffs and mountains of southern Bahri they retreated to the lowland plains of Semhar.

The Soviet advisers didn't expect the strategic retreat and immediately knew their plans to encircle the EPLF forces were doomed to fail. They expected the EPLF to stay put in the towns and fight them in a conventional way to the end; to their dismay that didn't happen. Their war plans were discarded, but still they kept drawing new maps and thus fell into the traps of the war plans designed by the EPLF. It was then that the Russian generals and Derg authorities realized that the situation was transformed into a prolonged war of attrition based on a new strategically crafted EPLF war plan. The units of the EPLF forces retreated step-by-step and took position around Nakfa, the symbol of perseverance, and spread to the east up to the hills of northeastern Sahel, and to the west up to the hills of Halhal and Melebso and were able to defend the Nakfa stronghold.

The EPLF units behindthe enemy defense lines converged around Badme and its environs without sustaining any losses. We located ourselves inside Badme, and in cooperation with the commanders of the other departments we held seminars to calm the people and rebuild their confidence in the revolution and to convince them that they should not despair and panic because of the retreat. We managed to stabilize the situation of the people and went about our normal activities. The people stood by the side of the fighters and supported us by doing whatever was within their capacity. The new place that we entered into was previously a territory under the ELF administration and influence and winning the people's hearts and minds to support the EPLF was not an easy task.

3.1.1 Badme and the Tigray Peoples Liberation Front (TPLF) During the Strategic Retreat

During the time when the Badme area was under the control and administration of the ELF, both Eritreans and Ethiopians from the surrounding areas were squabbling over the small village of Badme. The ELF was educating the people from both sides that in addition to Badme, it claimed other places deep inside Tigray, including Enda Lilo (Adi Hageray) to be Eritrean territory. On its side, TPLF was campaigning hard to convince the Tigrayan residents in the area that Badme was an Ethiopian territory. There was also intermittent shooting between the two sidesmilitias of the surrounding areas.

From time to time, both sides were moving the border markers that were erected during the Italian era to suit their respective claim. When the EPLF units camped in Badme and its environs, the TPLF combatants in the area started to campaign and lecture the people claiming Badme was theirs and thereby instigating the people to agitate. And on the side of the EPLF, though we tried to explain to the TPLF cadres that the border issue should wait for the proper time and be resolved after a joint study, and that we should at the moment focus our combined efforts towards the Derg's offensives, they did not heed to our appeal for restraint.

That was the time when the Derg regime strengthened its forces and organized the units in a new restructure of task forces--a military centralization of many divisions--and by accumulating a large number of forces, in order to stretch the forces of the TPLF and the EPLF and encircle them in a cordon. For the EPLF at the time, igniting a confrontation with the TPLF was like putting a noose around your own neck and jeopardizing the struggle of the Eritrean people. When it was possible to mobilize as your allies on your side the four million strong people of Tigray against the common Ethiopian enemy army, it was thought inappropriate to direct your focus at them in such a difficult time. Because of that, the case was discussed by senior officials from both sides. Sebhat Negga the Chairman of the TPLF at that time led the team of TPLF cadres from the area, and on the EPLF side, the team was led by Solomon Seyoum, the head of the local EPRP branch, with the attendance of department directors who met behind the frontlines at Adi Hageray in mid-1982.

Before that meeting the commanders of the EPLF rear areas met with Arkebe and reached an unofficial agreement based on the maps which were drawn and agreed upon by the Italian and Ethiopian governments. The TPLF leadership did not, however, stop the agitations that their cadres were carrying out on the ground and they also had other internal problems. Later on, during the meeting held in Sheraro, (Adi Hageray), that was led by Sebhat Negga, they were asked about their reason for raising the Badme issue when the circumstances are not suitable for that. Aboy Sebhat said that they only raised it because they were pressured by the people and not because they wanted to. I was not convinced by the reply and remarked, "do you lead the people or do the people lead you?" However, since the issue was raised by their cadres, and they couldn't stop it, an agreement could   not   be   reached.

The meeting was reported to the leadership of the EPLF, and to avoid a possible conflict as a result of the disagreement, it was decided to postpone the resolution of the Badme border case to a later date so as to give it enough time. We carried out a campaign among the people to calm the situation and avoid confrontation and we moved away from the Badme area. Our troops camped by the Mereb River in the area of Zaid Akelom at Sefra Genet, Geza Mebrahtu, Fawlina, and Ekub Hamed. The people, particularly in Badme were unhappy and didn't accept the way we handled the case. They didn't want to be administered by TPLF and were displeased. However, in a short time the task force organized by the Ethiopian forces came to the area from Tigray, and the forces in the area behind the frontline retreated to Sahel.

3.1.2 Badme and the Democratic Movement for the Liberation of Eritrea (DMLE)

While we were in the environs of Badme, the Movement for the Liberation of Eritrea DMLE, a group that split from the ELF and was moving in western Eritrea, met some cadres from the EPLF's department of agriculture and presented a request to unite with the EPLF based on its call for a united front. The leaders in the Gash and Mereb area representing DMLE were: Haile Gebru military commander, Mezgebe in charge of the political office, and Gebrihiwet in charge of administration. Though the EPLF in 1975 was advocating for the formation of a united front with ELF against the ELF position which was advocating for a total unification in one front arguing that the field cannot accommodate more than one front, the EPLF now reversed its position when it rejected the proposal of DMLE for the formation of a united front. In addition to that, they were given an appointment for a meeting for dialogue and were detained on the order of Sebhat Efrem, the commander of the behind enemy line area and member of the Political Bureau of the EPLF. The EPLF that was accusing the ELF as reactionary and hegemonic because of its position on unity, after 1981 when it defeated and outnumbered the ELF it became the only strong force in the Eritrean struggle, changed its position and argued as did the ELF in the past that Eritrea cannot afford to have more than one front in the field.

The DMLE members who were detained in Badme stated that they voluntarily came to the EPLF to dialogue about unity based on an appointment they set with cadres of the EPLF, and when they arrived they were kidnapped. During the time of strategic retreat those who expressed their willingness to fight alongside the EPLF and strengthen its capacity were arrested. The EPLF, changing its color like a chameleon, turned its guns against those who demanded formation of a united front in order to monopolize the field as the only front in the country.

That didn't take long. Soon, a member of Halewa Sewra nicknamed A'ades, who was a cousin of Haile Gebru the DMLE military commander, sneaked him out of detention and they both escaped to Sudan. The kidnapping that was done in a secluded area in the forests of western Eritrea was exposed in the streets of Kassala. The entire world found out that the kidnapped leaders of DMLE were in detention under the EPLF. They were soon transferred to Sahel and were finally released. The EPLF made sure to silence A'ades, the Halewa Sewra member and the relative who helped Haile to escape from the detention, and made him disappear without trace in the Sudan.

The EPLF, which in the past accused the ELF of being reactionary, clannish, a sectarian organization, and anti-unity, itself adopted anti-unity position after achieving military supremacy. And in order to monopolize the Eritrean revolution, it raced against time to eliminate any organizations that could be a threat to its monopoly of power in national affairs. The EPLF couldn't tolerate any other entity: good or bad, an organization that intends to help or compete, be it an organization inside the EPLF or outside it. In order to monopolize the Eritrean revolution and move unhindered by using a secret party which was known at first as EPRP, and later renamed as the Eritrean Socialist Party (ESP), gradually embarking on a single party power monopoly and system of governance. Whether Menka'a or Yemeen, be it ELF or DMLE, all eliminated, one after the other, thus the Machiavellian Isaias changed his colors and became dominant and a powerful individual in Eritrea.

After the units that were behind the enemy defense lines retreated to Sahel, we established a temporary camp in Adobha, at Ella-Ababu and we stayed there for a while. When the Derg's task forces advanced from Tigray, crossing Gash and Mereb, and reached the surroundings of Barentu, we started to plan to return behind the enemy defense line areas. The retreat was tense and time consuming. It was not a situation where one could work calmly. There were some who couldn't resist the pressure and left while the majority of the fighters challenged the situation with resolve.

At the time of the retreat, Tsgereda Gual Signora was pregnant. Though there was an attempt to abort the pregnancy, but since unit 17 was established to take care of pregnant mothers, the abortion idea didn't get acceptance. After she stayed in Sahel for three months, the pregnant Gual Signora could not return to behind the enemy line areas and she was assigned to the units in Sahel.

The revolution had intermingled social and political problems. At the time I was in western Eritrea I was very engaged in organizational and party activities. Particularly in the party activities, when I secretly left my unit to participate or administer several party-related meetings and to evaluate the developments of the retreat. Gual Signora started to look at the situation differently, and suspiciously, and there were incidents that she secretly followed me to the places of the meetings. Though I made excuses to leave for the meetings, she was not convinced by the excuses I gave her. The topic was alien to Tsgereda Gual Signora, and it was natural that she became suspicious since she didn't expect us to hold a secret meeting that she or other fighters didn't know about. Because of that we started to have a misunderstanding and frictions. I tried hard to calm down the situation which continued in that manner until we reached Sahel where we almost reached the breaking point, I left her in Sahel and returned behind the enemy defense line areas.

That was not the only problem. In addition to the suspicion, her pregnancy also forced us to stay separated from each other and the situation worsened. One cannot accept separation from a person that provides warmth and one is used to and goes to a faraway place in such a tricky situation. There was no problem that the Eritrean revolution didn't cause. "A given name leads to one's identity and a torch lights the way ahead," is a Tigrigna saying that was not uttered in vain; the Eritrean revolution was a deep cliff with noble intentions. Some of those who discovered the existence of the secret party and later became members evaluated the situation of those who have become members before they did and found out they were not better than them andthat made them feel bad. And those who were not members observed the movements and they became disillusioned. And given the strict rules of the party revealing the existence of the party to non-members was a serious punishable crime.

When I returned behind the enemy defense line areas, I didn't go to Sahel for a long time and in the meantime Tsgereda Gual Signora had given birth to Yohanna, our daughter; I found out about that from people who came from Sahel.Behind the enemy defense line areas, we first camped at Geza Mebrahtu and then moved to Shekha Gurja, on the banks of the Mereb River, a virgin forest area. The medical department camped by the Faytet river, in a place called 'Sheramut'. According to legend, many years earlier some women became outlaws and were stopping and robbing men in that place, called Faytet. The surroundings of the western rivers of Eritrea are lush, filled with so many trees and wildlife, including lions, tigers, and elephants.

The western rivers are Gash, Mereb and Tekezze and they are landmarks in the Ethiopian Eritrean boundary. Mereb River runs from its source in the central highlands of Eritrea, and it runs along the Eritrean-Ethiopian border until it reaches the environs of Fawlina, Shekha Wedi Khulala area where the Kunama ethnic group resides. Here its name changes to Gash and it continues westward until it enters the Sudan. The border runs in a straight line from Fawlina and leaving Badme on the Eritrean side and continues to the west.

The place has remained a hide out of bandits and outlaws. When the EPLF units first arrived in the Mereb area, at once it became a dwelling of bandits; there were times when we were sleeping close to one another side by side when we slept on the open, while the bandits were in the woods. We were new and we were not familiar with the area, whereas the bandits knew all the ins and outs of the Mereb area like the back of their hands. However, since they didn't want to disturb their abode they didn't provoke the fighters.

Slowly, we studied the area and mobilized and organized the people and gradually managed to control the area as well as banditry. Most of the cases concerning the detained people were related to firearms which found its way to Eritrea from Ethiopian arms markets. Also, whether they were armed by the TPLF or ELF, or were militias and Bandas armed by the Ethiopian government, they would sometimes quarrelwith those who armed them or they would be overtaken by greed, and embark on banditry to rob people and live off it without working. Thus, most of the cases we were handling were related to banditry and murder.

The Ethiopian Bandas were mostly 'Wedo Geba', elements of the Eritrean struggle who surrendered to Ethiopia. The enemy Bandas were given wheat grains and money and were ambushing fighters and causing damages. They would also rob people, collect money and return to their homes. The Ethiopian army knew what was happening but didn't question the Bandas as long as they accomplish their mission on its behalf.

Generally, the majority of the cases were spying and banditry, including cases of murder and rape. In addition, there were revenge killings which increased the number of murder cases. There were also cases of Prisoner of Wars (POWs), or surrendering soldiers; these were a major source of military secrets and general intelligence.

There were times, when we were crossing the Mereb River and were retreating to Goboyezghi in Tigray, that we had confrontations with Ethiopian forces who were marching from Barentu, or from the Qola Seraye, from Qenan Qobia'a. Even the connection with Sahel was a wide loop that crosses Tokombia, then Forto Sawa and passes through Zara River to reach Sahel. At the beginning of 1983, I went to attend a meeting in Sahel and on that occasion I bought some baby clothes from the surroundings of Shelalo and I had a chance to see my daughter Yohanna for the first time.

Immediately after I reached Sahel, I first went attending my meetings until it was finished, then I proceeded to the camp of the mothers. Tsgereda didn't receive me warmly as she used to. The relation cooled down; and a long separation followed, and as they say, 'out of sight out of mind'. We decided to separate. Yohanna was about six-months old at the time. I took pictures together with Yohanna and Tsgereda Gual Signora, and I gave Tsgereda the things I brought along and promising that I will send her what she needs in the future and we parted ways.

Sebhat Efrem called Petros Solomon on the radio and asked him to take me along with him from Hishkeb on his way to Zara. He informed me on the radio to get ready for the next morning. Local Beer (Siwa) had been prepared for Halewa Sewra members who had come for a meeting and he came in the middle of the party and took me along. When I reached Zara, I found a car that Sebhat has sent and immediately we continued to Girmayka. We ate breakfast there and we continued to Mereb. Before I reached my destination we stopped and ate lunch with Samson Mehari, Sebhat's driver, under a rich Arkokabay tree. We drunk from the liquor that the members of the trading department offered us in Girmayka and then I reached my destination.

There I was to deliver an educational seminar for all cadres, as my first task. After reading the papers that I prepared from my interviews with the soldiers and officers who were captured or who surrendered from the Derg, and with spies who were either kidnapped or were captured, and re-reading the studies and papers of incidents that were prepared in Sahel and related studies, I was ready to hold the seminar on the next day. The seminar contributed to raising the overall security awareness of the cadres, and the reports of accusations that were presented against suspects became qualitatively better.

A body known as the 'intelligence family' was formed from Military Intelligence, Halewa Sewra, the Communication Department, and the Commando Unit, and regular meetings were held. There were repeated requests to hold a seminar after evaluating the Halewa Sewra seminar, but I saw that such a serious seminar could be sensitive. I told them that after assessing the military situation, the seminar would only be held once in a while. Just like the planning of the commando operation at the Asmara airport, which was planned by the tri-partite intelligence body and was decided to be handled discreetly by the commando and communication units, in order to avoid leakage of secrets and to prevent the enemy from evaluating the security awareness of the EPLF, we reached an understanding that activities should be carried out after thorough and meticulous study.

The effectiveness of the military intelligence of the EPLF increased very much after the formation of the body of intelligence family and the military confrontation it was engaged in became less haphazard. In addition to the intelligence that was gathered from soldiers and spies, the organizing of collaborators inside the cities, and the activities that were carried out by sneaking behind enemy defenses and camps, made the military command more efficient. It became common to see the units prepare in advance to ambush the enemy well before the enemy campaign started. However, though the activities against the bandits and outlaws were not that many, they were also carrying surprise attacks on property and EPLF fighters.

Considering the heavy military and political activities, sport and cultural activities were introduced to save the forces from boredom. Football clubs were formed in the west and in the sport field that was set on the lush plains of Mereb, activities that attracted spectators were carried out. And to entertain the forces, cultural activities were carried out. To ameliorate the shortage of supplies and improve the lifestyle of the fighters, on top of the development activities that were carried out by the Agricultural Department, each unit struggled to become self-reliant by developing plots for gardening. Growing vegetables and legumes became common, the health of the combatants improved, the only enemy to the health of the fighters remained to be the Mereb Mosquito, and it was weakened by anti-malaria pills and sleeping mosquito nets. The units in Mereb started to brew beer and invite each other; they almost became one family and their relations went beyond unit relations and created strong bonds outside the respective units.

Politically, we prepared cadre school refresher courses for the cadres of behind the enemy defenseline areas. The activities in Mereb skyrocketed and each unit designed political and academic courses and enhanced the level of skills of the fighters. However, the situation didn't continue as it was. Whenever there was news about appearance of 'Wedo Geba' or bandits, taking fighters from the units to pursue them became extensive. And by choosing better defenses against the repeated campaign of the enemy, the units were made to retreat to the dry and thick mountains of Jarbet and its environs. Moving from Mereb to Jarbet felt like being tossed from the laps of a mother to the laps of a stepmother. What can be done! Our fate dictated that we move from a cold to a hot situation and back again from a hot situation to a cold one.

While we were in Mereb, I tried to establish some romantic relations but the situation, not only didn't allow it, the struggle hindered me and I didn't succeed. The social structure of the units as noted earlier had wide gaps of class, ethnic, gender and economic status. Accordingly, the choices were limited. In the EPLF there were many university students, even bachelor and masters degree holders, who got married to individuals who only went through basic literacy education in the struggle. But this doesn't mean that those who grew up in the countryside and those who grew in the cities, or, the educated and uneducated, could not have relations. It is an attempt to illustrate the different and abnormal decisions one takes when pushed by the prevalent socio-political situation. It was inevitable that the incidents of divorce to be more frequent.

It was common for fighters to be at any time transferred from one unit to another, based on the requirement of the organization and not based on the priorities or choices of the individual. Meeting one's spouse was just like a workplace that allowed in limited days only, one month every year. But there were instances that a commander of the unit could allow fighters to meet their spouses if the situation was convenient. The distance that separates the spouses also limited the frequency of the meeting. But there were also lucky ones who were working in the same unit. Apart from that, there were many instances where the chances of spouses strengthening their bonds were in the hands of their commanders; if the commander allows it the spouses meet frequently and if the commander didn't, then the meeting is limited. It was in such a situation that I met my colleague and wife in Jarbet.

Before she joined the revolution, Almaz Kahsay was a second year student in the University of Santa Familgia when her father pushed her to get married to a man many years her senior; she interrupted her school and fled to Addis Ababa where she worked for a while and returned to Asmara, from where she was travelling through the field on her way to continue her travel overseas. But she was caught in the lowlands of Seraye and was sent to the training camp at Molqi. After she started military training she was sent to Halewa Sewra in Mereb to be debriefed because her work while she was in Addis Ababa gave her the ability to know the military structure of the Derg. After her debriefing she was assigned to the Medical Department.

We started a close conversation in Jarbet, when she came to visit us from the Medical Department, the Pharmacy, which was located close to the place where Halewa Sewra was stationed. In the struggle I spent most of my free time reading and listening to music. I joined the unit after work and brought along a big stereo tape recorder that I used at work, to entertain them with some songs from the seventies, and other traditional party songs. After a few slow songs, they were excited and wanted to do some dances, and we played Wedi Tukul's songs and the entertainment party continued. Towards the end, Gebrihiwet Wedi Belih tuned his Krar, a harp like traditional instrument, and started to sing,'the good spirit makes me dialogue with my brethren, the bandit spirit... to obliterate me and to take away my properties'. Hearing the wild drums, the residents of the area came and joined the party. Almaz liked the songs that she heard at the party.

The fighters, who were still under the spell of nostalgia for Mereb, forgot about it in the new barren lands. The love and happiness were unmatched, the fighters always accepted the dire situations and tried to change it into good times; it wouldn't be possible to achieve the goals if not for that patriotic attitude. Jerbet was located in a difficult terrain; let alone the enemy, even the bandits could not challenge it. Only the fighters who compare themselves to the mountain monkeys could overcome it. In such a barren land is where I established the romantic love relation of the forest and married and produced three beautiful children after I was separated with Tsgereda Gual Signora.

On the evening of the next day, as Almaz was about to return to her place, a magnificent event occurred: on the west the sun was covered in the colors of a red hot fire, and on the opposite side, on the east, the crescent moon appeared. A micro tape in hand, and listening to songs of the seventies, I escorted Almaz to her place. Tesfay Gebreab 'Gomera' her commander had asked her to bring him cigarettes and when we sat to rest on the way, I fished a stick of cigarette and lighted it, and she realized the packet was full. Almaz has big eyes; her complexion was not yet ashen with the heat of the sun and the harsh wind. She was beautiful and tall, whenever she accidentally passed by, her physical appearance enticed the eyes of the beholder to watch. Our stars met and we had to formalize our relations; I made Tesfay Gomera aware of our relations, and until she was in that area, whenever work was slow, she had the chance to frequently come to my place. But after a while, in order to be able to take a pharmacy course she was assigned in the central pharmacyand she had to leave for Sahel. We were thus physically separated.

When I reached Shelalo to escort Almaz, I accidentally found members of my unit on their way to Sahel, and I found Jime'e who was a member of the surveillance unit behind the enemy defenseline areas. I asked him to carry some clothes for my daughter Yohanna and he gave me the sad news that she had died. Yohanna died in her first year, considering the situation of the struggle, it was not easy to investigate and identify the cause of death. It was the fate of the struggle: my first child died before I could have enough of her or see her for a second time. I saw Almaz off and returned to my usual routine work in Jerbet.

After Almaz left, I stayed behind the enemy defense line area for a while and left along with someone who was a member of a select group of fighters who had a satisfactory educational background and were being trained in a secret location in Mereb to be assigned to foreign countries to carry out intelligence activities abroad. They were being dispersed to different countries and locations. We went together to Kassala where I bid 'Wedi Birri' goodbye and returned to Girmayka before going off to Sahel. The cadres who were gathered at the secret camp were assigned to carry out intelligence activities and were spread across Africa and Europe. EPLF, and particularly the military intelligence activities that was under the command of Petros Solomon and in collaboration with the unit that was managed by the Communication Department, which had clandestine cells inside the cities where it carried its activities through members of the mass organizations. It had established a sophisticated network that spread from inside the enemy occupied territories all the way to the international arena. The EPLF was able to spread beyond Eritrea and nurture a satisfactory intelligence gathering apparatus and personnel that it deployed in the Horn of Africa and the world beyond.

The operatives were getting into many situations and passing all sorts of critical information back to the field; the members were not known to all fighters and at times, even their spouses didn't know their whereabouts. By stage-acting fake surrenders of fighters to the enemy they were sending intelligence information from inside Asmara or other parts of Eritrea and Ethiopia. These dedicated combatants were considered traitors by Eritreans in the city who thought they berayed their comrades not knowing that they were on missions. However, they had to withstand the accusation of being traitors in order to accomplish their patriotic mission. There is nothing the Eritrean struggle didn't do; it faced all kinds of challenges to open the gates to independence.

3.2 The Life of Freedom Fighters in Sahel: Intra-Party Squabbles

Towards the end of 1984 the combatants and leaders were reshuffled and I was transferred to Sahel. After eight years of guerrilla activities behind the enemy lines, I was pulled to the relatively calm EPLF base area. I planned to rest a little, look after myself and allocate time to read. I accepted the transfer positively because I believed it would give me an opportunity to be close to enlightened cadres who could help me develop my capacity, and because my girl friend who later became my spouse was in Sahel. I was assigned as head of the interrogation unit along with Rezene Seyoum, thus duplicating one position. My childhood friend Isaac Rezene was appointed as personnel officer of the department and we met at the central location of Halewa Sewra.

I was assigned to work in the cells of the EPRP that were already formed and there I met Isaac Rezene. After the meeting, we went alone to a secure location and talked about the party. He reflected on the past situations and how the party that he was active in was dissolved, and he was then working in the secret party that the existence of which Btsay Goitom confided to him about. He had arrived at a stage where he was working for and talking about a party whose very existence was denied. He said that it was not clear to him in which direction that party was leading him. Based on what he experienced, he was not happy about the nature of relations among the members of the party.

The leaders of the cells in the rear base camps were rarely moved from their positions. Positions rarely needed replacement because martyrdom was rare, and the positions were almost taken as a private domain; there were a lot of scheming and maneuvers to be assigned to higher positions. Both the military units and the units behind the enemy defense line areas suffered a lot because they suffered from high number of casualties and martyrdom that led to higher turnover of assignment to different positions. Because of that, mutual respect, love and care were highly valued since the guiding principle was, "let me die in order for you to live." But in the calm base area of the stronghold, where there was not much enemy action, the relations between the members was characterized by watching one another, rivalry, mundane competition; the motto and principle was almost changed to, "you die so that I can live."

Those who accused the Menka'a movement as a movement of petty-bourgeoisie, the secondary school and the freshmen and sophomore university students, had convinced themselves they were the "enlightened revolutionaries." After the Menka'a movement was liquidated, they went deep into competition and were at one another's throats.

Isaac Rezene told me the reason for his acceptance to be a member of the party. He didn't' want to abandon the struggle because of his discontent with the party. He wanted to contribute his part and try to mend things, and since he decided to continue the struggle, he preferred to be inside the party rather than outside it. He was afraid he could reach a stage where he cannot defend himself and be at the mercy of others; at least he wanted to be inside the party and defend himself, particularly since he confirmed that he cannot be safe after knowing about the secret existence of the party.

He also said that the party that was formed by Btsay Goitom had been the same as the party they created but had been brought so low that it had to be condemned for causing an organizational damage. Even though the party leaders were pretending to be gentle, they were at logger head because of the unproductive rivalry that focuses in outshining one another. He couldn't understand how the party members saw themselves.

In the rear base camps of Sahel, except when occasional planes bombed the area when one had to hide in the caves for a short time, there was nothing that would compel you to think about martyrdom. Even the martyrs were remembered at the closing of meetings only. But the time available to think about oneself is limitless. It was very difficult for those who were transferred there from the frontlines to understand the situation in the rear base camps.

About a month after we talked with Isaac Rezene, Abraha Wedi Kassa, one of the committee members of the party in the base area, came to Halewa Sewra to hold an election and he gathered the party members. He said that we would elect a party sub-branch leader. I didn't like the situation and didn't want to be engaged in the squabbles.

94

In order to show that I will not take sides I explained to him that I did not want to take part in the voting since I was new in the place. Abraha Wedi Kassa told me that I must take part and vote in the election and he gave me an election card. He didn't seem to understand that there was a right to abstain, or maybe he wanted to demonstrate his authority. When the votes were collected he noted that there was one card missing and said it should be presented. Again, I told him the missing voting card was mine and I was not willing to cast a vote and he went ahead counting the votes in his possession.

The situation was new to me and I preferred to follow and evaluate it; I did just that without taking sides while doing my work. Whenever I had the time, I would go to the pharmacy at the camp of the Health Department and meet Almaz. Likewise she would visit me whenever she got the time and we became closer to each other. When I went to the pharmacy, since I knew almost all the members there, starting from my brother Isaias, I felt that I was a member of their unit. Isaac Rezene had started an informal relation with Gidey, a member of the Halewa Sewra and she got pregnant; that created misunderstanding in the unit and criticism was heaping on him. The situation calmed when the relation continued. He didn't take sides in the groupings of the cadres and there was no one to defend him.

The work at the central location of Halewa Sewra was not difficult. Two of us were appointed to one position and when one goes away the other would do the job. My assignment to Sahel was a good opportunity for me. There were three interrogation squads in Hishkeb. The first squad investigated serious cases of spying, murder, banditry and rape; the second squad investigated different cases such as cases of theft, embezzlement etc; the third squad was responsible for cases that concerned fighters and cases that mainly related to escapees, abandoning position, and other serious cases of murder, and light cases related to discipline and the like.

At the time, the secret party had fully controlled the organization and there was no political power inside the organization that threatened it; there were no cases identified as emerging political trends. Outside Hishkeb, there was a place in Adobha where the accused would go after being investigated to be rehabilitated; and there was a branch that investigates war crimes in the camp at Ararib where Ethiopian POWs were kept.

In the camps of the rear base area there was no consistent movement and that offered an opportunity to do research and be

95

prepared. It was possible to consult reference books and documents and produce material and pamphlets that would help improve the performance of the department and I was myself able to produce some reference booklets for the Department. When I was behind the enemy lines, in an unstable situation, on top of the usual informative reports I was preparing, I also produced a reference booklet entitled 'Introduction to Elementary Security', as well as a report on banditry in Eritrea prepared in conjunction with members of my team.

The booklet about banditry was prepared by referring to the story of and consulting with the bandits, who were in detention and were being investigated, and by interviewing older people, known bandits in the past and who were described as ruthless by the residents in the area. One of the bandits who provided detailed information about banditry in western Eritrea was Tekle Gilagabir, the bandit who held hostage the son of theItalian businessman named Taligiero, who waskidnapped by Abraha Tagliero. Tekle Gilagabir was known in the region for his marksmanship as a sniper and people said he wouldn't shoot and miss a thread. He had once killed a lion in Tekezze near a well that now bears his name, Ella Tekle. In the interview that was carried out with Aboy Tekle, he explained everything he did and the cooperation he provided to Abraha Tagliero during the time Tagliero's son was kidnapped.

Together with the cadres whom I found in Sahel, we collaborated in an attempt to make our operation more scientific. We were able to prepare two documents, i.e.: 'Basic Interrogation Guidelines'and 'Basic Criminology'. I also served as a board member of the Department's magazine named Halewa.

In 1985, after a short period in Sahel, I took some members along and went to participate in the mobilization efforts to attack Barentu. When I was on my way to meet the Commander of the battle, Petros Solomon, we met Isaias on the way and he took the vehicles we were travelling on before we could reach the place where the forces were converging, and we were compelled to continue the rest of the journey on foot. And because the vehicles were needed to tow heavy military equipment we handed over the car without an alternative. However, in order to get directives and request logistical needs, I went to the command center in Sawa to meet Petros Solomon and I found Isaias with him. I made my arrival known and waited outside.

After he was finished with Isaias, Petros called and informed me about my task and provided the logistics that we needed. He gave me orders to work in collaboration with the military intelligence squad and informed me that I will be told about the zero hour of the planned attack through a radio. I prepared my work plan and returned to my colleagues and gave them the necessary directives. Later on I went to the military intelligence members and we agreed to operate in a coordinated and collaborative manner and we waited staying close to each other expecting the zero hour.

Though Barentu was believed to be tough considering its terrain and previous attempts to capture it, in the 1985 battle it was not as we feared it would be; we didn't have much losses. The approach of the zero hour was announced earlier and all units were given time to get ready. When it was zero hour, we marched on and Barentu was fully captured on the third day. Though there were some soldiers who remained hidden in foxholes in the town and were shooting, it didn't take much time to clean them up. The plan was to proceed to Akordat after Barentu.

Immediately, together with the members of the military intelligence, we took control of all the offices of the Ethiopian Peoples' Labor Party and Security, as well as the police stations. Our forces encircled Barentu and prevented anyone from gettingout of the town, and by referring to the documents that we seized from the offices we were able to detain all the civilian operatives who were in the service of the enemy in Barentu. We took the necessary information from them and then sent them to Sahel. We then gathered all the POWs in Barentu, provided them with first aid services, and they were sent to Sahel; we kept the officers with the rank of first lieutenant and above in Barentu for further interrogation in order to use the information that we obtain from them.

After searching for the suspects in Barentu, we went to the environs and to the villages around the town to investigate and do the same. The investigation was based on evidences supported by enemy documents which contained names and addresses of the wanted people, some indicating the amounts of money they were paid for their services, and be it salary or something else, for which they signed, documents that clearly showed transactions. Thus, presenting the suspects to face the law after investigations was not difficult. In addition, some of the sponsors of the spies were officers who were in detention, and based on the information they gave us, almost all the spies except those who escaped with the retreating enemy forces were caught.

Compared to other towns in western Eritrea, Barentu is built on a high altitude, its climate is temperate; it looks as if it was built to be a garrison town. Since there were many soldiers in Barentu, there were many bars and restaurants to cater for them. Though the activities in the Barentu market slowed as the shooting began, it didn't take much time for it to return to its normal situation with the advance of the EPLF. The respect and high esteem with which the people held the freedom fighters was great. The fighters started to carry out tasks and campaigned among the people; we reached a stage where we brought a cultural musical troupe to campaign in the town.

The Ethiopian authorities didn't accept the loss of Barentu and were determined to recapture it at any cost. They mobilized troops from everywhere and carried repeated counter attacks. On the part of the EPLF, the intention to continue to Akordet could not be carried out as planned. The Ethiopians kept increasing their forces and the front was overstretched. Ethiopian commanders gathered superior number of soldiers and equipment and wanted to defeat the forces that defeated them, by stretching the frontline to spread the forces of the EPLF and encircle it. In addition to that they tried to pressure the EPLF forces; they moved to Nakfa and opened a front hoping to further spread the EPLF forces and then hit it when it is thinly spread. They were determined to recapture Barentu at any cost.

In such a frustrated attempt by the enemy to recapture Barentu whatever the cost, by reckless attacks, the EPLF leadership instead of waiting there to face the enemy, chose to retreat from Barentu and relieve the pressure and challenge on the Nakfa front. We left Barentu after occupying it for fifty days. Not only was the time given to prepare for a retreat short but even the facilities were not adequate.

When we entered Barentu, Idris, one of the famous spies of the enemy, was not there and we were not able to capture him. And after Barentu was captured he was continuing his spying activities behind enemy lines and after identifying where he stayed we prepared a plan to kidnap him. However, since there were other priorities we decided to defer his kidnapping for some other time but three days before retreating from Barentu Petros gave me an order to put everything else on hold and to accomplish the kidnapping of Idris in a limited number of hours. For the given task he provided me with a Waz car, a type of car that can move efficiently in the rough terrain. In the evening just after sunset I took members of the mass organization who knew the area well and we sneaked behind enemy defense lines. By the next day we accomplished our mission and returned with Idris; Petros again ordered me to take the captured officers along and to retreat. Idris was a very dangerous spy who caused the jailing of many members of the mass organizations and he had also led the enemy to a hidden arms cache belonging to the ELF.

I requested for vehicles to help in the retreat, but there were none other than the ones assigned to transport the wounded, the sick and captured supplies. Petros assigned a large number of the forces to guarding the POWs and we agreed to retreat towards Tessenei. We set up a special radio line to monitor the developments and to coordinate the retreat. In addition to the problems that may be created because of the scarcity of vehicles the situations didn't also allow enough time for the retreat. We left all the excess stuff and we retreated ahead of time. The retreat started on foot with the senior Derg officers who were used to comfortable means of transportation.

Before we began retreating from Barentu I sent Ghebrehiwet Wedi Belih behind the enemy defense lines to Jerbet to prepare a few things and I was worried that he would return and unknowingly go to Barentu and fall in the hands of the enemy. I radioed Jerbet to warn his group but I found out they have already left. There was no other choice but to hope they would listen about the retreat through the Dimtsi Hafash broadcast but unfortunately Dimtsi Hafash didn't broadcast the news. However, the next day as we were marching Dimtsi Hafash did broadcast the news announcing: 'today our heroic liberation army retreated from Barentu'.The news came too late since Wedi Belih and his group had already gone to Barentu without listening to it but to their credit they observed abnormal activities. Then they saw Derg soldiers behind them and they opened fire on them; they were able to escape the danger and retreat. They ultimately caught up with us on the way to Tessenei.

We started to follow the movements of the forces through the radio and we learned that they had not left their positions on the second day. But soon, Gerezgiher Wuchu the Division Commander informed Petros that the forces will leave their positions. We were not very far from Barentu and I asked Petros Solomon for clarification in relation to Gerezgiher Wuchu's information about the forces leaving their positions. He put the situation into consideration and told me to wait for a while, he left the radio conversation and after half an hour he returned and told me to set the captured Ethiopian officers free and let them go to wherever they wish to go.

The rationale of the directive was not new. When the EPLF captured POWs, with the exception of war criminals that it presented to face the law, it used to educate and enlighten them and then set them free. Based on that instruction we took the POW officers away from the highway through which we were marching and to the side of a mountain to rest. When they were told to get off the highway they were fearful and started to whisper to each other.

The officers, who were intoxicated with the Derg propaganda and were spreading news that the EPLF is a petro-dollar mercenary army, were now afraid that we were taking them off the highway to execute them. Some began to look to the sky and pray and others were cursing the day they were born; they imagined and dreamed many scenarios. The Derg regime officers that oppressed and eradicated Eritreans cannot think beyond similar actions; however they soon discovered the situation was not like that. The secret of the success of the struggle of Eritreans was not founded on eradication of human beings but liberating them. Therefore, to fall into what they dreamed and did was very shameful.

I gathered the officers and told them in Amharic, 'From today on, from this minute, EPLF is letting you free to go to wherever you wish to', but their ears that are used to hearing Amharic could not understand it and asked me in Amharic, 'what is that you said, could you please repeat it?' They didn't expect that and they had difficulty believing it. I explained to them in detail that if they wished to return to the Derg or go to the Sudan, or return to their home country and to either do their private affairs or join any of the Ethiopian opposition organizations, they will get support to reach their respective destination.

Many of them were suspicious of my explanation and others were breathing a sigh of relief while others were confused and had difficulty deciding where they wanted to go. I gave them time to think and thereafter they were divided into groups based on their choice of destination. Most of them wanted to go to Sudan or return to their country but a few decided to join the Ethiopian opposition organizations. Only a few of them decided to return to Barentu. We gave them flour and other supplies, most of it to those who wanted to go to Ethiopia, and the least portion to those who were going to Sudan. Those who were returning to Barentu got a portion enough for one day and all were seen off to their destination.

It was difficult to tell what would be the fate of those who were returning to Barentu, but according information obtained from some sources, the soldiers who were captured by the EPLF and later released were either detained or some even executed by the Derg. The Derg authorities,who were spreading false propaganda on how the EPLF handled prisoners in order to prevent its troops from getting caught or surrender, were not allowing the freed POWs to interact with other soldiers for fear they may tell the true story of their life as POWs and the humane manner they were treated. It was difficult to tell the fate of the officers who returned to Barentu.

As the officers were returning to Barentu, they were met by our retreating forces and they asked them where they were going, to which they replied that the EPLF has pardoned them and allowed their return to Barentu, and nothing happened to them. This is because the policy of handling captives was very clear to all the fighters. No one suspected the veracity of the explanation given by the captives, and to be fully certain, and to avoid some suspicions, after some commanders found answers to their questions, the Ethiopian officers were able to reach their destination without facing problems.

I had to return to Sahel quickly and I left my Kalashnikov with the squad who were in a harvesting campaign and were to accompany prisoners to the surroundings of Ali Ghider. I headed to Kassala from where I went to Port Sudan and on to Sahel. Beer was abundant in Barentu but it became as the saying in Tigrigna goes, 'as scarce as a female's beard' when I entered the Sudan, the country under Sharia'a, Islamic law. In Barentu we controlled all the security offices; we almost controlled the entire officers club. After taking control of the military offices and arms depot, the forces started to look for clothes. But we carried all the beer from the club and moved it to a spare hut at the Halewa Sewra Office; we had planned to quench our thirst with it until we captured Akordet.

Late afternoons after work the fighters strolled on the narrow streets of Barentu to enjoy fresh air. By then the heat of the day gets milder and a breeze of cool air takes over. If they found little money, or if someone invited them, the fighters spent their time in restaurants and bars drinking and chatting. Sometimes an unexpected situation unfolded and they entertained themselves and became happy. Fighters who have been far from normal human life started to return to life of normalcy. Many fighters from Sahel started to come to Barentu either on duty or for leisure to relax.

The martyr Ashaal Wedi Zere, who at the time was in charge of the POWs branch of the EPLF, came to Barentu and we met at the office. I took him to our resting place and told him that later on we would stroll in the streets of Barentu. After he took a shower, he insisted and told me, 'what do those who sleep benefit, let's go and visit the town, it may not be much but I have a few Sudanese pounds and if you can exchange it, let's have some drinks'. I brought beer cooled under wet burlap and I wanted to leave to go to the office. He stopped me and said, 'Let's leave this beer for later, now let's go and drink beer in its place, in the bar'. I agreed and told Girmay Shawl where we would be, and I took Ashaal and we headed to 'Adey Aytereren's' place.

Around 4PM in the afternoon we found Deldul and Ghebrihiwet Wedi Belih drinking beer at Adey Aytereren's place. They were embarrassed to see us because they were drinking during work hours and they considered Ashaal not only a colleague but as their elder and they respected him. They left their table for us. Ashaal raised the beer bottle and talked to it, 'O beer! Do you remember me?' The bottle didn't respond because it can't; he smashed it onto the wall. Adey Aytereren was scared and exclaimed, 'what is wrong my children?' Ghebrihiwet Wedi Belih told her not to worry because he is used to doing that, and they calmed her down. Once at Mersa Gulbub, fighters found drinks that were buried during the Italian era, Ashaal found wine and drunk to the extent that he raised his Kalashnikov and began to shoot at the mountain, 'O mountain, now you should talk!' He ordered more beer and he kept asking the bottle if it knows him. Adey Aytereren opened the beer and the gas made a sound as it got released from the bottle and Ashaal said, "Now you saved your life, I am Ashaal Wedi Zere, master of beer and master of Anice!" He then finished the bottle in one go.

Adey Aytereren sold local beer (siwa) in Barentu and her product was very good and would be sold out instantly. The next day when customers who came to drink and asked for beer she would say, 'Aytereren' (meaning not mature enough), and the fighters baptized her as 'Adey Aytereren'. They liked the place and suggested to her to sell beer when she runs out of Siwa, the local beer. She started to do that. We finished our beer and we took Ashaal to Gira Fiori, to a restaurant to eat. But at the doorstep, Ashaal was reluctant to continue and stopped for a while, but later he followed us in.

Inside the restaurant we found a battalion commander nicknamed Derg and we sat with him and ordered anice. As we were chatting, Ashaal called the owner of the place by her name and she looked at him in surprise. The young Ashaal that she knew has changed and she couldn't recognize him. She asked him how he knew her name, he told her that he knew her a long time ago, when her breasts were tight and she was young not old as she has become now. Before he finished his talk she screamed in excitement. She was the friend of his child's mother and she used to sell beer in Aba Shawl. She took us to a private room and she slaughtered a sheep and treated us very well. Beer and liquor were mixed in our system and we were very high when we left. When we stayed in Barentu she became like a second mother; we used to spend our time in relaxation between Adey Aytereren's and Adey Gebriela's places.

After about a month, Barentu run out of beer and what was coming from Asmara could only reach as far as Akordet and the festive times came to an end. Adey Aytereren's work was doubled, Adey Gebriela also run out of beer and started to sell liquor that she had hidden for bad times. The local beer houses, even those that sold Dagga, a version of the local beer, saw their business increase and earning good income. Once we went to Adey Gebriela and she said she missed beer, we took her to our place and offered her beer. She asked where that came from and we pulled a joke on her and told her it was bottled in Sahel. She had done many favors for us, and in return we offered her a crate of beer and escorted her to her house.

Tsa'edu Bahta, the head of the cultural department of the EPLF spent all of his time with us when he stayed in Barentu. After work, the leaders of the mass organization department, all of us Asmarinos, including Solomon Wedi Amanuel would grab our beer and chat, and Tsa'edu brought some members of the cultural troupe over with their musical instruments to our place. We really had spent good times. Tesfay Gomera, the head of the pharmacy branch behind the enemy defense lines, brought a plastic bag full of condoms and while having fun with us he said, "Good life and too much fun leads to problems and these condoms are my gift to you." The worry is not about fighters who may get killed in battles only, to protect the life of the fighters care is needed even in the sphere of social relation --those who turned cliffs into plains, and replaced difficulties with prosperity, the fighters who do not think of the bad, but only of the good need to be protected from unexpected danger.

After leaving Barentu to Kassala, I remembered the entire situation: the hardships and difficulties, the wounds and martyrdom that we passed on one side, and the caring and love, the camaraderie on the other side. I was so irritated to leave it behind to be stationed with the opportunist leaders who have only crooked thinking and who are at each other's throats. Those who are away from martyrdom by many kilometers, --to be with them again in the Sahel base area camps didn't please me.

The relations of those "enlightened revolutionaries," the relations of Halewa Sewra leaders can not be left without mentioning because it is an interesting example of how they behaved. Even if my closest friend, my comrade Isaac Wedi Rezene, whom I loved and respected, was there in Sahel, so was also my sweetheart Almaz, only their presence in Sahel was like a small paradise in the middle of a huge hell.

I didn't spend much time in Kassala and went to Port Sudan from where I bought a few items, like cigarettes and soap bars for my colleagues in Sahel, and tapes with songs that Almaz loved, and arrived in Sahel. Before I reached my unit, I went to Arareb and I spent a night with Almaz after which she took permission and we both went to Hishkeb andI didn't like what I found there. After a few days Almaz returned to her place, and I presented my report about Barentu and returned to my routine work.

Those who led the department were better educated cadres who attended university or were at least high school graduates, but when compared to what prevailed among the frontline troops, the love and camaraderie among them was as different as the sky and the earth. When you talk to each one of them privately everyone gossips about the other. On the contrary, they talk good about a leader or an ordinary combatant whom they consider are on their side, they exaggerate and elevate their status. Slowly you see the various groupings clearly. Sadly, the reasons they mention as the cause of the differences are inexplicable and are based on what Isaias once in his speech gave an exaggerated account about nepotism to damage the reputation of others in his bid to assume power and have total control of the organization. He exaggerated and presented minute shortcomings as if they were major problems.

The leaders in the valleys of the base area enjoyed a better lifestyle; they had their private offices and bedrooms. They do whatever they please in their offices, but they approach the ordinary fighters who sleep on the trenches and whisper, so and so is getting close with so and so, monitor his move; where are the cigarettes coming from?; the homemade liquor is getting abundant, and in that way they make everyone suspicious about the specific leaders they consider as competitors and want to inflict damage by making the fighters biased about them; they were engaged in cheap political wrangling.

And those who became tools in the political squabbles were the innocent but disciplined combatants who would follow any order because they lack political consciousness; they act only based on the directive given to them by a leader. Just like Isaac Rezene said, if you are not a member of the secret party, you reach a point where you cannot defend yourself after you have been evaluated in a secret meeting during which already a judgment has been passed on you. Even if you were a member of the party, if they campaign against you in secret and convince the other members it would be difficult to defend yourself.

Let me refer to a simple example: Dawit Habtu, who helped shape Halewa Sewra from the beginning and who led it as a member of the party and a senior officer and who became the editor of 'Halewa'the magazine of the department, was targeted in the political squabbles by Musa Naib 'Hargaf'(which means greedy in Tigrigna), the head of the Halewa Sewra Central Office and by Tewelde Wedi Andu the head of surveillance, both of whom lined up members of the party and accused Dawit of being unreliable in his work, and because they said he was demoralized they recommended for him to be transferred to another department...etc, he was as a consequence of such character assassination campaign replaced by elements who in comparison didn't contribute a small fraction of what he contributed. This was only because they depended on damaging people and making them fall as a means of clearing the way for their ascendency to power by eliminating more capable and potential competitors. They create excuses to control the power and monopolize it.

I witnessed when Wedi Andu criticized Dawit Habtu's report while he himself did not produce any report at all and he exited from the meeting without being criticized for not submitting a report! Before the meeting was closed, Dawit Habtu completed his job and was criticized for minor shortcomings in the work, but the member who, whether he worked or not, didn't even present any report was not criticized at all when the meeting was closed. This was something I have never seen before and I was compelled to intervene. I directed my criticism to Musa, the chairman, and I raised his mishandling of the issues, and I asked him to allow me to continue, though Tewelde Wedi Andu tried to end it by saying, "the point that Tsegu raised is correct" after Musa raised his criticism, I explained the mistake was from both of them and owing to my protest the conspiracy hatched to damage an innocent person failed. However, the organizing activities became wider and extensive and they continued their targeted attack like a ping pong ball ultimately kicking Dawit out to the information department.

The conflict continued now between Tewelde Wedi Andu as head of the party and Musa representing the front; the competition between them and their respective followers intensified. Finally the number of Musa's follower grew larger and Tewelde Wedi Andu was defeated and Musa ultimately represented both the party and the front. And in the Second Organizational Congress Musa was elected a member of the Central Committee. After they were done with Dawit Wedi Habtu, they tried to damage Rezene Seyoum who was devoted and focusing on his work. They started a secret campaign against him; I met Musa and told him, "You have before expelled the talented individual and what you want to show us now, we will go as far as we can." He withdrew the case.

In general, I was disgusted for returning to Sahel, and just like we evaluated it with Isaac Wedi Rezene the issue was centered on personal interest and I realized that it was very unhealthy. Knowing the question would come to haunt me, I was prepared ahead of time. To be there to liberate a country and be willing to sacrifice your life and then be immersed in such muddy situation was sad indeed. However, the needs of human beings are limitless and it can go as far as riding on the back of others to promote the interest of someone else. I witnessed that clearly. But are they imitating? Of course, the one who was using the same tactics and holding the steering wheel of the front, Isaias, the student of Machiavelli is there in the forefront.

***

The attacks of the enemy continued under different campaign names: Red Star, First Campaign, Second Campaign, Stealth Invasion, etc, and the rage of the battles went on intensifying. Whenever the situation became tense, individuals were pulled out of the departments and sent to the frontlines to cover empty patches on the defense lines, and the Derg was weakened. The Derg was weakened by the EPLF forces which were able to defeat it by sacrificing about a fifth of its capacity. Towards the end of the 1970s, the EPLF had changed its views on the mobilization strategy and policy. This was because the general indiscriminate mobilization was weakening its capacities, and putting into consideration the need and the contribution of the technically talented and professional individuals they were relieved from being mobilized to the war fronts. This new policy and practice of mobilization increased the competition among those who considered themselves the 'enlightened revolutionaries' and they developed a tendency of avoiding sacrificing their lives. However, those who consider themselves as 'enlightened revolutionaries' used it to send the undesired educated and potential competitor ones to the war front where the risks of martyrdom are high. It was under such a condition that Isaac Wedi Rezene was sent to the defense of the Nakfa front from where he never returned.

Before he left, he came to my office to see me and we went for dinner where we found Tewelde Wedi Andu and Wedi Rezene made a sarcastic comment at Wedi Andu by saying, "what happened today, you are here for dinner--didn't you find someone who could bring you dinner up to your office." Most of the time he would call and say, I am working; I have a guest, etc and annoy the cooks. He continued, "Up there would certainly be bottles of drinks to wash down the food." I didn't like the situation and I interrupted him by saying, "I have a gallon of Dmudmu in my place, later we will wash our dinner with that," and that way I changed the subject. After dinner, I told Tewelde Wedi Andu to follow us to my sleeping place and we left. I admonished Isaac Wedi Rezene, and told him, "What happened to you today? As if you were not saying these people have to be faced with due diligence!" Isaac Wedi Rezene said, now there is no time for a civilized method and I wanted to finish a small part of the task of facing them. I didn't understand and asked him if there were new development I didn't know about. He said that they have told him to gather the group who were supposed to go to the front the next morning at dawn. He said it is good to be away from this faceless place, may you have the same opportunity to leave it.

Isaac Wedi Rezene was very smart and intelligent and was physically fit. He used to be a basketball player at the YMCA in Asmara. He tried all kinds of indoor sports, and he had contributed a lot to the Hishkeb Sport Committee. Not only that, he was among those who worked in the department for many years and knew and understood the operations of the department very well. He played an important role in developing and changing it, he was among those that one would not want him to leave his position. I was dumbfounded and asked him when they told him to leave. He said they told him that same day a moment ago in his office and that he immediately came to meet me.

They know the policy of the organization but asking Isaac Wedi Rezene to be mobilized at that time was not an innocent decision, but what could be done, it was already decided. At any rate, before he left, Isaac Wedi Rezene wanted to know my view on the topic that we didn't finish last time and he asked me about my evaluation of the situation. 'I expected your situation and I understand things that could happen to me... I expect it, if the issue goes beyond acceptance, it can lead to confrontations, and the alliance among the powerful will arrive at a time like a knock out game of football, but it will eventually end. Just like the saying, the revolution eats its children, and a hen plays with the guts of its offspring'. I stopped when Tewelde Wedi Andu came and I changed the topic. Tewelde Andu left after drinking one cup of Dmudmu.

'Who did you call powerful! Are you comparing the group of Tewelde Wedi Andu with that of Musa? Tewelde Wedi Andu and his likes will be used to go along for a short time, but the group of Musa was initiated by Isaias and came down to them through Ali Saed, the showoff of Tewelde Wedi Andu's group cannot cross the Halewa Sewra gorge.' He added, 'I want to appeal to you, since martyrdom follows us wherever we go, if you live after me, please take care of my son Ephrem: Ephrem. Alas! Hilal, Amanuel, Hasebellah, Fitsum, Michael... are lost and they will be replaced by other Ephremes, Amanuels, Haseballahs -- and now Isaac Rezene is gone and will be replaced by other Isaacs so that other will not be orphaned, because his son has inherited the name of one of our colleagues who was martyred, and I appeal to you again so that this history will not evaporate but be passed to the next generation.' He packed his things and went to join the squad heading towards the front.

Fighters are not cruel at heart, when Isaac Wedi Rezene left; my eyes became watery. However I know that a fighter, who is ready to offer his life for his people, could pass away at any moment. But the special circumstance of Isaac Wedi Rezene left a never fading scar on my memory. In our last meeting, we couldn't talk comfortably because the situation was not ripe and we couldn't identify issues clearly, the time to talk about critical issues would preferably be after giving it due time for reflection, and after being certain. It was not the proper time for that. In general, we had a common observation and understanding about the situation. The person who would understand me in that valley, the one that could see trends and see their final direction, my dear colleague was separated from me. Though as a person I was affected by the feeling, and realizing the rationale that was presented by the leaders of the revolution with whom I was left, and since it was an incident that I expected from the day I joined, I tightened my belt and prepared myself to challenge any situation that may arise.

The next day I woke up early and went to the kitchen to eat breakfast and I discovered that Tewelde Wedi Andu had ordered breakfast to be brought to him in his office; I knew he was up and went to his office. I mentioned the transfer of Isaac Wedi Rezene and asked him in what manner and how the decision was reached. Tewelde Wedi Andu said, "you know our organization is pressuring us not to send the talented individuals who could contribute here, but sometimes it is good to blend some talented ones with the others, and send some and he was the only one who could be sent from this office."

I mentioned there were others who could be sent and that the frontline doesn't require spicing by sending Isaac Wedi Rezene as if one is putting onions and tomatoes to spice up a dish--and that we should use the talents that we have wisely, and that there were individuals who do nothing but limited to guard duties and it was not wise to send talented people so that the number of guards would not be decreased and that he should stop making decision that he cannot reverse by regret-- and better still, the talented individuals could double as guards and stay close where their skills are most needed and could be used. I was loud. Tewelde Wedi Andu assessed the situation and attempted to make an excuse that the decision was taken without enough thinking and that a grave error was committed. I found the excuse worse than the decision for which he was making the excuse, I was inflamed. I told him that we will be together and we will revisit it slowly in our journey. I left from his office.

Chapter 4. **TREATMENT OF ETHIOPIAN PRISONERS UNDER THE EPLF**

After the Second Organizational Congress, a Justice Department was established under the leadership of Ramadan Mohammed Nur. Law students and graduates like Rezene Seyoum, and others who had interrupted their law studies and were in Halewa Sewra, including Dawit Habtu, were pulled out of their respective units and they staffed the new Justice Department. As a result of losing several talented staff members, Halewa Sewra underwent restructuring. I was appointed Head of Interrogation and Gebrehannes Bashay Aineta became the Head of the Prisons. Halewa Sewra's talent pool suffered a lot and the gaps were filled by military commanders while political commissars filled the vacancies that required talented professional people.

The reorganization and the allocation of personnel were deliberate. The military commanders most of whom had no experience on the type of work of the department only executed orders from the Department Head without question. They put pressure on the more educated and the talented individuals in order to have them controlled. The new personnel in the department carried out campaigns and political organizations among the masses and were recruiting supporters and followers. The prime mover of the process Ali Saed, who was the highest authority and in order to protect his power he appointed Musa Naib as his deputy who managed the department that was staffed with his followers. Ali Saed Abdalla was the trusted right hand man and a loyal soldier of Isaias whose directives he accepted and executed without question.

I didn't want to continue in my position as head of interrogation because I didn't like the overall situation. Therefore, I wanted to be released from my function and be assigned to any other position. I applied through Musa Naib, by now a member of the central committee, and I received a negative response. Then I brought my application to his superior Ali Saed Abdalla and told him bluntly that I will not work in my current position and I was ultimately assigned as Commissioner of the Department of Ethiopian Prisoners of War (POWs). I was transferred to the POWs Department a short while after hearing the news that the Department Head Asha'al Wedi Zere had committed suicide and was replaced by Fisahatsion Shekha, 'Kurue Dummu'.

Asha'al was not educated when he was growing up; he was one of the Asmarinos who were so confident of their strength, such as Gebrezghi Arej, Rezene Ukket, and Yemane China. He grew up in Villagio Giunio and was a famous character in Asmara. Asha'al was often involved in fights and he was once accused and charged with murder and was jailed. He joined the EPLF and was assigned to Halewa Sewra in northern Bahri but was subsequently transferred to the central location and finally became the Head of thePOWs Department.

Asha'al didn't like Marxism, he followed a personal philosophy of his own and admired Digano, the Italian philosopher. Neither did he believe in the equality of women, nor much of the policies of the organization. He had a low self esteem and used to say, 'people like me can only contribute in this field of war and after liberation we do not have a role.' Though so much was said about his suicide, regardless of how true it was, according to Gaber the commander of the prisoners guard force, who was in the area with him at the time, Asha'al was intoxicated with liquor and had depression which finally led to his suicide.

After I was assigned to the POWs department, I wanted to improve the work, and I asked an academician among those who used to frequently visit the field, who happened to be my maternal uncle, Dr. Bereket HabteSelassie, to send me books on international law and books and documents that could help me in the handling of war prisoners. I among other documents wanted the Geneva Conventions and other documents related to war prisoners and references that show the experience of other countries. He sent me some books that helped me acquire new knowledge and insight about the new job. The EPLF didn't sign the Geneva Conventions; however, although the handling of prisoners was dictated by the requirements of the military strategy which focuses on how to weaken the capacities of the enemy, our handling of the war prisoners was fairly humane and just and meets the standard set by the Geneva Convention. In contrast, there were cases when minor mistakes of Eritrean freedom fighters have been blown out of proportion in order to incriminate them and make them appear big that could lead to the destruction of the organization. Such incidents have at times resulted in passing death sentences on individual offenders. But when it comes to the cases of POWs the EPLF was transformed into an angel, and for those who do not know the nature and character of the EPLF from inside, it could be deceiving.

When war prisoners are detained, they do not cause problems or incur damage except the manpower that guards them. To make sure that such prisoners were treated humanely and taken good care of, and be able to show the world that they are handled humanely, it is natural and would not be surprising that different charitable entities took notice and admired. Because of the way POWs were handled many countries and NGOs that advocate for human rights were willing to be involved in the affairs of the prisoners. Thus handling POWs humanely has yielded huge international diplomatic and material benefits for the EPLF.

It was understood that there would be no benefit to be gained from lining up the prisoners who pose no risk to the organization and summarily execute them. On the contrary, treating them in a humane way was rewarded with material assistance that was not only enough to sustain them but also contributed greatly to the sustenance of the fighters and the civilian population who were under the front's administration. Moreover, the EPLF also made good use of the labor of the prisoners. It used them in building roads and in undertaking agricultural projects, and they contributed to their own well-being and also to the well-being of the organization and the struggle. And as a matter of principle mistreating war prisoners inhumanely is not only prohibited under international norms and is a shameful act of inhumanity but it also doesn't yield any benefit.

One may wonder as to why the leadership of the EPRP/EPLF treated humanely the Ethiopian POWs who were armed and had com to attack it, while it was killing the nationalist Eritreans who were part of the national struggle and who made themselves available to fight the common enemy? This question doesn't require much thought; it is clear and is the A, B, C of power politics.

Since the Ethiopian enemy soldiers were the prisoners of the Eritrean people, it was unthinkable that they would agitate and organize Eritreans and make them work for the advancement of their interest of seizing political power. Isaias had nothing to worry about concerning these Ethiopian war prisoners. However, the Eritrean freedom fighters, who were willing and ready to fall alongsidetheir compatriots and who are entitled to engage in any dialogue on issues of concern to Eritrea, and who stood for the rights of the Eritrean people by showing their disapproval of certain undemocratic decisions and policies, and had the ability to mobilize and convince the other fighters, were seen as potential threat and eliminated. Isaias realized that they can even create a situation that could effect change in the leadership structure of the organization, and because he did not want to risk any change of leadership, owing to his selfish interest of maintaining power, he chose to eliminate them rather than engage in dialogue and accommodate their demands for reform and move ahead.

Isaias and his cohorts could not think beyond their egoistic interest of monopolizing power. They are selfish, opportunists who are blinded by their hunger for power, and who put their interest ahead of the Eritrean people. They are a backward thinking lot. Ofcourse, this doesn't mean that because the fighters were not treated humanely the prisoners should not have been treated humanely.

After I was assigned as a head of the POWs Department, the lower Hishkeb office was a bit far from where the prisoners' camps were located. In order to be able to follow the work closely I shifted my office to Arareb. There were about ten thousand Ethiopian and hundreds of Eritrean prisoners. The number of the Eritrean prisoners became relatively small compared to that of the Ethiopians they were held in separate places. After taking academic and political education, except for a few, most of the Eritreans were recruited to the ranks of the EPLF. The location of the prisoners'camps was widely spread extending from Nakfa until a place called Beref inside the Sudan. But the largest prisoners' camp was at Ayteway inside Sudanese territory close to the Eritrean border.

In terms of authority structure, the Military Commander had the highest position of command at the camp while the Commissar was in charge of mobilization, records keeping, monitoring and surveillance. After I came to the camp, the committee that investigated Ethiopian war criminals was shifted from the Interrogation Department to the POWs Department.

The group that was in charge of rehabilitating and conscientizing the POWs was publishing a bi-weekly magazine called Ewnet. The primary objective of the magazine was to educate the prisoners but it soon expanded and was made to reach the Ethiopian soldiers of the Derg. It was smuggled and distributed inside the defense lines of the enemy and it contributed greatly to disseminating news of POWs. A cultural troupe called 'Ethiopian Prisoners Cultural Department' was set up by the prisoners and it entertained them and contributed to changing their quality of life. A healthy atmosphere of entertainment was created and they became harmless up to the time they were released. To prevent their physical conditions from deteriorating, and to invigorate their minds, to prevent them from undesirable thoughts and engaging in disputes due to idleness , as well as an entertainment and a participatory sport activity were created for them. Though preparing a volleyball field was easy and the prisoners liked it, they played different sports in different facilities that were made available depending on a specific location. In addition, whenever they wanted they could play indoor sports like checkers, chess, and playing cards that were all readily available.

Since the prisoners stayed in detention, in order to make better use of their time academic classes were organized and offered to them. Classes starting from basic literacy going up to elementary school education were prepared. Some teachers were identified from among the POWs to teach and the academic level of many prisoners was improved. Moreover, those who had higher education were encouraged to teach each other and elevate their knowledge base and many of those who were interested made use of the opportunity.

In addition, in order to help them develop skills, instructors were assigned from among them and also from the fighter pool to train them in handcrafts and other life skills. They were able to produce tools for their daily use. And the principle of self reliance, that was so much advertised by the EPLF and other leftist organizations and which often is not translated in reality, but seen through the eyes of those who came to visit the prisoners, journalists and representatives of humanitarian organizations, the prisoners' work was much admired and self reliant in the true sense of the concept.

They were able to produce tools: wooden and metal combs, extracting wires from discarded vehicle tires and melting plastic containers, large bowls and pans made from canned food cans, couches, beds, drawers and other furniture for daily use that were made from ammunition boxes, and paintings:--activities that showcased the policies of the EPLF and how it handled the war prisoners. But when such well developed handling of prisoners is compared with the way the imprisoned Eritrean freedom fighters were treated, it is not difficult to identify the diplomatic motive behind the humane way POWs were treated. As Machiavelli said, the EPRP, and particularly his student Isaias, believed in the notion of 'the end justifies the means', and he was determined to stay in the position of power that he was occupying, and he used any means to maintain and preserve his power. He was well aware of what he was doing. In order for him to reach his aim, hindrances that could appear in the way, particularly threat from among the freedom fighters had to be eliminated.

It was not possible to maintain acceptable living conditions for the fighters and prisoners or to defeat the situation and improve their living conditions with limited resources at the disposal of the front. Therefore, it was decided that the POWs should be involved in agricultural production and become self-reliant. The resources that were deployed to guarding the prisoners were helpful in making the prisoners productive, change their living condition and that of their surrounding, because they led by example by becoming productive themselves. Though the productivity of the agriculture activities differed from one place to another based on the natural resources endowment of a given region, different activities were carried out in accordance with the nature of the regions, and in line with the availability of spaces and the characteristic of the terrain of the area.

The terrain and climate of Sahel where they were camped, except for some places of high elevations in the surroundings of Nakfa and the camp where they were located, in the surroundings of Arareb, and small and temperate areas on the mountains of Hager, the rest is all dry and arid land, and the inhabitants of these areas were nomads who don't depend on agriculture for their livelihood. The mountains of Sahel, on top of them being badly eroded and with no top soil, the water was also salty. Even the seasonal streams that run down from the gorges to the rivers on limited period of the year, let alone to help in agricultural projects, they were not suitable for domestic use. Moreover, it was not possible to use irrigation because it required specialized skills and capacities.

In such a situation, the members of Halewa Sewra and the prisoners achieved qualitative change in their living conditions. Those who were in the central location in Ayteway were mainly involved in animal husbandry and poultry engaged in raising cattle, goats, sheep, chicken, and ducks and were successful. Though the area was dry and the water salty, they made terraces on the mountains that preserved more top soil, made small irrigation channels and were able to cultivate and produce green peppers, tomatoes, eggplants, and other vegetables. The prisoners' camp near Nakfa prepared satisfactory farming lands and cultivated all kinds of vegetables and legumes. The produce was adequate enough to meet the needs of the prisoners, of the sick, and even of the fighters situated in the area.

The largest handcraft production unit that the prisoners and fighters used was located in Arareb. However, another self-sufficient location was also established in Ayteway. All sorts of household utensils were produced there. In addition, POWs were engaged in weaving and woodwork. They made ploughing tools, and tools for road and house construction, like hammers, spades, pickaxes and levers. The source of raw materials for making tools were recycled items: old tires, shock absorbers, ammunition boxes, oil and food cans, oil jerry cans, flour and grain sacks, and wood and clay soil from the surrounding areas.

The political and diplomatic gains were enormous. In addition to freeing the POWs from the Derg's political propaganda that they brought with them they also gained firsthand knowledge about the history and nature of the Eritrean struggle. Some of them considered the EPLF a mercenary army paid by the Arab countries to cut a piece of Ethiopia and sell it to the Arabs. To change their twisted historical understanding, they were taught world history and related topics, and they became aware that the propaganda that they were fed by the Derg or even previously by the Haile Selassie government was not correct. On top of the Eritrean and Ethiopian history, a platform was created for them to discuss the rights of Ethiopian ethnic groups and nationalities and their movements for self determination. Their political consciousness was elevated and many of them joined the Ethiopian opposition organizations.

Nevertheless, it doesn't mean that there were no problems among the prisoners as they were engaged in all of these productive activities. Let alone the salaried soldiers, even those who voluntarily gave their lives to become monks, even the fighters who were willing to sacrifice their lives faced certain challenges. Naturally there were difficulties related to the sexual urges that the prisoners could not subdue as human beings. The urges tested the prisoners who had no women among them because the women who were deployed to serve the Ethiopian soldiers were immediately pardoned and released after they were captured and were sent home. Though they were not fed nutritious and tasty food that would increase their urges, they were not able to control their biological urges. Because of that, homosexual behaviors occurred among many of them.

Traditionally, homosexuality is one of the most rejected and abhorred behaviors in the Eritrean society. When an Eritrean is found in such an act, he is completely excluded and isolated from the society. May be it is as a result of such tradition and prevailing social norms that the EPLF laws on homosexuality were stringent and harsh. In the military law of the EPLF it is articulated that, 'homosexuality is punishable by death.' Not only that, it is said that in the initial stages, the EPLF apprehended fighters who were accused of homosexuality and after proving the accusation, it immediately executed them without trial. In view of the fairly widespread practice among the Ethiopian Prisoners of War, if the EPLF military laws were applied, many among the prisoners would have been executed. Thus, the EPLF laws didn't find practical application as concerns the Ethiopian POWs.

Red Rose was the commissar in charge of the prisoners' camp that was close to my office. Influenced by the perspective of the organization, he had a lot of hate for the homosexuals, and he wouldn't have objected to have them tried and punished. Red Rose was smart and intelligent; he had mastered the Amharic language to a level of proficiency equal to that of the prisoners. He had also studied and learned their culture. At night he would cover himself in blankets like they used to do and sneak among them to observe and witness what was going on inside the camp. He saw what happened and heard the conversation; he didn't need someone to present him with a testimony. He knew in details who was who, who thinks what, and who wants what, among the prisoners. We were also carrying out similar monitoring and follow up in the other POW camps.

Because the guards knew the condition of the prisoners in minute details, it was helpful to them to be ready and prepared to prevent actions and deeds that could unfold and cause an unwanted situation. Often they were able to correct it and stop it before it happened. However, inspite of the intensive mobilization activities undertaken within the camp of POWs and the considerable success achieved, it would be impossible to control every activity of the enormous population of prisoners. If one is able to change a few prisoners, to transform the other into harmless individuals, what remains is monitoring the few stubborn individuals. Monitoring was carried out by recruiting prisoners from among them, or by sneaking own members inside their circles and noting additional observations. Getting a clearer picture of activities was not difficult and expected damages were aborted on the basis of the information obtained.

Many sabotage activities were tried and had failed during execution. One major attempt was carried out by one of the regiment of prisoners that were camped in Ayteway. They planned to beat the guards and snatch rifles and then proceed to the other prisoners 'camps to free the prisoners and escape. The operation was conceived by an imprisoned officer who was under treatment at the central hospital with the participation of other prisoners who were transferred to the central hospital to receive better medical treatment. The operation was secretly planned by the prisoners who trusted each other very much. They didn't accept the fact that they were prisoners. Preparing the tools that would help them in executing the operation was their top priority. They prepared the tools they needed from the material they used for making utensils. They made knives from the different metals, and sculpted stones and other sharp objects to be used to overpower the guards.

However, although the prisoners were able to prepare some of the tools that they needed for the operation, their plans were being followed and strictly monitored by the security guards. As a result all of them were apprehended before they could move and the operation was foiled before it started.

This particular operation was attempted by a Major who was captured in Barentu and pardoned and because he chose to return to Barentu he was escorted to the town. He planned the operation. When the Major was captured in the battle of Barentu, he was a Lieutenant, but due to his loyalty to the regime and his contributions, he was promoted to the rank of a Major. The movement of the prisoners that he planned and led was being monitored by the surveillance and security guard members. It was stopped before they could take the final steps.

When the Major was presented in front of a tribunal, he said, 'I have observed the EPLF seriously. I understand your struggle for self determination and it is right. However, what will happen in the end, Eritrea will be separated from Ethiopia and my conscience could not accept that separation. I couldn't swallow it, that Eritrea will be

119

separated from Ethiopia and be self-reliant, and Ethiopia will be strangulated and choked without an access to the sea. Because of that, I ignored the great pardon that the EPLF bestowed on my life and I was captured again with a higher rank. Though the decision of the pardon was taken under the pressure of war, if it was not guided by its policies, it could have shot us and left us in the gorges.' He added, 'I have observed and witnessed, different Ethiopian national movements come to our camps and take selected prisoners who were pardoned, to join their movements if they so chose. I am also an eyewitness that some were set free to go to their respective villages. I, when I was with the senior officers, you have allowed us to form any political organization that we prefer. However, to be captured fighting the EPLF again, with a higher rank, after I was pardoned, made me give up hope on life--I was afraid that if you discover I was captured for the second time you will not pardon me-- This mission was my attempt because I wanted to be free from the life of a prisoner, by any means.'

Answering a question about the fate of prisoners who were set free by the EPLF and return to Ethiopia, and how the Ethiopian government handles their case, he said, "that the Ethiopian authorities treated their issue as a special case. First, their decision to return to Barentu though they had choices, to face any eventuality, it assured them of the officers loyalty to Ethiopia. What followed was the EPLF policies on POWs and the influence that those who were pardoned would have on the Ethiopian army, they explained the situation as if the EPLF was militarily pushed and was escaping and it left the prisoners without taking any action against them because the Ethiopian army was chasing them and about to attack, and they had to leave the prisoners. Concerning the general issue of other prisoners who were freed, they were worried and believed that if the news spread among the people, it would cause a dangerous situation and they took steps they considered necessary to stop the spread of the news, they went to the extent of detaining and killing."

There was one partially successful attempted escape plan by the Ethiopian prisoners. Once when armed guards were accompanying a number of prisoners to a harvesting work, after they reached a considerable distance in the mountains, and the leader of the guards started to go down the slope of the mountain, the prisoners and the guards were separated into two groups. When one group had already reached the peak and was descending on the other side, the rest were ascending the slope. When they reached the high range of the mountain, the prisoners who were at the back overpowered and choked the fighter who was guarding at the rear end took his gun and hit the other guard who was ahead of the line and tried to escape. However, the mountains of Sahel were on the side of the fighters— the prisoners couldn't find their wayin such difficult terrain. Some of the prisoners returned to the camps on their own, while others died of hunger and thirst. Still others were apprehended by other fighters. Dispersed, they couldn't accomplish their plan.

The EPLF divided and separated prisoners according to their nationality and ranks. They were categorized as Eritreans, Russians, high ranking Ethiopian officers and senior authorities, frontline officers and ordinary soldiers.

Chapter 5. THE ERITREAN LIBERATION ARMY'S SECOND INITIATIVE

5.1 The Second Organizational Congress and the Nadew Offensive

Shekha Gurja camp in Mereb rivals Filfil in northern Bahri the one that is endowed with a temperate climate and lush trees and gardens. It is adorned by Arkokebay (coconut) trees and wide streams; the underground water level near the banks of the river is high and only a shallow digging is required to dig a well for irrigating gardens. The love among the fighters was very warm; they moved within and between the units and departments and still felt at home wherever they went. After I was separated from Tsgereda Gual Signora, though the environment was suitable for establishing other romantic relations, I didn't rush to start a new one. Every once in a while I tried, but the conditions were not favorable and I didn't get steady with anyone. It was in such a situation that suddenly I started a brief but intense love affair story that I kept to myself.

Here name is Yemisrach, a tall beautiful girl from Asmara. Her big eyes looked as if she was tearing up, so big they mirrored large reflections and made one do away with mirrors in Mereb. God stopped making other eyes after making hers. Her hair was silky and dangled down reaching her lower back. Though I saw her in our Asmara neighborhood as a child, I didn't make acquaintance with this Asmarina girl of Emba Galiano. Her elder brother was my schoolmate and I remember his beautiful younger sisters.

When I returned to my location after attending a meeting, I found her in the kitchen with a mixed race Italian young man. I greeted them and sat down. Yemisrach looked at me and said that she thinks she knows me, speaking in Tigrinya with an Amharic accent. I told her that I also know her, Yemisrach! She hasn't changed much since I last saw her. She corrected me on her name saying that it was Nbserat, and she didn't like her actual name, Yemisrach. I didn't understand why she changed her name. She introduced me to her sister and her brother-in-law but I didn't know why they were there. I preferred not to say anything and I made an excuse and went to my office. I checked some files on my table which were opened in my absence and I now knew why they were there and I returned to the kitchen and continued chatting.

The human traffickers/smugglers who were accompanying Yemisrach and her group to the Sudan abandoned them and fled when they saw freedom fighters. The freedom fighters that caught them sent them to Halewa Sewra. Yemisrach started to talk about Emba Galiano and mentioned all the buildings starting from Officio Gondrand until Santa Familgia; she drew a picture of my neighborhood that I left a long time ago. For a while I forgot I was in Mereb, I envisioned all my childhood friends. Most of them have either joined the revolution or travelled overseas, and those she left behind were too young for me to remember. I asked Yemisrach why she was going to the Sudan. She said, "I don't know, but my brother- in-law has an Italian citizenship and he was taking his wife along with him to Italy; they told me to join and they said they will do everything to have me travel with them but I am not sure if I will succeed or not, I joined them with no plans."

In the evening, they went to the guest resting area and I went to my bed until we met at breakfast the next day. I asked her where she slept and she told me she slept with her sister and her husband. I joked, "Were you a good referee, why didn't you ask for a separate place?" She smiled, "Referee! You will see, I will blow a whistle on you."

I was listening to music and working when Yemisrach unexpectedly came to my office, "you are listening to the music alone, and you don't even invite others?" The comment was not in vain, I think she wanted to make me blow a whistle. I told her that I will finish the work in my hands and will call her and as far as the music is concerned it is just like being in Mocambo club and thanks to the traders who pass bymusic is abundantly available.

I couldn't continue my work. Her big eyes appeared to me on the pages of the papers I was working on and I repeatedly questioned myself. Though it was natural for me to be interested in a girl when I lived alone; she was there because she has a case and I started to think of a relation that I was not sure where it will lead and how it will end. I advised myself, "Tsegu, don't rush, what will happen will happen naturally, handling such an issue carefully saves you from unnecessary risks." I went into deep thoughts for hours, but when I checked my watch time had not moved at all. I realized there was something within pushing me. I was patient for two hours in my office and then I went to where she was and I met Yemisrach. "Now the music that you love..." She interrupted me saying, "I am coming...." and she stood up and we left, she didn't want her sister or her brother-in-law to come along.

My office was a tent pitched inside a forest of Arkokebay trees, it was a quiet place at some distance from the kitchen and guest places. Inside were a table, a chair, a guest stool made from Arkokebay ropes, and a filing cabinet. Behind the stool was a rolled sponge mattress on which I slept. When both sides of the tent are opened, there comes pleasant breeze, and sometimes even rain droplets, it made the tent comfortable. A large stereo tape recorder was on top of the filing cabinet.

When I brought her to the tent, she sat on the stool and I went to where the tape recorder was and asked her what kind of music she would like to hear. She asked if I had tapes of the Beatles, and I played 'Don't Let Me Down'. Then she asked for John Lennon's 'Imagine' followed by Etta James' 'I would rathergo blind; these were songs we used to play in tango dances. Yemisrach's mind went away and she floated on a different planet. She evenforgot I was sitting next to her.

She said, "Sorry, I was thinking about Asmara, I see you cannot live without music and I am even more like that, God has dropped me in an unknown place!" She leaned on my chest and my heart beat increased. I had convinced myself not to be hasty, but at that moment I totally forgot about that.

"Are you seriously with me or with the one in Asmara?"

"It is the nostalgia of the music, it took me back. Otherwise, I have left the one in Asmara behind; I was not worried what I will encounter. Please don't take me into that, I have finished with him when I left."

"Did you finish with him to travel overseas?" I continued my questions.

"No. It's only because I had enough. I didn't have plans to travel overseas, my sister pushed me to that, I do not have any idea where I will end up."

I murmured to myself, "Holy Mary, rewarded you well Tsegu, by getting you an Asmarina girl in bandit-land." I slipped my fingers in her hair and put my lips on hers.

Yemisrach was so happy at that unexpected happening of the moment. It was a stormy Situation. I was dumbfounded where and when all that started, and at first I didn't know how to handle it. Though she grew up in Asmara, Yemesrach's parents were Ethiopian. And we met in a place where I was struggling to push out the Ethiopian occupation authority and establish an independent Eritrean system of government. Many freedom fighters who knew nothing except Eritrea, though they had Ethiopian ancestry, fell fighting in the ranks of the liberation fronts. In addition to that, the EPLF has educated and rehabilitated Ethiopian POWs to join its ranks. Many were martyred and some were even able to survive and witness the liberation of Eritrea.

I asked her, "Now, what do you plan to do?"

She replied, "I will remain with you here."

"How?"

"I will join the struggle."

Her body is lighter than cotton, her smell is enchanting, I loved Yemisrach and whatever the consequences, as far as it is her wish, I decided to let her stay with me. When we stayed together in Mereb, we enjoyed a brief but beautiful love story. In the land of the bandits, in a place we unknowingly slept close to bandits, no one knew about our love and we enjoyed ourselves without hesitation and rolled on the meadows of Mereb listening to romantic music. When she noticed that I gave her all my love, Yemisrach said she had never before experienced such intense love.

After about two months, I confided about the affair that was going on to my colleague Girmay Shawl, a member of the Interrogation Department. He was supportive and encouraged me and suggested that we should send her to the training camp. At that time I had on one hand an assistant, a "comrade", who came from the political cesspool of Sahel and who immediately reported anything happening in the behind enemy defense lines by spicing it up as he pleases, and on the other side was Yemisrach. The fact that she will stay behind her sister who will be leaving, bothered me, making me feel uneasy. In the end, I and Girmay Shawl agreed to explain to her sister and the department members about the decision and then send Yemisrach to the training camp. It was at that time that I left for the base area in Sahel to attend a meeting.

People were sent to Halewa Sewra for different reasons: there were those who did not have cases against them, the Ethiopian soldiers who surrendered, foreigners who were caught trying to sneak out to the Sudan, and Eritreans who could not join the struggle for different reasons and who wished to go abroad. All these were kept in the Halewa Sewra camp until their numbers were enough to be sent to Sudan. After I left for Sahel, the number of those going to Sudan had reached the required size and my assistance who in my absence was deputizing as head of the department called Yemisrach's name with the group who were leaving for Sudan and told her to prepare herself. She told him she had decided to remain and join the struggle, but he insisted and told her she cannot remain. Girmay Shawl tried his best to persuade him but he was not willing to listen.

When I returned from Sahel, I expected that Yemisrach would have been sent to the training camp, but a day after I returned Girmay Shawl came to my office and handed me an envelope that was left by Yemisrach. Though she was not willing to leave, she left to the Sudan after she was told that she cannot join the struggle. It was a shock and painful to me. I played Temane Gebremichael Barla's song, "Nea'akhi Z'habe Girma." My colleague Girmay explained to me about the situation in which Yemisrach left and that it was outside his control; he also told me that she didn't have any bad feelings towards me and she accepted taking the matter as a destiny willed by God.

I couldn't open the envelope and I asked Girmay Shawl to accompany me for a walk to the football field. We walked silently for a few minutes.

Shawl broke the silence, "You brought us a weird person."

I asked, "I have never seen anything like it, did you tell him, by the way?"

He was disturbed, "Told him! I wish I didn't tell him. Why would someone who wants to struggle be denied a chance? This is not his father's domain."

I lighted a cigarette at the football field and opened the envelope that she left me. Shawl reached to his pocket and gave me a ring that Yemisrach left for me. I started to read the letter, I read a few lines and went into thoughts, then I resumed reading and when I finished reading I burned the letter.

The letter read, "My missed and beloved brother, Tsegu! I can't express the sadness I felt writing this letter. The love that we had would not leave my memory, I never slept well after you left, I missed you a lot. But that was fine, now I am facing a more difficult situation. I grew up in Asmara, but now I feel I was not a child of Asmara, I don't know what I have done. They told me I cannot join the struggle, all the things you told me was erased in its entirety and everything turned to its opposite. I wish I didn't know you. I can't say you wronged me because I know what type of person you are, and there is nothing that you did, I am just bitter at my fate, my brother Tsegu. Keep the picture that is attached to the letter so that you don't forget me, and so that you don't take me out of your memory, I am leaving you a ring with Girmay Shawl. I will try to console myself by listening to Yemane's song.

From the one who loves you from the heart."

Yemisrach.

Ah! Gedli Oh struggle! What a deep abyss you are! A freedom fighter bears everything thrown at him, including separation from his/her sweetheart. He/She is also separated from his colleagues who are martyred. No one wants separation; it is fate. Girmay was disturbed more than I was, about the unfinished love affair. I found myself lost for words. Silence is more eloquente.

"I haven't seen such a crooked mind in my life, is the 'comrade' all right in the head?" Girmay asked.

I was upset, "its good you didn't see the thick headed people who sent him here, but this 'comrade' is not even educated enough! He is dumb and wouldn't understand even if he is educated."

"I have never seen anything like that; I don't think there is a worse creature than him." Girmay didn't know who ordered the guy to do what he did.

"All right now, enough, we cannot possibly talk enough about this." We stayed in that place for an hour and we didn't notice the passage of time.

The leaders who sent the 'comrade' to be my assistant in the areabehind enemy defense lines were the same dumb people who deployed Wedi Rezene to the frontline with no justification. They did everything they can to stretch their sphere of influence; whoever was considered a hindrance to them had to be removed at all costs. The re-organization was made to remove the freedom fighters they thought would be a threat and hindrance to their aim. Isaac Rezene didn't live long after he was deployed to the frontline, the brave man whose physical fitness and selflessness was much talked about in the front, was martyred in the struggle to which he was not compelled but volunteered to offer his blood. We hadn't finished the discussions that we started when Isaac left to the place from which not many return alive.

It was after this sad incident that Almaz came to Mereb to console me. Almaz's eyes looked similar, but Yemisrach's eyes were special not given to any other creature after her. Maybe it is the culture of Amhara people that taught their women how to approach a man, they are equal on that. I have never prayed for myself, but I prayed so much for Yemisrach to find another Tsegu, I had nothing else to do but wish her well in her future life.

I didn't find any news about Yemisrach before Eritrea was liberated. Fast toward after independence, I went to the airport to find out from the security office when a certain visitor from overseas entered Asmara. I was checking the passengers' manifesto and suddenly I saw Yemisrach's name on it. I checked her entry card and found out she was staying at the Keren Hotel where I immediately went after work. They told me she had travelled to Massawa a day earlier; I returned to my work without meeting her.

Back to Sahel when I shifted my office to Arareb, I was meeting with Almaz frequently because she was stationed there. In order to solidify our relations we decided to get married and the wedding time was set for 1986 at Adobha-- a group-freedom fighters' wedding, where several couples shouted "Victory to the Masses" and entered a covenant. In place of a tuxedo, we were given a Milano military uniform, and instead of neckties and crowns, we were given sarongs which we wrapped around our shoulders and heads. But the love was purer than water; it was different from traditional weddings. Goats were slaughtered, dmudmu the freedom fighters' drink was brewed and after the invitees ate and drank, and it was time for singing and dancing. Six couples of newly weds danced together--we were our own best men and bridesmaids--there was no need for someone to lift the brides' dress/vello, or to open the limousines' doors. There were no priests or sheikhs; we signed on a paper, on a simple table, and vowed to never betray each other and to multiply. No jewelry and gifts for the bride was asked, after the Milano uniforms, the brides' families didn't ask for a dowry, the organization took care of the expenses of the wedding, good food and drinks were prepared by the freedom fighters. It was a magnificent wedding.

The wedding was special because it was attended and graced by three elders: Zegenfo, a fighter, Aboy Araya, EPLF militia, and Aboy Debessay, member of the EPLF mass organization. Zegenfo andAboy Debessay came fleeing from the highlands, and my aunt's husband, Aboy Araya Abraham who was jailed by the ELF and who was released after it was pushed by the EPLF and moved out of Eritrea, into Sudan made the wedding exceptional. Zegenfo and Aboy Araya came to Sahel through Sudan and happened to be there by chance. Aboy Debessay had been involved in the reconciliation efforts between the ELF and EPLFin the highlands, and when the ELF wouldn't leave him alone and sought protection at the EPLF's Solomuna camp, he was invited to attend the wedding. He wrapped his Netsela (Shawl) and started to dance and he switched the dancing that was known as "our fighters or our children'sdance" to its original traditional style. Zegenfo, who was used to Qechech (Anice) liquor, didn't admire the dmudmu much; nevertheless he excused himself stating there was no other choice. They gulped the drinks all night until they spread their blankets and went to sleep.

Late at night, each bride and groom went to their respective small tents, the size of a doghouse, which was prepared for us to spend our honeymoon. But after sunrise when it became too hot inside the tents we had to go out and sit under the shade of the trees. A man approached our tent and asked, "Did you see a camel?" Almaz replied, "We didn't."

It was our colleague, a fighter Saleh Hamed Omer who was dressed like a pastoralist civilian. He came to join us under the shade and said, "It is burning hot inside the tent, but Khedija (his wife} has turned into butter and she is still there." He added, "But I am not thinking about Khedija turning into butter, I am worried what will happen to the children who will be born here!"

I laughed, "Maybe they will be born as worms!"

Almaz joined the laugher and said, "You are crazy, change the subject."

"Liar, you like the chat." I saw her laugh hysterically.

"Aren't you talking about the children who would be born?"

Saleh remembered my daughter Yohanna, "No problem, they will not be born as worms, God is there, and that is if they don't die of hunger."

"What you just said is even worse; you want to get my husband sick?" Almaz left to check on Khedija.

After the honeymoon of two weeks, we left for Arareb. Almaz stayed with me for a while and then I escorted her to her unit and returned to mine and started to catch-up with the work. Meanwhile, the organization was preparing for the Second Organizational Congress.

Towards the end of 1988, Gorbachev, the then leader of the Soviet Union introduced a general restructuring and reorganizing of the old Soviet system in a project that came to be known a 'Glasnost'. Though the Soviet Union didn't change its position regarding the Eritrean revolution, the fact that the East-West polarization and the cold war was normalizing, the assistance that used to be given to Ethiopia to weaken the Eritrean struggle at the end of the 'Red Star Campaign' when they attacked, had been reduced considerably. Even the leftist socialist ideology has been weakened, and the socialist-oriented secret party within the EPLF had also to change with the rest of the world. The party was forced to adjust its policies and transform itself by even changing its name so as to be in tune with the time and adjust with the new developments to avoid alienation from the global leftist community.

To advance along with new development that was unfolding in the international arena, the orientation that was given to the freedom fighters of the EPLF was presented in an improved manner. Even the seminars were conducted in a different style and the contents were much more sober and different than before; the leaders had decided to move away from the Marxist dogma of the past by adopting a much milder philosophy they termed 'social justice' in place of socialism. The secret party, EPRP, taking into account the changing global reality as well as recognizing the potential internal dissent and conflict that could emerge, became willing to organize the Second Organizational Congress which should have been convened three years after the first one but had been deferred for ten years. It unusually rushed to furnish the required logistics and complete the preparatory activities and set a convenient ground for convening the congress.

The secret party held its election secretly and came out with a list of names of those who were proposed and 'mandated' to become members of the EPLF Central Committee and was distributed to all party cells. Based on that, at the Second and Unification Congress, the ELF splinter group called Saghem became an integral part of the

EPLF. Those whose names were presented by the party, the leaders of the organization, including Isaias and his clique, were elected as leaders of the EPLF unopposed. As was also the case in the first congress, the secret party congress was secretly held before the organizational and unity congress of the front. Just as Adhanom Gebremariam remarked at the first congress, the homework was already finished during the second congress of the secret party. After the completion of the first organizational congress the leaders did not wastetime to destroy the Yemeen movement which was the only one left and since it was defeated at the first congress it remained with no political support base to defend it.

In the EPLF, congresses were never held in time as required by the congress resolutions; this was one of the methods that the party used to extend its stay in power. The attempted reform movements within the organization were eliminated and there was no reason that could cause delaying the holding of congresses in time. The case of the ELF was resolved in 1981, and there was no organized power that could threaten the EPLF internally. But because there was no internal excuse for not holding the congress in time, the leadership was using the international situation as an excuse to delay the congress. However, though all the excuses were not acceptable because there was no threat within the organization the leadership decided when the congress would be held and approved the resolution already prepared at the secret party congress.

At any rate, after ten years, the second organizational and unity congress of the EPLF was convened in 1987 in Arareb. The exceptionality of the congress was the fact that a faction of the ELF that was called DMLE that was camped at the Eritrean-Sudanese border at Rasay changed its name to Saghem and became part of the EPLF. The second part of this faction that split from the ELF, didn't trust the EPLF and had opposing views to its vision and it adopted the name of Saghem-Qetsel and crossed over to Tigray, Ethiopia, to continue its struggle after rejecting the call for total unity. It is still active in Tigray against the PFDJ, and though it has the TPLF's support, and carries out sporadic activities, for over twenty five years it has been limited to the forests of Tigray and western Eritrea and until now there is no visible achievement that it accomplished. Still, it doesn't seem to be aware of the reality.

Saghem that joined the EPLF was small in terms of numbers and the number of leadership positions that it asked for in the EPLF.

Considering the expansion of the organization that unfolded in 1987, was not worrisome; an agreement was reached for the allocation of limited number of leadership positions to Saghem and were united with the EPLF. Based on that arrangement, in addition to those who were nominated by the EPRP to become members of EPLF Central Committee, five senior leaders of Saghem were made to join the leadership as members of the central committee. They were, Ibrahim Toteel, Dr. Gergis Tekhlemariam, Zemehret Yohannes Abrahaley Kifle and Ahferom Tewelde. Beyond that, Dr. Gergis and Zemehret were elevated to membership of the EPRP and thus were bound by the directives of the party and were fully controlled. On the other hand since they didn't trust Toteel and couldn't accept him becoming a member of the party they monitored and limited his movements, thus controling whatever risk that he may pose.

In the second and unity congress, EPLF passed resolutions that heralded institutionalization of the rule of law and the respect for the democratic rights of the Eritrean people. Everyone who read the resolution felt that we were almost getting ready and preparing to 'enter heaven'. The resolutions were designed to give the impression to the people that what took ages for the western government to achieve, we would accomplish through a shortcut; it was so hopeful and optimistic. The promises looked like they were like dispensations written in gold and a ticket to heaven. Even the government of USA was astonished by that, and after independence, it hoped for the emergence of a "New Democratic Country"; the USA wanted Eritrea to become their partner; Hillary Clinton came to Asmara and participated in a public dancing ceremony.

During the Second Organizational and Unity Congress, an incident happened in the form of an unusual announcement by the EPLF: The martyrdom of Ibrahim Affa, member of the Political Bureau and Commander of the Military Training Department and Chairman of the Military Committee was officially announced. The announcement that was kept secret for a few years, explained that an enemy military unit sneaked into our base areas and attacked him and his colleagues. Ibrahim Affa was sleeping behind our defense lines near Arag at Agamet along with his senior assistant, the freedom fighter Major Mebrahtu Tewoldemedhin and a few others. An enemy squad named "Sergo Geb" (stealth forces) sneaked in and crossed to the northeast frontline of Sahel, and went behind the EPLF frontlines and executed the operation where Ibrahim and his comrades were killed.

There had been rumors that Ibrahim Affa and Isaias, long time companions, had developed differences. But not much is known about the relations between Isaias and Major Mebrahtu Tewoldemedhin who was an experienced senior ex-officer of the Ethiopian Paratrooper forces.

If the above mentioned fighters were killed by the enemy behind the EPLF defense lines, it was not clear why the incident was kept a secretfor so long, and it doesn't seem there was any benefit of keeping it a secret. The special handling of the incident had left many people to speculate about the real causes. Considering the history of the leadership of the EPRP that claimed the lives of many freedom fighters in its ascent to power, and which has not been transparent, and applied different tactics at different times, it was natural that the announcement created suspicions and speculations.

In the second and unity congress, all those who were members of the political office in the first organizational congress, except for Mesfin Hagos, Ogbe Abraha, and Berhane Grezgiher, all the rest were elected as members of the Political Bureau for a second time. What happened during this congress was exchange of leadership positions in which the former chairman, Ramadan Mohammed Nur, who was during the first congress nominally elected as chairman of the organization as a cover up, was stripped of his position since his usefulness as a cover up had ended. Isaias came to the open, satisfied by his political design and assumed the ultimate authority as a leader, and Ramadan became the head of the newly established Justice Department. Sebhat Efrem replaced Ibrahim Affa in the Defense Department, Cadre School and Information was fused into one department under the joined leadership of Haile Derou and Alamin Mohammed Saeed. Sherifo became the head of Public Administration; Ali Saeed became in charge of the Foreign Affairs Department; Petros Solomon continued to head the Department of Intelligence and Security and Mohammed Saeed Bareh in charge of the Social Affairs Department. Isaias Afwerki became the chairman of the organization and the secretary of the secret party; he became the alpha male leader.

Isaias made sure to elevate himself and created a special position that would keep him above the members of the Political Bureau. He established a system where any contact with him as the chairman of the organization had to go through the newly established Secretariat under the Office of the President where Saleh Kekya, Abraha Kassa and other members of the Central Committee were appointed to manage it. The special resolutions that were passed in the congress were similar to the beautification of an ugly girl with the help of plenty of makeup so as to make her face attractive and shiny. The resolutions were passed as a make believe to deceive the freedom fighters and the people that the leadership was visionary and progressive.

After the Second Organizational and Unity Congress, the military committee of the first congress that was led by Ibrahim Affa was transformed into an expanded committee consisting of Sebhat Ephrem, member of the political office and in charge of defense, division commanders, and some members of the central committee such as Mesfin Hagos, Teklay Habtesellassie, and Haile Samuel 'China'. By that time, the military supremacy of the Derg had been significantly weakened and the EPLF had begun to have the upper hand in the balance of forces. Partly because of the political resolutions, the image of the EPLF became more attractive. On top of the heightened morale renewal of the EPLF in the field, the Eritrean struggle became better recognized worldwide. Isaias exploited the favorable conditions in order to appear as caring for the Eritrean people; he concealed his true nature and character. He found good opportunities to deceive and win the trust of the people and was ready to reap benefit from it. He became the highest authority in both the organization and the party. Isaias, who doesn't consider and value the views of others but only his own, became intoxicated with power. His cohorts, cheered and applauded him, which helped him to inflate his ego and to become a dictator.

The war of attrition that continued after the retreat caused the balance of power of the enemy and the EPLF to shift from one side to the other. Particularly after the Second Organizational and Unity Congress, the military confrontations were carried out on advanced military strategy and tactics. Military operations were carried out after collecting refined intelligence information and thorough research and studies. The successive military victories were a result of the command teams which were composed of well educated leaders with military and intelligence expertise and experience. In parallel, the EPLF had the resources of combatants whose dedication and readiness for martyrdom was exemplary.

The counter attack offensive waged between March 17 and 20 of 1988, which was aimed at removing the Nadew Command Garrison stationed in Afabet caused a major shift in the balance of power of the waring parties. The situation was thoroughly studied for a long time before the offensive was carried out and was undertaken after a meticulous planning. In that battle the Nadew Command and Control Center was destroyed and the enemy forces were in disarray. Though the previous major attack on Wqaw Command in 1984 made the Soviet military plan get lost in the plains of northeast Sahel, where the enemy's division commander and many other officers were taken prisoners, the psychological pressure that it caused on the Derg army was not comparable to that of Nadew. They brought consultants from the Soviet Union, accumulated swarms of tanks and heavy equipment, and confidently camped. The destruction and the capture of prisoners and equipment signaled to them and the world the shift of the balance of power.

The battle of Afabet frustrated the Derg. Before the March 1988 attack, the attempted attack on Afabet on December 8, 1987, in which the EPLF attacked the 22nd force of the division on the second day had inflicted serious damages on it. After the initial battle of Afabet in which many soldiers were killed or taken prisoner, Mengistu Hailemariam, the Ethiopian dictator, who was desirous to eliminate his rivals, scapegoated some of his commanders for the defeat and dismissed about twenty officers. And though the commander of Nadew, General Tariku Yayne, was sick during the battle in which his command was defeated, Mengistu blamed him for the defeat and had him shot in the environs of Asmara in March 1988.

The counter attack that began on March 17, 1988 happened not much later after the attempted attack of December 1987 and the changing of leadership within the Derg. The EPLF advanced its forces from three direction and started its initial attack by engaging the 14th Division that arrived later on and which tried to retreat but couldn't. The battle continued and the enemy called support forces from Keren. The road to Keren was blocked and the mission became unsuccessful. The EPLF encircled the Nadew Command garrison and forced it to either perish or surrenderand as a result only a few escaped from the battle zone, including the Commander of the Second Revolutionary Forces who put on civilian clothes and escaped on a camel, while Colonel Getahun Haile and some of his colleagues who were outside the Nadew encirclement also escaped.

In the battle of Afabet, over 22,000 enemy soldiers were either killed or taken prisoners. Of these, more than 6000 were taken prisoners. But their biggest loss was the exceptional quantity of armament and equipment that they accumulated in Afabet with the advice of Soviet consultants to attack the EPLF, and which fell in the hands of the EPLF after the swift attack. Though they tried to burn some of the equipment, the tense battle situation didn't give them a chance to do that. The killing of one Soviet officer, and the capture of three others advising officers from the Soviet Union, was the first such incident in the history of the Eritrean struggle. And that exposed to the world the active participation of the Soviet Union in the war, which they had been categorically denying until then.

The attack on the Nadew Command was a battle that contributed greatly towards making the EPLF known internationally. The late Basel Davidson, the famous British historian, who was inside the field near the battle front at the time, compared the EPLF victory in Afabet against Nadew to the celebrated Vietnamese victory against the French in the battle of Dien Bien Phu.

5.2 Coup Attempt in Ethiopia and the Liberation of the Port City of Massawa

In November 1987, as the preparation for the initial attack of Nadew was underway, my first child Pitias was born in the Arareb Hospital Maternity Ward. When he was four-months old, Almaz brought him along when she came to visit me in March 1988 as the final attack on Nadew was being waged. The senior Derg officers who were taken prisoners in 1984, among them the Deputy Commander of the Wqaw Command, Colonel Girma Tessema, Major Bezabeh Petros a Mig 23 fighter pilot, (whose airplane was downed twice, and he was captured twice, the first time with the rank of a major, and on the second time with a rank of a colonel), Brigade Deputy Commander Captain Deggafe, and lieutenant Wendemu, were released from prison and were staying in a waiting area close to my office. We were chatting when we heard on the EPLF Dimtsi Hafash Radio that Afabet was liberated.

These officers were the founders of the 'Free Ethiopian Officers Movement' (FEOM) and were given an opportunity to campaign among the POWs to recruit members for their organization and were able to mobilize quite a few members. Though the obliteration of the Nadew Command Centre, in which thousands of soldiers were taken prisoners, gave the founders of the movement an opportunity to recruit many officers, they were, not happy to see the Ethiopia for which cause they bled and were imprisoned, weakened and

137

fragmented, particularly Colonel Girma and Major Bezabehwere saddened by the news. They were, however, aware that the Derg regime didn't make any attempt to secure their freedom and instead campaigned within the army against them and they as a consequence developed hatred towards the Derg. On top of that, because they had been released from EPLF prison and freed they didn't rule out the possibility of them being able to be competitors in the new system of government that would be established after the demise of the Derg.

After he was freed, Captain Deggafe was given a chance and assistance to tour overseas and he carried messages about the humane treatment the POWs were receiving to the world community in general and to the Ethiopian Diaspora in particular. In an interview they conducted, Colonel Girma and Major Bezabih explained the hate they developed towards the Derg that defamed and branded them as traitors; they explained the goals of the EPLF highlighting that it was an organization struggling for justice and not to delink Eritrea and sell it to external bidders; they explained that the EPLF took good care of the POWs and treated them humanely in a manner not outside what the standard of the Geneva Convention on POWs required.

After Wqaw, and the great Nadew attack that followed, the number of officers who were taken prisoners increased substantially. The Soviet advisers who were taken prisoners in Afabet were kept in a secret place not known to anyone except those who were involved in their case and those who were appointed to guard them. They were kept in a secret special place in Hishkeb, near the central office of Halewa Sewra and were not allowed to meet with any unauthorized person. Their guards were also almost prisoners like them; they were not allowed to meet with any combatant or civilian, except the Russian prisoners whom they were guarding. This was done because, on top of the organization being closed and secretive, it was also an attempt to prevent the leak of information about their whereabouts; because however minimal, there was a risk that attempts could be made to free them through Soviet Union intelligence agents. The poor fighters who were guarding them became equally prisoners in the process of fulfilling their duties.

The majority of the prisoners were taken and dispersed in the camps of Ayteway where the officers were put with other officers and the Eritreans with other Eritrean prisoners. Those who were below the rank of a lieutenant were put together with the ordinary rank and file soldiers. It took the new prisoners time to adjust to the life of a prisoner, and adjustment period created a lot of dissatisfaction and unhappiness, but when they arrived at the mountains and gorges of Sahel, where one cannot see anything except burned rocks and the sky, there was nothing they could do but accept their fate. However, they were treated just like the freedom fighters if not better. They engaged in productive activities that helped them change their living conditions. The only company that didn't receive new prisoners was the company of the free prisoners who were set free after a given time and waited until they were seen off to their respective destinations. The company looked after prisoners who were engaged in productive work in many places, from Nakfa to Ayteway, until they left for the destination of their choice.

This company of our department took care of both Eritrean and Ethiopian prisoners who were kept separately. The reason for keeping them separated was for national interest considerations, particularly the Eritreans who were unconsciously becoming tools of the enemy and who were given awareness raising education to enable them to repent and come to the side of their people. The Ethiopian prisoners had been exposed to the side of Derg propaganda only. Their circle was being penetrated by EPLF freedom fighters to influence them to change their views and attitude against the propaganda of the Derg and also make them engage in open debates, to encourage them to ask about issues they did not understand, to create a platform for arguments, and to help them take part in the establishment of a people-oriented representative System of government in Ethiopia.

The prisoners who asked to join the liberation organizations like the Tigray Peoples Liberation Front, Oromo Liberation Front, EthiopianPeople'sRevolutionary Party, or other Ethiopian organization were escorted to the Ethiopian-Eritrean border. Sometimes the organizations sent their members to escort them to Ethiopia. The EPLF had adopted the policy of allowing prisoners to join and strengthen the Ethiopian opposition organizations that were struggling against the Derg in order to exert more pressure on the enemy by stretching its forces.

Major Dawit Weldegiorgis, who during the time he was with the Derg was the representative of the Ethiopian Workers Party in Eritrea for three years starting in 1982, and who was also previously the head of the Ethiopian Relief Commission, tried to be active against the Derg.Though his activities were overseas, considering the fact that he was a senior Derg official, and as a commissioner of relief agency he dealt with officers and commanders of the war against Eritrea, both in Eritrea and Ethiopia, therefore he had good knowledge of and acquaintance with senior Derg authorities.

He depended on his past relations with the senior authorities and exploited the conflicts and reservations of the Derg officials. The EPLF assisted him when he agreed with some senior military commanders in Ethiopia who were planning to overthrow the Mengistu regime. And to accomplish the mission, he started meeting with senior EPLF members led by Petros Solomon, member of the Political Bureau and head of the Intelligence Department. He also met with representatives of the TPLF and EPRP (Ethiopian People's Revolutionary Party) to solicit their cooperation in the planned coup attempt. It was then that he came to the field and met the FEOM.

In Port Sudan, one of the transportation officials in charge of dispatching vehicles made room in one vehicle which was heading towards Swakin on its way to the field. One of them was Major Kesete; (Brigader General in independent Erirea), a senior military intelligence official of the EPLF who was accompanying another person who wore dark, shaded glasses. He heard the man speaking in Amharic with Major Kesete and guessed he was Ethiopian. He asked the Major, what have you brought to us today? He didn't reply. But Major Kesete was discussing about his days with Major Dawit when he was an Ethiopian Army Officer. They were mentioning names of people who were with them in the army. After travellingfor a long time, the driver and Major Dawit recognized each other and he explained to him that he knew Major Dawit in prison when he was detained by the Derg security agentsin Asmara. He was detained because he was accused of being a member of the mass organizations and tortured, and when they searched his house, they found a guide bookon espionage. In addition, they suspected that he was going to send the guidebook to the bandits and they tortured him.

But because they couldn't prove anything apart from finding the guidebook, they presented him to the senior authorities alleging that he was going to send the book to the 'bandits'. They asked him how he got hold of the book. He said that his relative, an officer of the Ethiopian military forgot it in his house. They released him because the book was used to teach at the Ethiopian Officers' Academy.

When Major Dawit heard the story, he said, "you would have decayed by now, I saved you!" The driver said, you didn't let me go because you were compassionate, but because you couldn't find any proof to keep me. Major Kesete interrupted him, "change the subject, but how did you recognize him?" The driver used to see Major Dawit frequenting Mariam Gmbi and sometimes in the streets of the city. He couldn't forget him.

When they stopped the car to rest, the driver didn't talk much, but many thoughts went through his mind. The man who introduced Maggalet (exposing those you knew were involved) and Self-Maggalet to Asmara and made the members of the mass organization expose and spy on each other, and in order to pressure those who didn't want to be exposed, he declared that those who are exposed by others will not be pardoned, but if they admitted and testified on their own, 'the revolution' will pardon them because it is its characteristic. The man who was a senior official of the Derg and who played a big role in weakening our mass organizations was now being taken to the field by the EPLF. He couldn't understand that and he was astounded.

He wouldn't have objected if Major Dawit got the most severe sentences in the world, he was the man who helped expose educated mass organization members and turned them into important tools in the service of the Derg--and now he was entering the field! The torture he went through in Mariam Gmbi had left a scar in his memory. Since he couldn't think beyond that, he chose to suppress his anger and ignore the issue. The EPLF doctrine, "don't try to know secrets that don't concern you," hindered him from thinking and expressing his views freely, and the remark of Major Kesete, "Change the subject," made him uneasy. He didn't want to argue with Major Dawit. Like all freedom fighters, he respected the directives of his superiors in the organization.

After sunset, they continued their journey at night and reached Arareb by dawn. After a short sleep, they met colonel Girma, Major Bezabih, Captain Deggafe, and Lieutenant Wendemu and started their discussions. Their plans were based on the communication that was conducted overseas with the idea of forming a three-pronged cooperation. Major Dawit was to act as a bridge to coordinate between the two antagonistic parties, the EPLF on the one hand and the high ranking Derg officials who were plotting a coup against the Derg and the Free Ethiopian Officers' Movement operating with assistance of the EPLF on the other. Additionally, he came to the field to solicit and ascertain the support of the EPLF.

While Mengistu Hailemariam was trying to destroy the Eritrean revolution and the opposition movements in Ethiopia, by getting support from the Soviet Union which was a rival super power of the USA, the USA started to carry out some diplomatic initiatives and rapprochement with the Eritrean and Ethiopian opposition movements in order to overthrow the Derg. It also exploited the opposition movement of the senior officers that was unfolding within the Derg in Ethiopia. And to broaden the internal rift it made it possible for the officers' movement to cooperate with the Eritrean revolution. To accomplish that plan, the USA guaranteed the safety of Major Dawit in the field in spite of the allegation that he had committed crimes during his time in Eritrea.

The senior officers could not tolerate the arrogant and the dictatorial character of their external representative who looked down on them; he rejected their advice and expert recommendations causing disharmony among them. Mengistu like all other dictators could not tolerate any educated and talented person that was superior to him and he wouldn't hesitate to squash anyone whom he considered a threat. Though the senior Derg officials who overthrew the regime of Haile Selassie didn't have a different character than his, they were superior to him in educational attainment and rank, and they looked down on his leadership that they were forced to accept. The differences between Mengistu and the elite officers kept growing by the day until it culminated in their attempt to overthrow him and take over power.

Among the senior officers who led the coup were: Major General Mered Negusse, Chief of Staff; Major General Fanta Belay, the Minister of Industry and ex-Commander of the Air Force; Major General Demisse Bultu, the Commander of the Second Revolutionary Army in Eritrea; and Major General Abera Abebe, and all of them recruited other officers to join them. Major Dawit and the Free Ethiopian Officers' Movement were hopeful for the EPLF to arm the POWs in order to support the force in Ethiopia that was planning to overthrow the Derg. The POWs appointed Major Dawit to liaise and coordinate the relations between them and that of the forces that would lead the coup inside Ethiopia.

After the meeting, Major Dawit and I met at the office of the administration of the POWs. He characterized the Derg as a dictatorial regime that oppresses the Ethiopian people and tried to present himself as an innocent person. All the wasted lives of innocent Eritreans and his activities in Asmara didn't appear to him as a sin. He mentioned Red Tears, the book he had just authored, and wished that it would have been better if it was written after his trip to Sahel. As the saying goes, "Seeing is believing"; I believe he observed there were many things that needed improvement concerning the Eritrean Revolution.

The coup attempt against Megistu Hailemariam took place in May 1989. In its first day, it was exposed and overpowered in Addis Ababa and it came to an end. The leaders had lost trust among one another, and couldn't decide and agree whether to hit Mengistu's airplane in the air when he was on board, or to force it to land in Asmara. They also differed on who should lead the operation. Some senior Derg officers who were suspected to have been displeased with the plan leaked the secrets and betrayed their colleagues and sided with the Mengistu side of the Derg. The leaders of the attempted coup who were in Addis Ababa were killed and the coup failed.

After the coup failed in Addis Ababa, General Demsee Bultu, who was stationed in Asmara, received erroneous information. He wanted to continue the coup from Asmara and form a government that would replace Mengistu's Derg. He didn't find anyone to listen to him. At that moment, the EPLF had offered a cease fire for 15 days to give an opportunity to the organizers of the coup. General Demisse's forces that were sent from Asmara to attack the palace in Addis Ababa, and the forces that were expected to join in Addis Ababa were neutralized before they could move. At the end, most of the senior officers of the movement were killed, the plan was aborted, and many soldiers were put in detention.

All the EPLF plans hit their targets. The plan was to cause the Derg army to attack each other and be weakened. In actual fact, the two sides had almost identical views as concerns the Eritrean revolution; replacing one side with another would have been more of the same as far as the Eritrean case is concerned. Many Eritreans who heard about the incident were not only dissatisfied but thought it was a risky move.

The bloody liquidation that was unleashed by the Derg on the senior military officers during and after the coup attempt, and the imprisonment of hundreds of officers, weakened the Derg. They are believed to have been some of the main factors that brought the Derg closer to defeat. Following the defeat which came just after the Nadew blow, the Derg army that was in conflict within itself became more vicious in its internal conflicts and hastened its own demise.

At that time Isaias started to prepare his agenda to establish a government that would ensure and secure his stay in power. In the first half of 1989, when the Mengistu regime became shaky, Isaias circulated a memo to all members of the secret party, and unceremoniously ordered the freezing of all party activities. In February 1990, the port city of Massawa was captured and the balance of power shifted to the extent that every freedom fighter in the struggle started to be sure that Eritrea would be liberated within one year. Isaias had already noted that because in an interview with journalists he confidently declared that Eritrea will be liberated within one year. Isaias based his conclusions on the expert assessment and efforts of the experienced and skilled senior intelligence and military commanders, and on the martyrdom of the dedicated fighters, but he frequently said, "according to my thinking," as if it was his individual assessment and tried to get credit for the inevitable eventual victory.

After the attempted coup against the Derg failed, the army expected the EPLF to attack Keren. However, the second major and surprise operation was Fenkil which was undertaken in February 1990 to liberated Massawa. The operation was led by the experienced and skilled intelligence and military commanders. On February 8, the EPLF forces cut the Asmara-Massawa road and severed the logistical transport nerve-line between Asmara and Massawa. By afternoon the next day, in a surprising swift speed, the EPLF forces held positions around Massawa; by the third day they were able to control the entire naval base of the Ethiopian Navy.

The enemy forces were locked inside Massawa and had to endure bombardment by the heavy artillery equipment. They held the people of Massawa hostage and prevented them from getting away from the field of the battle. The EPLF was worried about the safety of the civilian population and it sent two Ethiopian soldiers who were taken prisoners, carrying a white flag with a message to the senior commanders of the Ethiopian army and navy in Massawa asking them to let the hostages free. But the enemy commanders were not willing to release the hostages, and the battle continued. This time, unlike 1977, the battle to capture the Red Sea port city was different because the attack was carried out simultaneously from the sea and the land.

The EPLF naval force that was being developed for the purpose of attacking Massawa attacked with speedboats and opened cover fire for the advancing fighters. The tanks couldn't cross Sigalet Qetan, the causeway that links the island port city of Massawa from the main land of Edaga and environs. Three EPLF tanks were destroyed there and on the following attempt, the EPLF forces crossed the narrow causeway that is no more than 15 meters wide and surrounded by sea; Ethiopian army soldiers were killed, wounded, or taken prisoner. Massawa fell under the full control of the Eritrean liberation army. The tanks that were hit at Sigalet Qetan were after independence mounted on a special place in Tewalet as a testimony to the gallant bravery of our martyrs.

About ten thousand Ethiopian soldiers were killed in the battle of Massawa. When the EPLF freedom fighters controlled Sigalet Qetan, some senior Derg commanders, who realized that the battle was over, attempted to escape through the sea aboard a battleship. Their ship was hit and many onboard drowned and ended up becoming fodder for the fish. General Ali Hajji and General Telahum, the senior Commanders of the Ethiopian army were taken prisoners alongside thousands of naval officers, including commander Tesfaye.

Realizing their defeat, the Ethiopian Air Force in Asmara resorted to bombing the civilians with napalm and cluster bombs and killed the old, the young, and mothers with their children who were residents of Massawa. Nothing less was expected from the Ethiopian army notorious for its cruelty, especially now when many of their troops perished and they were totally defeated; the same act of cruelty was also experienced in the past towards innocent villagers of She'eb which they ran over with tanks. Not only that, they had killed villagers starting with Adi Qontsi and of Wekidibba, and others like Ona and Besekdira whose innocent civilian inhabitants were shot and stabbed with the bayonets of the barbaric army.

Musa Naib, who was born and raised in Massawa, and who used Ali Saed as a bridge to be in the good books of Isaias, became administer of the port town which was liberated in February 1990 after many fierce battles. He handed his position as head of HalewaSewra to Naizghi Kiflu who is known for naming the 1973 movement as 'Menka'a', which could mean leftist, a bat or crooked. Naizghi came from overseas, where he worked within the foreign relations section to take over Halewa Sewra. As per Isaias' plan, the position passed over from the greedy Musa to the crazy Naizghi. When Naizghi was in Algeria, he was not a member of the secret party. It is said that one time the Algerian government asked Naizghi for a meeting with the secret party; considering his position, and since they didn't realize the party was secret, they assumed him to be a member. Naizghi claimed he was a member and held the meeting. That resulted in controversy regarding the secret nature of the party, but later on he was admitted to the party as a member. Finally he was brought to the field and appointed as the head of the Department of Halewa Sewra.

Naizghi's mother, Weizero Emuna, explained that when he was growing up Naizghi had a problem. He was hyperactive and troublesome. She said they nicknamed him 'Esher' (tithe,10%) because he was uncontrollable. In a political education class for freedom fighters while explaining who the enemies and friends of the revolution were, Algeria was somehow mentioned. A participant asked the teacher if Algeria was an enemy or a friend. The teacher responded, "As long as Algeria keeps Naizghi there, it is our friend." He explained it in a humorous way but clearly described Naizghi's character.

On the first day that Naizghi took over the responsibility of Halewa Sewra, dmudmu was brewed in his honor at his reception during which time he and I disagreed and the situation ended up with each of us at each other's throats until Fitsehatsion Sheqa came between us and ended the fight. There was no reason for the fight but solely because Naizghi just wanted to fight; it was over a tape recorder and over playing the reverse side of the tape. They pulled me off the place with the excuse that Naizghi was drunk.

In the EPLF, every freedom fighter is bound by strict adherence to the directives and the code of conduct of the organization and by the military discipline. Whoever violates the disciplinary regulation is punished, and if the violation is grave it may result in detention. However, the troublesome Naizghi used vulgar words to insult and abuse freedom fighters but nothing happened to him. Once, when he was in charge of the Economy Department in Sahel in Fah Bleqat, a freedom fighter that came from the highlands was returning to his place and asked Naizghi for jackets to carry to his colleagues. Naizghi didn't only deny him that but worse still he called him son-of-a-bitch/prostitute. The combatant went as far as the location of the top leadership known as Zero One in Fah, and complained to Isaias who called Naizghi to talk to him. When Naizghi arrived he found Isaias sitting with the combatant he insulted and told Isaias, you son-of-a-bitch/prostitute, you called me for this! Isaias looked at the freedom fighter, "See! He even insults us." The freedom fighter was dumbfounded and left in utter surprise.

Why was Naizghi able to move as loose as he pleased in an organization that followed strict discipline? Why was he not punished for falsely telling the Algerians he was a member of the secret party and held a meeting when he was not a member? Let alone for minor transgressions and violation, Naizghi was never punished for even major offences.

The freedom fighter that was close to him made excuses for his behavior saying that Naizghi is crazy, don't hold it against him, he is unpredictable, etc. But many other freedom fighters like him were severely punished for minor violations. The reason is because Isaias and Naizghi were two faces of the same coin that is one and the same. As long as Naizghi did what Isaias wanted he was confident that nothing would happen to him. Problems could only arise when his relationship with Isaias was severed. Trying to find out the nature of their relations, one could only discover that their relations went beyond their common views and stand on the leaders of the movements of 'Menka'a and Yemeen'. It appears the two of them share a secret and that aspect should be seriously investigated.

When Naizghi took over the leadership at Halewa Sewra, he started his relations from the archive unit of the department. The archives were directly under the Department Head of Halewa Sewra. According to Naizghi, the guards and secretaries have to be dumb and ignorant persons who would not go beyond implementing the instructions they are given. They shouldn't be inquisitive and observant. It appeared he had something to hide. Those whom he appointed at Halewa Sewra, be it as recordkeepers and registrars, or individuals working in the office, like secretaries, were ones who had no self-confidence, who are obedient and cautious about not to veer out of the directives they receive. In short, they were people who were very cautious and fearful.

After Naizghi arrived, the activities of the secret party had slowed down and the conflict among the members cooled off, as well. But that doesn't mean Naizghi sprayed the department with holy water. Since the arrival of Nizghi, the members of the secret party who used to mingle with the common freedom fighters and spread defamatory information about a specific person they wanted to damage by confusing and biasing the freedom fighters, and who used to promote others by inflating the character and dedication of those they wanted to promote, were denied the usual platform. Meeting began to be limited to organizational matters and related activities. The military cadres didn't like the new arrangement. On the other hand Isaias took the struggle in a different direction without worrying about the squabbles that were going under his watch. He focused on the senior leaders who were capable and could ally with him and he avoided those he considered a risk to his power designs for the future.

Isaias temporarily denied a platform for all those who acted whether on lofty ideals or to advance personal interest and he started to organize loyal party members and others who were not members but vetted as loyal cadres whom he will groom to become loyal allies in the future. But the committed freedom fighters who were focused on the liberation of Eritrea, and who were offering their sweat and blood did not have the time to think of what will happen to them or how they will live in the future independent Eritrea. But Isaias, pursuing his homework on the party level, began to marginalize the experienced and knowledgeable freedom fighters who were previously his allies which he thought could be competitors in the future. He raced to create new crop of recruits who would be obedient allies who would accept and implement what he instructs them without hesitation:--in the parlance of Isaias, the 'new warm blood.'

Therefore, the reason for stopping the party activities was that the objective situation was getting ripe for the liberation of Eritrea, and the leadership of the party that has stayed together for a long time might assume power and be unwilling to perform as per Isaias' wishes in the government system that would be established in the post independence period. He froze them all and accomplished his personal homework in order to monopolize power in the fast approaching future independent Eritrea.

Before Musa was transferred to Massawa, he used the support of the military commanders that he appointed to the Halewa Sewra Department to not only stay in the leadership position, but they also helped him during the elections in sidelining his rival and competitor Tewelde Wedi Andu. The group of Tewelde Wedi Andu, which Isaac Rezene described as spineless and untrustworthy by the top leadership, was slowly weakened and it became almost non-existent due to the intra-party activities. Musa was transferred and appointed as administrator of Massawa, the biggest port city that was captured during the February 1990 offensive. His appointment was chiefly because of his status in Halewa Sewra and also because he hails from the Massawa region.

Naizghi Kiflu became the highest EPLF authority in the Department of Halewa Sewra. The competition that might have surfaced in the party was cleared before his arrival enabling him to use his authority as he pleased. Naizghi found a space, but he was not a fool and he understood that everything he does requires the blessing of Isaias, his patron. Isaias was not ignorant either; he gave Naizghi a position because he knew that Naizghi who was treated just like a messenger boy during the time of the 'Menka'a'movement will stay a loyal messenger boy throughout. There were things Isaias wanted to do through Naizghi. Appointments to a position within the EPLF were decided after a thorough study and those who were not considered ready after the study were made to stay on the sidelines until they met the threshold. If they didn't meet the criteria they were completely removed.

5.3 The Liberation of Asmara, Keren, and Asseb
a. Eritreans and the Independence Honeymoon

As the EPLF was preparing to enter Asmara, all the departments were engaged in various activities in support of the military campaigns. Within the Department of Halewa Sewra, except for a few who were not familiar with the city, the rest who grew up in Asmara knew the city very well including its culture and society.

When Asmara was liberated, the entire Eritrean people received their children, the freedom fighters who struggled tirelessly and paid dearly to defeat darkness and bring the dawn of freedom, driven by the love and care of their people. Recognizing that the lives of the 60,000 martyrs who sacrificed their blood were not in vain, the people respected and saw us as angels. The suffering was over and the dream was that all Eritreans will be equal first class citizens. They thought that they will be engulfed with prosperity and peace, and they will be relieved of their burden; the chains of occupation will be broken and the people will be able to work and earn a living with no discrimination. The youth will grow and mature and contribute to the growth of the nation, away from the threat of war, and to peacefully go to school. In short, Eritreans had abundant, optimistic and pleasant dreams.

The first few days in post-independence Eritrea were like a honeymoon, and at the same time worrisome for the Eritrean people who were not sure of the whereabouts of their children whom they had missed. The freedom fighters who survived the struggle were not in a rush to see their parents and families; after so many years of absence, they thought a few more days will not make it any worse. They focused on the tasks at hand; they knew they would soon have enough time for family reunions. They didn't even disarm themselves in haste in order to relax. On the third day, I rolled a sarong on my head and together with some colleagues passed in a car by the house in which I was born and raised. When I pointed that to them, they suggested we should stop for a few minutes but I didn't allow them to stop.

Surprises are not good; I didn't want to meet my parents whom I haven't seen for years in such a surprising manner. I wanted to send them an advance message telling them that I will come on a specific day in order to prepare them before I show up and hence I passed by the house, the house of my parents that I love so much because I was afraid my surprise visit might hurt them.

Raucous parties of music and dances overwhelmed Asmara, people didn't return home until very late at night. Young women were told to go wild because their brothers have arrived, and went wild like unleashed puppies and active like overfed calves. Their trust in their brothers and sisters who brought freedom was extremely high. Eritreans had never experienced such happiness before. The day, whose arrival the Eritrean people awaited for many years but had difficulty forecasting its actual arrival, became a reality at long last. However, since Eritreans realized the heavy price that was paid for the independence of Eritrea, they concealed their sad feelings and chose to enjoy the wild nights. Every family had at least one fighter in the struggle. It was in some sense an incomplete happiness. Everybody wanted independence, but martyrdom was a reality. The sufferings and difficulties that were paid dearly have ended. And the sacrifices produced the joy. The bitter sacrifices can only be swallowed when it is accompanied with the sweet taste of independence. It was the end of the bitterness of colonial occupation.

The sacrifices were not paid to achieve independence alone but also for freedom and social justice. The struggle that followed is a continuation of the initial phase of the journey that required more sacrifices. The goals of the struggle were not fully accomplished; one chapter was closed and another opened that would show the limits of the honeymoon. The Eritrean people were expecting a peaceful life in a prosperous and developed Eritrea. Thus, the people were not prepared for the second phase of the struggle for liberation. They transferred all their loads onto the shoulders of the trusted freedom fighters who sacrificed so much to achieve independence. They never doubted them even for a day. It is a pity! Let alone the people, even the fighters didn't suspect the leaders who led them to independence would betray and let them down. When the people saw it themselves they started to move away from previously held beliefs to which they subscribed and religiously followed.

It was not in vain that my grandfather had said, "We will see all those who reach for each other's throats, the EPLF and the ELF, when they come to govern the people." He had experienced the authorities of different foreign powers and he had no difficulty guessing how those who were waging guerrilla warfare in the forests will behave when they transform themselves into statesmen and govern. When the powerless gain power they are often blinded by it.

When the freedom fighters were asked about the whereabouts of a certain fighter, they would lie and say that they were still in Sahel, or in Ethiopia, or in the environs of Addis Ababa. They lied until the honeymoon ended and the eulogy for the martyrs was read. The unfortunate news about those who were martyred or wounded at the eve of independence in Asmara, Keren, Asseb didn't only sadden their families, it saddened those who knew there was martyrdom in the final stages of the struggle, the fighters couldn't taste the sweet flavor of independence in their mouths.

The freedom fighters who were left behind after the Fenqil operation in Massawa wanted to be done with their mission; maybe because they felt they had roamed enough in the forests, or maybe because they evaluated the new situations critically. But the political activities in the base area were slowed down drastically; the EPLF was engaged with the prevailing military aspects or engaged in different diplomatic and propaganda activities. Isaias was doing his homework alone by covering himself with the military and diplomatic activities that were underway to cement the independence of Eritrea. He was engaged in organizing new institutional structures, tools that he would utilize in the future. The structuring was narrow limited only to the upper echelon, involving only his old trusted allies and new recruits he chose as tools for the future. He embarked on the task of changing the experienced camels with the newly tamed horses.

The US government was watching the Mengistu Hailemariam regime very closely and knew its collapse was nearing. Though it was in full agreement with the idea of removing the Marxist regime, the US government was not in favor of the independence of Eritrea. The US government comes on top of the list of countries that advanced its own interests and wanted to again disregard the wishes of the Eritrean people by bonding Eritrea with Ethiopia. The historical proof for that kind of US policy is found in the words of the US Representative to the UN John Foster Dulles, who in 1950 was instrumental in federating Eritrea with Ethiopia:

> From the point of view of justice, the opinions of the Eritrean people must receive consideration. Nevertheless the strategic interest of the United States in the Red sea basin and the considerations of security and world peace make it necessary that the country has to be linked with our ally Ethiopia. (Martin Plaut, "Eritrea: From Annexation to Independence, 14/12/2012".)

After Jimmy Carter was replaced as president of the US in 1981, a year later he formed a non-governmental organization named public policies and international studies to work on resolution of conflicts that might arise in different parts of the world. His NGO was formed as a facade on behalf of the US government that could not be involved in certain activities due to limitations by international laws and charters. After the Eritrean revolution became an important factor, and reached the doorsteps of independence, as if the US was not the chief advocate for the federation of Eritrea with Ethiopia, as if it didn't say the Eritrean case was an internal Ethiopian issue, the US took an initiative and got involved in what it previously considered an 'internal Ethiopian affair', thus closing the doors to prevent the world from being engaged in it. The USA started to knock on the Eritrean door through Jimmy Carter.

The Eastern Soviet Union block countries that were cheering on the side of Ethiopia and had good relations with the Derg regime were at some point engaged in peaceful talks. In 1978 the EPLF met with the Derg in Berlin East Germany and also in different European cities between 1982and 1985. But the talks had pre-conditions and denied observers from participating; it was believed by analysts to be solely a military maneuver by both parties intending to buy time.

Carter became a mediator and between March and May 1989 he travelled to Africa and held three meeting with Colonel Mengistu Hailemariam, the leader of Marxist Ethiopia, and with Isaias Afwerki, the then secretary general of the EPLF and made them engage in peace talks. In the talks, Isaias told President Carter that as long as the talks reflected the wishes of the Eritrean people, there should be a referendum after which the people can chose to be either an independent state, a federal arrangement, and beyond that option or can chose an autonomous government on a limited scale. They parted after stressing that the meeting could only be productive when it remains open.

The US government had reservations; it feared that after Mengistu's regime was removed the direction of the country might go against its preferred ways and wanted to influence the talks. But the reality on the ground was different from its wishes. In August President Carter stated that the two warring sides have agreed to meet in September and they were invited to send their delegates to Atlanta: the EPLF's office in Washington DC, and the Ethiopian Government from Addis Ababa, formally announced they will send their delegates and both sides declared their formal acceptance to engage in the talks. The statements praised and expressed gratitude for ex-President Carter who took the initiative to uphold peace and human rights. The TPLF stated it would have liked to participate in the talks, but ex-President Carter realized the difference, and didn't want to mix the issue of self-determination of Eritrea, with the TPLF's goal for regime change.

On September 8, 1989 at a meeting that was held in Atlanta between the delegates of the EPLF and the Ethiopian Government under the sponsorship of ex-President Carter, the EPLF delegates explained that beginning in the 19th century Eritrea had gone through a period of Italian colonization but it was denied independence during the decolonization period of the 1950s and 60s unlike in the cases most of African countries. Instead of independence it was temporarily placed under British Military Administration (BMA) by agreement of the Four Allied Powers until 1952, when it, with pressure from the US became federated with Ethiopia. And in 1962 Emperor Haile Selassie abrogated the federation that was provided for under a UN Resolution and unilaterally annexed Eritrea and declared it a province of Ethiopia.

Dr. Ashagerie Yigletu, the head of the Ethiopian Delegation requested that, "The talks should be conducted without taking sides," while the EPLF head of Delegation Mr. Alamin Mohammed Saed, said "the talks should be handled without stretching time and creating political confusion." Diplomatic and political acumen was required of the delegates. Both sides had shown their wish to have president Mubarak of Egypt participate in the meeting. Though Carter didn't mind to have the meeting held in Geneva, London or Cairo, based on the choice of the interlocutors they decided to hold the meetings in Atlanta.

After the Atlanta meeting, though an unannounced ceasefire was held between the EPLF and the Ethiopian government forces, sporadic clashes between the two forces didn't however stop because the attacks inside Ethiopia were being carried out jointly by the EPLF and TPLF.

In November 1989, ex-President Carter, together with International Negotiations Network and with the experts of the Carter Center, went to Nairobi at the invitation of the Kenyan Government. Based on the initial meeting in Atlanta and the Nairobi meeting that followed, the warring sides reached an agreement on 13 basic procedural issues that could help facilitate the following year's meeting.

The two sides agreed to appoint president Nyerere of Tanzania as assistant to the chairman, ex-President Carter, and to have other countries participate as observers. Five countries were agreed upon and invited: Kenya, Sudan, Tanzania, Senegal, Zimbabwe, and the Organization of African Union (OAU). The continental body accepted the invitation while the UN didn't accept it claiming the issue was an internal Ethiopia matter, and saw it in conflict with its Resolution of 1952. After several meetings with Mengistu Hailemariam of Ethiopia, and Isaias Afwerki, the EPLF Secretary General, President Carter expressed his happiness saying that, "the two sides reflected honest wishes for the peace and prosperity of their region's people." However, the EPLF delegation accused President Carter that he leaned towards the Ethiopian side and sympathized with it concerning the choice of invitation of observers.

In Eritrea, the Derg forces were confined to Asmara, Keren, Dekemhare, and Asseb, and in Ethiopia, the opposition forces assisted by EPLF army were marching towards the center of the country. At the end of September 1989, it was officially announced by the government of the Soviet Union that the remaining 2000 Cuban forces were going to be pulled out of Ethiopia. The Soviet Union also announced that it would stop funding the Cuban forces, in addition it officially announced it was going to stop the support it gave to Ethiopia in terms of arms and other military equipment. Hence the Ethiopian government went into panic.

Starting in 1989, joint attacks by the EPLF and TPLF exposed the nakedness of the Derg regime. The Nadew assault that was unleashed on Afabet was followed by attacks on other garrisons and convoys, and armament was captured on the Asmara-Massawa road or inside Massawa; the derg forces were literally disarmed, and particularly when the Asmara-Massawa road was blocked. The supply lines of the Derg were choked and the troops were forced to depend only on supply by air. In addition, the TPLF offensive on Shire shook the forces that were positioned in southern Eritrea and Tigrai, even the forces that were confined to Mai Chew and Mekele camps were forced to abandon their position and leave the whole of Tigray due to the intense attacks.

The February 1991 attacks in Gojjam, followed by attacks on Gonder on March 8 and 9, and Shewa on May 19, and 21to 23 in Addis Alem and Debre Berhan, broke the Derg's limbs and paralyzed it forcing it to be confined in Addis Ababa. The military attacks that were carried out, in addition to the internal conflicts that were raging within members of the Derg, caused the Derg forces to feel lost with nothing to hold on to; they left all provinces to save their skin and fled towards the center of the country, towards Addis Ababa. The number of Ethiopian soldiers who perished in the final days of the war was staggering.

Mengistu wanted an exit from the chaos and immediately started to change his stance towards Western countries. Though the American administration knew it couldn't rely on Mengistu, in October 1990 and February 1991 it made a few agreements with him for the benefits of Israel. Diplomatically, the US was unable to prepare a system that would represent its interest. After providing unlimited support to the forces that attempted to overthrow Mengistu failed, they didn't find another force to replace it. However, as the interview that Ambassador Herman Cohen conducted with Ethio-sat explains, to enable Israel to move about 300,000 Fellasha (Bete-Israel), the US asked the cooperation of Mengistu Hailemariam, and through Israel, they provided him with 100 T-55 tanks, arms and spare parts for the use of the air force, and $35 million was deposited by Israel in the Derg's bank account in New York at the Federal Reserve. This diplomatic appeasement was aimed at helping their ally Israel to get what it wanted. However, the support that was given to Mengistu was limited and insignificant. In general, the situation on the ground forced even the US policy makers to do nothing except run after developments. To the US, the Ethiopian situation resembled the Eritrean saying, which goes as, "why worry about the health of a person who is already dead."

In the middle of May 1991, after the Central Office of the 3rd Revolutionary Army in Dessie and Kembolcha came under the control of the TPLF, the road to Asseb was closed cutting the Derg from any access to the sea. After a few days, by May 21, Mengistu Hailemariam was sure his time in power had come to an end; he left a caretaker government that would take over and administer the country until the TPLF enters and assumes political authority. He escaped to Zimbabwe, through Nairobi by plane, where he was ahead of time guaranteed political asylum. In the final days of the Derg, the caretaker government under the leadership of General Tesfaye Gebrekidan was supposed to meet with the EPLF and TPLF after one week based on the outcome of the meeting that was sponsoredby the US Assistant Secretary of State for African Affairs, Mr. Herman Cohen, and a week before the EPLF entered Asmara. The EPLF was tied up in activities that should be accomplished, thus, it hastened the meeting time by one week.

On May 24, while the EPLF forces controlled Asmara, its delegates headed to the London mediation conference of 26-28 May 1991. The developments on the ground entirely dictated the outcome of the meeting. The TPLF was also getting ready to enter and control Addis Ababa. According to Mr. Herman Cohen, the London mediation conference was basically to make sure that no destruction follows the EPRDF entry to Addis Ababa, and to bless the EPLF's quest for self-determination, to replace the Derg government by EPRDF, and to encourage it to establish a democratic government.

On the meeting of 27 May, the EPLF, TPLF and the US Government agreed on the nature of the system of government that would be established; The EPLF said it will require three years to prepare for a referendum, while the TPLF, declared its intention to form an all-inclusive transitional government. It was agreed that Eritrea and Ethiopian will work towards building close economic cooperation, and for Ethiopia to freely use the port Asseb. Both countries agreed to move together and to establish democratic systems. Prime Minister Tesfaye Dinqa, the leader of the Derg Delegation, objected to the US support of the TPLF to occupy the Menelik Palace and also for the US acknowledgment the self-determination of Eritrea, and thereafter withdrew from the meeting. However, developments on the ground had already made a statement of their own. The proposal by the Oromo Liberation Front for the right of self determination was rejected. Based on the final agreement of the London meeting EPLF attacked the Derg garrison in Asseb and TPLF entered Addis Ababa. It heralded the conclusion of the peoples' wars.

After the end of the cold war the Eritrean-Ethiopian conflict came to an end. In a conference that was held in Addis Ababa between 1 and 5 July 1991, a transitional Ethiopian government was formed in the presence of a senior UN representative. In that conference, the EPLF which defeated the Ethiopian army and entirely took control of Eritrea participated as an observer and talked about the future relations between the two countries. Based on the outcome of that conference the Ethiopian government officially recognized the Eritrean peoples' right to independence to be ascertained through referendum. The referendum was carried out in April 1993 and was observed by the UN and other regional observers; almost all Eritreans voted for freedom that is 99.8% of the total votes cast. On 28 May 1993 the UN formally accepted Eritrea as a new member of the international community of nations.

In the meantime, Isaias continued to organize his new party: the camels had finished their mission and should be sidelined, and to be replaced by newly groomed horses to take over responsibility of the party and government that would accomplish Isaias' wishes. They were given a task to actively direct the party to where Isaias wanted it to go. However, in order for the new party to reach a stage where it would enable Isaias to lead, the agreed Eritrean referendum must be implemented so as to legitimize the independence and give the nation international acceptance. Yet, while Eritreans were moving in unison with the world to secure an international recognition of Eritrea as a free country, Isaias was also crafting a structure that would guarantee him control of the state machinery and thereby control and monopolize political power.

b. A Family Reunion and the Anxiety of the People

Adey Marta called Weizero Bisrat on the phone, "Your son Tsegu has come, our boss saw him in the city, and he said he will come home tonight, I just wanted to give you the good tidings." I didn't go straight home because I didn't want my parents to be shocked by the surprise and suffer a heart attack. Instead I first went to our neighbor Aboy Bahta's home.

I and Adey Marta heard the happy ululation on the other end of the telephone.

She told my mother, "I am coming over," and she picked her netsela (shawl), and said to me, "I will wait for you over there, wait a little bit here before you go in." She went to our house ahead of me.

Before leaving the doorsteps, she turned and asked me, "How about your brothers, did they return?" She was disturbed because she didn't receive news about her own son.

I explained, "We were with the advance forces, the rest will follow." She walked fast towards our home.

Many thoughts crossed my mind at that moment, on the one hand the happiness and ululation and on the other the anxiety and sadness of my parents, and the rest of the Eritrean people. There was no Eritrean family that the calamity hadn't touched. My brothers, those who grew up with me, my comrades, who were the cream of the struggle, almost all were left behind. I knew that the questions I heard at our neighbor's house would face me again in our house. I also knew I had nothing to say but lie.

Standing at the doorsteps with the colleague who escorted me we rung the doorbell, Miriam my youngest sister, the only one left with my parents, opened the door. When she saw me she screamed. Adey Marta and my mother knew it was me and my mother hugged and kissed me. The neighbors came and started beating the drums, they sang the song, 'the lions of the forest' and none of them had any idea of what will eventually become of the affairs of the city.

My father arrived from outside and he heard the cacophony. He suspected and couldn't wait until he got inside the house. He saw me and immediately he looked up to the sky and thanked God and said, "I am glad I was not denied at least one child." He hugged and kissed me and my colleague. As a reception for the guests drinks were brought, food was prepared, and conversations started. When the people asked me about the whereabouts of my colleagues and my childhood friends I made an excuse for smoking and went outside.

I had to use the usual replies of: they are still in Sahel, or across the border, on a military campaign in Shoa (Ethiopia), etc, but such was not convincing them. I tried another one: the field is so wide we meet once in years. I created other excuses to avoid answering. While smoking outside I told my friend that I used to be interviewed by journalists many times in relation to my work and never had a problem, but now for the first time, may be because I was lying, I was troubled by the questions, because a lie cannot be repeated.

My mother asked me where I left my brothers. But since I was prepared for that I told her that I left my older brother Isaias, who was martyred after independence, a few days back in Sahel.Regarding my other brothers who were martyred during the struggle, I told her that Amanuel is around Addis Ababa and Mussie is in the surrounding of Keren. My mother was hopeful but it appeared she must have heard whispers about the martyrdom of her two sons. She would say, "May

God protect them, otherwise where were all the bombs falling! They didn't fall on water." She expressed to me her old anxieties.

I and my colleague didn't like the situation the anxiety of the parents disturbed us and we started to remember all our fallen colleagues. We excused ourselves and said we have been busy and are too tired and needed to rest and went to the bedroom. I decided to sleep before I could see enough of my parents whom I had missed so much. We went to sleep just to avoid the disturbing questions.

In the morning, we washed up and dressed with any clothes we could find, ate breakfast and said we have to go to work and that we will return in the evening. We had reserved a place of residence near Nyala hotel, a house that belonged to General Getachew who was the chief of Dehnenet, the Ethiopian security organization. Our temporary office was at Agip. After we entered Asmara we found all the enemy documents intact. The major task we had was to screen and filter the documents in order to take necessary decisions, a task given top priority in which all the members of the department were involved. The inhabitants of the city also did their part and assisted us by picking and presenting the individuals who were recruited by the enemy and were abusing the people to face the law.

The over ten-thousand Ethiopian POWs were brought to Asmara in small numbers and they were repatriated to their country through Tigrai in coordination with Red Cross. Though it was cumbersome to handle their massive size the fact that they longed for their country prevented them from complaining a lot. The senior officers were given rooms at the Ambassador hotel where they were gently treated until they returned to their homes.

Those who were taken prisoners at the end of the war in the surroundings of Dekemhare, Asmara and Keren were directly repatriated to Ethiopia. Thousands of prisoners escaped towards Sudan but though most made it successfully, many died on the journey due to thirst, hunger and exhaustion. The smell of the decomposing bodies of the soldiers who were killed in the battles had caused a lot of problems; the stench was ameliorated only after the corpses were buried.

Once the prisoners were repatriated, we completed the task of searching, reviewing and filtering of the documents and a few cases were referred to the concerned authorities for investigation and surveillance. A task force was formed and delegated to study as to how the Halewa Sewra Department could better fit into the national

159

government structure and prepare a proposal of departmental structure suitable for the future Eritrean internal security portfolio. The last reorganization of Halewa Sewra that was done in the field in 1973 was mainly aimed at purging the movements that unfolded then as well as to prevent similar occurrences in the future. And following that, its task was to weaken the enemy of the revolution and to be a punishment and rehabilitation entity for the 'crimes' that occur in the journey of the revolution. Every once in a while it underwent changes but the changes were not made within the framework of a national or government context.

The security structure of the Halewa Sewara during the struggle had served its purpose but in the post-independence era creation of a modern national security structure is indispensable and its improvement would require research on available alternatives and review of the experience of other countries. We started the task by reaching out to the dedicated members of the mass organization who were residing and worked in Ethiopia and to the retired senior Eritrean officers who were at that time living in Ethiopia and Eritrea. Since any security apparatus protects the authority for which it works it considerably expresses itself by depending on the political system that the government establishes. No country can function without a security establishment; however, when a popular governance system is established the security apparatus is expected to protect the interest of the people of the country. But if the government is neither popular nor democratic it more often than not is directed against the people.

Based on the resolutions of the Second Organizational and Unity Congress, the initial task was to create an institutionalized system of governance based on transparent and accountable institutions. Checks and balances should be put in place so that governmental bodies do not operate as they please, and the three branches of the government- -the legislative, the judiciary and the executive--ought to have an internal control system within and between them. That should be the starting point and basis for the envisioned democratic governance structure.

The government institutions that are responsible for the administration of justice--the courts, the office of the attorney general, police and security establishments, prison administration and correctional facilities--should be clear about their relation with other entities. All of these units should clearly understand and recognize their respective mandates and responsibilities as well as limits to their authorities. The task force was launched with that in mind. To prevent the police and other security establishment from arbitrarily detaining people, a law was enacted requiring the accused being presented to a court of law within 48 hours and it was further provided that in the absence of concrete evidence the accused should be released from detention. The criminal procedure code also provided that an environment should be created where people are not detained wrongly and where the accused will have the right to be represented and present complaints, and that the courts freely undertake their duties and pass judgments without any interference by the executive branch of the government. That formed the basis for the attempt to build a viable institutional structure for the administration of justice. These were not the only initiatives but all government departments were also preparing structures and directives according to the nature of their work and operations. After the referendum a proclamation for the establishment of a Constitution Commission was enacted heralding the institutionalization of a constitutional system of government and adherence to the rule of law in the country. The Justice Department started to prepare laws and regulations that would ensure respect of the rights and obligations of the citizens' under the law and used the civil and criminal codes of Ethiopia as reference and source to draft the required laws. To provide a basis for the guarantee of the right of freedom of expression, the Department of Information worked to create an environment where the people could express their opinions and also prepared laws that would help establish independent private newspapers. In addition, in order to establish a system that the Eritrean people expected, party formation and election laws were being drafted.

While carrying out all of these activities, now that the independence honeymoon was over, it was time the human cost that was paid for freedom in the struggle since its infancy was disclosed to the people. Tents and halls were erected in different parts of Eritrea for that purpose. As the names of the martyrs was being announced, the national flag flying at half mast, no one could console another, every family was affected in one way or the other, the only difference was that some families have to count one martyr, others were counting in twos, threes, fours and fives. The entire Eritrean population had paid the price for freedom.

As the martyrs' names were being announced, the anxiety of some families was saddening; they had children who left to bring freedom but didn't know if they were martyred or had survived. The sorrow of those parents was heart wrenching. There were people who had visited their children or siblings during the struggle. Some of them didn't return, and they were not listed amongthe martyrs, and the parents could not understand the reasonfor the omission of their children'snames. Some tried to convince themselves that it must be a recording error, and the announcers must have skipped over the names. Those parents didn't know the real nature of Isaias because most of the parents innocently elevated him to the level of an angel above that of an ordinary human being.

Once after a fierce battle, a freedom fighter could not be found and his name was forgotten and was not indicated in the report. Asmerom Grezgiher (Hawi Bchir) remarked, "How the existence of a colleague could be forgotten? We will be accountable to our people in the future." Many of the unaccounted martyred fighters were not commodities that you can buy with money or use and discard at will. Very dear lives were lost. In lieu of martyrdom, they were falsely accused as subversive elements, labeled 'criminals' and executed. These fighters did not fall victim to the enemy but of those with whom they thought had a common objective. Families were going everywhere to find news about their unaccounted children because they believed their martyrdom was not in vain. If they were criminals, they wanted to know the nature of the crime their children committed. That was after they confirmed their names were deliberately excluded from the register and that it was not an announcement error. This was the first and the loudest bell that chimed on Isaias' ears after independence. He knew he didn't have an answer for that, thus, he tried to cleverly escape it by promising to inform them in due course of time.

Some WedGeba, ex-fighters of the EPLF or ELF, who betrayed the revolution and surrendered to Ethiopia to become the tools of the enemy and who had committed crimes against the revolution and the people of Eritrea were after independence hunted down and eliminated. Even after Eritrea was liberated and the freedom fighters were controlling the cities, Isaias was still applying the law of the jungle. Though it was possible to apprehend the alleged criminals and to charge and present them in a courtof law, extrajudicial actions were preferred and taken against them. Only those individuals, who happened to be overseas, or who escaped and went beyond the reach of the Front remained untouched. But those who stayed in Ethiopian cities and towns were summarily executed. This is not to suggest that they were not criminals but the questionis, why these people wouldn't have been brought before a court of law to face justice instead of summary execution.

Isaias chose not to present them to a court of law because he knew many among those people may expose secrets he kept hidden from the public. He tried every possible means to prevent his secret from being exposed. One of the reasons that pushed him to take such measures was the presence of Tesfamichael Georgio who when Selfi Natsenet (the precursor of EPRP) was in A'ala at its infancy facilitated meetings for Isaias with the Ethiopians and beyond. He arranged for Isaias to visit the Kagnew Station, US Communication Baseinside Asmara, to meet with American military officials. Tesfamichael used to talk about such secrets of Isaias' history; he was killed in Addis Ababa. If what Tesfamichael said was not true Isaias should have responded to the allegations and refuted them publicly, but instead he went beyond that and spoke with bullets. He made it an excuse to vent his anger, and concluded in a manner that satisfied him. That is not only irresponsible, but reprehensible. Violation of a law should be stopped by the law, a mistake cannot be corrected by a mistake, and neither should a crime with a crime.

Isaias is not only foolish, he is also a coward. He didn't try to listen to the wisdom of the Eritrean people attentively to find a solution. May be the cheering and praising, "Wedi Afom Birri", intoxicated him and he was not willing to listen to the advice of his colleagues. He didn't seem to realize that the era of militarism had reached its end and a new era has dawned and it is a different world. He didn't realize that he needed help to swim in the new sea of democracy. But he was overly confident of his experience in the field where he managed to prolong his stay in power by secretly organizing people. He also forgot that the pain of ignoring and letting things pass for the sake of a bigger cause has come to an end. He forgot that the lives of the people will hold the top priority, and that they will ask questions. Unfortunately, he remained stubborn, rigid, and inflexible. Even those who lost their children, sisters and brothers, were not given an explanation because he thought they can't do anything about it. He immersed himself in the reactionary path of oppressors.

The Eritrean people are patient, their tradition and method in resolving disputes and issues through dialogue is a significant cultural resource. Eritreans were rewarded for the loss of their children by the independence of their country, Eritrea. They would have forgotten and forgiven all about the past willingly in order to march forward.

Trampling over the patience of the people reflects Isaias' inflated ego, misguided self-worth and arrogance. The source of the refusal to accept advice from colleagues and refusing to learn from the experience of others is a reflection of Isaias'view that emanate only from disrespect and foolishness.

He was not even willing to learn from the experience of those who viewed the world differently, and for the sake of their societies chose to forget the crimes that were inflicted on them, and refused to go to a low level and abuse their enemies. The experience of the leaders of South Africa such as the exemplary Nelson Mandela who struggled for change was there to be used as a relevant lesson.

In the initial period of independence, before the new structures were finalized and implemented, for a short time the Intelligence and Security Department functioned under the able leadership of Petros Solomon, a member of the Political Bureau. At the time, there were issues that the 'President' wanted to be investigated urgently. He ordered a hasty formation of a committee composed of members from the Intelligence and Security Department; Petros Solomon formed the committee and sent the names to the Office of the President. The committee received the cases that he wanted investigated directly from Isaias. Simon Gebredingel, the head of the communication branch in the Intelligence and Security Department, became the chairperson of the committee. I was one of the members among the five mid-level managers of the Intelligence and Security Department.

One of the cases that we received from Isaias for investigation concerned the case of the freedom fighter Brigadier General Bitweded Abraha who was under house arrest in Radio Marina, former residence of US GI's at the Kagnew Communication Base. Before his detention, he was the Administrator of Asseb. Looking at it from the outside, the accusation against him seemed serious and sensitive since we were told that he was a corrupt administrator involved in theft, embezzlement, corruption, and regional sentiments. As we were leaving the President's Office, Simon Gebredingel who was in charge of the investigation was given a reference file concerning a radio communicationheldbetween Bitweded and Isaias.

'President' Isaias gave us full authority to collect information from anyone to help us investigate the case. When we asked him in what manner we should ask the senior military commanders and senior leaders of the organization who were in the area, he gave us a short answer, giving us authority to ask anyone who can provide information, even members of the political office.

The accusations against Bitweded were grave, and to investigate a case of that magnitude is not easy for the investigators even if it involved people you didn't know, let alone someone you know very closely, your colleague and a childhood friend. Before we joined the revolution, I remember Bitweded when we were growing up kicking football together in Emba Galiano around Bar Tiblets. During the era of the struggle, we made the journey together, and when he was in charge of the revolutionary school campaigning to eradicate illiteracy among the people in the area behind the enemy defense line we worked together to present the members of the revolutionary school to the people as good examples. I never imagined that he would fall into such a situation; I knew him very closely.

Bitweded was placed under house arrest in a house at the camp in Radio Marina (previously housing US GIs of the Kagnew Communication Base), and he was told not to leave it. The charges were presented to him and he had answered them adequately and clearly. Though the answers that he gave were correct, they had to be verified from other sources. For that, it was important to travel to Asseb to meet and ask those who were in the area and who knew the situation. In Asseb we asked Mustafa Nurhussen, the one who leveled the accusations against Bitweded, to tell us the basis. We soon found out that the case was based on rumors and hearsays and he didn't have any concrete evidence, but subjective reasons: consisting of I think so or I don't think so, etc.

Mustafa who leveled the accusations against Bitweded and who replaced Bitweded as the Administrator of Asseb exploited the differences and the bad relations that existed between Isaias and Bitweded. He presented an unsubstantiated and unreliable report so as to be appreciated by Isaias, and to claim credit for all the developments that took place in Asseb under the watch of Biteweded. The senior military commanders and senior leaders who were in Asseb at the time, particularly Sheriffo, were among those who admired and regarded the administrative activities of Bitweded very highly.

Concerning the accusation of regional biases, although most of the workers who were in Asseb came from Biteweded's region of Seraye, our research showed that though most of the women workers who came to Asseb from the highlands were from Seraye, it was a cheap ploy that Mustafa designed as a trap to get at Bitweded. The workers in question were actually employed by Gerezgiher Wuchu (Wedi Itay), the military commander, who hails from the Hamassen region. That proved that the accusation was false and defamatory. There was no evidence whatsoever to prove the accusations related to theft and corruption either. The accusations were far from the truth. Bitweded was found to be innocent on all counts and on the contrary those who accused him were found to be the criminals themselves.

However, the accused knew very well the reason for his arrest. He told those of us who were investigating the case, "I was arrested simply because I refused to accept whatever Isaias ordered me without a question, it is better that you stop going in circles." He was absolutely truthful. There was a point of contention between him and Isaias. After the Derg was defeated and left Asseb, the goods that were captured in the port city were being sent from Assab to Asmara through Massawa, but after sometime, Isaias instructed Bitweded to deliver it to the TPLF instead. Bitweded objected to that: reasoning how something gained by the blood of Eritrean martyrs could be given to the TPLF? That caused a conflict with Isaias who became apprehensive because Bitweded didn't obey his orders. That was in actual facts the reason for his arrest. And that was the reason why he is still being kept in prison in spite of the fact that at that time he was suffering from mental illness. The accusation of corruption was an excuse designed to incarcerate him by creating false accusation.

At the end, the radio communication file that was given to the chairperson of the committee showed that Isaias gave Bitweded an order to which he replied negatively and therefore the case was an excuse to punish Bitweded for his disobedience. Since the committee that was mandated to investigate the issue of corruption was not tasked with investigating political issues, it concluded that Bitweded was innocent on all counts of the accusation and it also noted in its report that its mandrate does not extend to investigation of political issues.

Though the report clearly indicated that Bitweded was innocent it couldn't however free him from the shackles of the government. The case was not only unjust it was also not resolved after the investigation was finalized. He tried to find a solution on his own and escaped from his detention and went to a place from where he called some people he thought would have the ability to listen, and he confirmed that he was around. Bitweded was caught and transferred to Carchelli Prison and kept isolated in a cell. The issue demonstrates that anyone who is not obedient to Isaias and doesn't accept orders without question could be removed from the way. Still, the Sahel behavior and mode of operation didn't change much after independence.

After we finished investigating the case of Bitweded, since the sea travel from Massawa to Asseb was tiresome, we returned to Asmara by air via Addis Ababa. In Addis Ababa I found news about the senior ex-POW officers who were under my responsibility in the field, i.e. General Ali Hajji, Colonel Girma Tessema and Colonel Bezabih. General Ali Hajji invited me to lunch at his house and I was introduced to his family. I didn't locate Colonel Girma and Colonel Bezabih. Since I had a few days more to spare I travelled to Dire Dawa and before I left the town I visited the Continental Hotel where Afewerki Teweldemedhin 'Bureaucracy' was shot and fell. I made my martyr's remembrance for the man who accomplished great tasks and who gave his life to the liberation of his country and its people from colonial domination and oppression.

The next assignment that was given to us by the Head of the Intelligence and Security Department was to reconcile the cash and other properties that were captured by the heavy artillery units from the Ethiopian soldiers in the last battles in Eritrea and across the border. These included US dollars that were given to the units that were operating across the border in Ethiopia to spend on expenses of the operation, but which were not properly accounted for after independence. In addition, since the social and political relations among the members of the heavy artillery units were not healthy we attempted to resolve it by addressing the complaints of the freedom fighters.

Our directives were to audit the money that was captured from the enemy. But since almost all the combatants--from squad leaders, platoon, and company and battalion commanders--have spent a portion of the money there was nothing that could be done. Thirty thousand dollars out of the money that was given to cover the expenses of the 'Cross Border Operation Campaign' was returned to the treasury of the organization. Major General Ramadan Awliyay, the Commander of the Heavy Artillery Division, had kept it in a safe in his house. The unhealthy social and political relations among the units were made to subside through advice and criticisms.

The introduction of institutionalized system of governance in the process of building a new country was not limited to governmental entities only. There were attempts to liberate the cultural, social, religious institutions from depending on the government and to be self-reliant by providing them with the necessaryfinancial and technical support.

And to reinvigorate Eritrean capacities, local talents were sought and specialists were brought from abroad. Research was carried out to find ways and means of enhancing the national skill pool and to achieve a qualitative and quantitative leap forward.

There was no nationally centralized system of administration for religious affairs, and to begin with apart from the financial assistance offered a study to assess the available level of skills among religious leaders was also carried out in order to enable the Muslims to develop an appropriate administrative system. The study was conducted to determine if there were people who can manage the affairs of the Muslim religion at the level of Mufti, so as to enable the adherents of the faith to self administer their affairs. A few months after the report was submitted, without the anticipated election being held, the local news media announced that a Mufti had been elected. The truth is, the Mufti was not elected but was hand-picked to sit in the position as a Mufti. Though some Muslims didn't like the selection of the Mufti and tried to challenge it, their complaints fell on deaf ears by the authorities.

As the situation was going on the wrong direction, a hushed displeasure surfaced, though the prevailing independence euphoria prevented the people from rushing to take action. Soon, instead of the situation getting better, inequality clearly appeared within the rank of the freedom fighters as varying living conditions were visible and widespread. Open complaints started to be heard from among the fighters.

After we entered Asmara, salaries were not apportioned for the fighters who were required to continue living just like they were during the era of the liberation struggle. Most lived off the rations they received from the EPLF supply unit. It was difficult to live in a city where some had rich parents and others didn't, and live among the society in disparity. Others were scattered all over the Eritrean countryside and remote towns; they were living in a society that thinks in terms of cash and they couldn't tolerate it with empty pockets. The freedom fighters had accomplished their national obligations and now lived in the cities and villages, and though they were on duty they couldn't earn a living like a common salaried Eritrean worker who earned a salary. Members of a typical squad during the era of the struggle were immersed in the society where some were able to adjust with the living standards of the society and moved on, while others were lost and started to be bitter with the situation they were in. A new basket that is no better than the field basket was created containing the haves and have nots. Even if it is in the cultural attribute of freedom fighters to be respectful, and they were used to share their food and drinks with their colleagues, it will be difficult to imagine for how long those from well off families can endure supporting their own children and their friends. The conditions did get worse.

One night we stayed late at Toto's Bar Diana with my childhood friends who liked to listen to stories from my time in the struggle and they wouldn't let me leave and we stayed there drinking until dawn."What are you trying to show us? You want to transform the freedom fighters into monks; you want them to live only off handouts?" It was a childhood friend who came from overseas and realized our pockets had holes in them.

I replied to him, "For us, our condition is better; people would say that our pockets have holes and thus they would invite us to food and drink. People do not think we get enough but you should worry for those who have no one to go to, we have colleagues who spend their days helplessly held in their house in the camps." I was tired of taking those friends around town one after the other.

"How will that be solved in the end? They don't even have anything to go to Aba Shawl! Even if angels descend down to earth they would not work without a salary." It was a friend who came from the U.S. He recalled how he used to host and hide the fighters when they came to Asmara on clandestine business.

I replied, "Indeed before those who were angels became devils." I was a bit high on alcohol and I was meeting the comrade seventeen years after I joined the Front; he had gone to the US by crossing to the Sudan through the field.

The naturalized American friend continued the conversation, "Those who were martyred for freedom are gone so that the srvivors would have a better life. Now, independence has come; I didn't think there is a reason for someone to crucify his life for others like Jesus Christ did."

When the night philosophy got intense, I asked him, "Listen, what happened to you! You pushed many people to join the revolution and then you sneaked out leaving the struggle behind?" He continued, "My friend Tsegu, as if we didn't show them the way to Aba Shawl, they knocked me down in the field. And to avoid their pursuit I zipped my mouth and left the country. I didn't tell you because I thought if you try it on your own, you will find out when the angels turn into devils." He got a chance to vent what he kept bottled inside him for a long time.

I told him, "As if you were not like a lion, you became a lamb, what have they done to you?"

He said, "I was not the only one who was imprisoned, they inserted a ball into my mouth and warned me not to talk about Menka'a, I was a lion to die for my country not to die in vain. I didn't tell you then because I wanted to live a little longer. Check it out about the past comrade Tsegu".

I replied, "Even now, we are comrades buddy, we don't have a fight over piece of a farmland, we received the farm together; now our farm is your farm, take it over."

We realized it was too late when the bar owner sounded the last bell and we parted ways each going to his own house.

It was during the time when a Referendum Commission was formed to carry out the referendum to legitimize the military victory of the struggle for independence by political means; but the critical question was: should the inauguration of independence include the concerns of the freedom fighters? For how long will they work without a salary? The combatants didn't like the way things were developing, and they started to ask about their rights. But when their demands fell on deaf ears they started to take matters into their own hands and take action of their own.

The fighters were given a small pocket money that would be spent in one evening's sitting in a restaurant or a bar. The amount was embarrassingly meager and one would not think of saving it. The government was not willing or able to pay the fighters and they asked to be demobilized from service in an orderly manner in order to be able to work and fend for themselves and to be rehabilitated and re-integrated in the society on their own. Their request was rejected. Instead they were told they had to serve another two years under the same conditions. They observed some of their colleagues who depended on their parents' resources and others abusing government resources and enjoying satisfactory lives, while they, let alone adequately supporting their family they couldn't even afford to provide basic needs for their family. Since they didn't get an answer for their grievances which they presented properly in the middle of May 20th 1993 the freedom fighters took to the streets and occupied the Asmara airport and a few other government buildings. They pressured Isaias who was then President of the transitional state of Eritrea and frog-marched him on foot to the Asmara Stadium. There he was compelled to respond to the fighters' legitimate demands with humility.

The Isaias who normally inflates his chest like a lion when he lectures in different meetings, was humbled by the bold actions of the fighters and was forced to answer their questions and was instantly transformed into a humble angelic Isaias. He was unusually polite and spoke nicely and promised to implement all the demands of the fighters within a short period: that is to initiate demobilization and resettlement, to adjust the salary scale and implement a new system of salaries, to allow the handicapped veterans to form their own association that would represent them and be able to elect their leaders and be active nationally and internationally. He also promised to enact a law to control the corruption of officials, and to hold the organizational congress within six months, etc. His promises were delivered in humility.

The 'mutiny', as the action of the freedom fighters was characterized, was not violent but extremely peaceful. However, the following day, on May 21st. 1993, Isaias appeared on national television and described the incident as follows: even if the questions were legitimate, the 'mutiny' was illegal and shameful. He confirmed that the promises that he made were meant only to calm the situationand would not be implemented. Subsequently, almost all the participants of the protest action of the fighters were arrested, and through a court-martial all of those who were considered ringleaders were sentenced to over four years of prison term while the rest were sentenced to prison term between one and three years. Isaias described the sentences as lenient; however, on the fourth anniversary of Independence Day, Isaias stated that most of the fighters were pardoned. In actual fact, most of them were made to fully serve their prison terms--the claim that the sentences were light on one hand, and on the other hand declaring pardon, were statements meant for propaganda purposes and for political expediency, hence they were deceitful.

Chapter 6. HIJACKING OF THE REVOLUTION: DERAILED JOURNEY OF STRUGGLE AND THE FORMATION OF A "NATIONAL COUNCIL"

In 1993 an election was held for the national council without the existence of competing political parties; all administrative zones elected their delegates. In meetings for middle level cadres and leaders that were held at the Teachers Training Institute and in Cinema Capitol, the Secretary General of the EPLF Isaias explained that the elected members from the zones will be added to the members of the EPLF central committee and will form a council that will lead the transitional Eritrean government.

During meetings held for the leaders of the Ministry of Defense and the Department of Intelligence and Security, I posed a question: "Isn't this outside the requirements of the law? What will happen when the third organizational congress is held and new members are elected to the Central Committee? Does it mean they will replace those who are council members now? I don't think the council should be beholden to organizational congresses and the work of the government and the organization should not intermingle." Isaias replied by arguing that what was done was dictated by the situation and it will not be affected by the organizational congress. Many cadres expressed similar objections, considering the proposed process to be a short cut to power. Isaias concluded the meeting by admonishing and threatening the participants.

In a meeting of the departments that was held two days later at Cinema Capitol, Brigadier General Tekheste Haile explained that the formation of the council was illegal and contravenes the provisions of the constitution and the charter of the EPLF. Referring to General Tekheste's question about legality, Isaias gave a lecture for about ten minutes and explained that he agrees with the comment, but at the same time he tried to confuse the participants by making an excuse that the decision was dictated by the prevailing situation. However, almost all the mid-level cadres of the organization and almost all the members of EPRP didn't object to Isaias' explanation because it appeared to serve their interest of becoming council members through a short cut.

After the conclusion of the meeting Isaias found excuses to imprison the cadres who objected to his proposals. Brigadier General Tekheste, who became a member of the EPRP towards the conclusion of the struggle, was accused of revealing the existence of the secret party and of divulging party secrets to the freedom fighter Stefanos Dagnew, and was imprisoned. Later, they released Brigadier General Tekheste explaining that there was no evidence for the accusation leveled against him and that he was jailed wrongly. The goal it appears was to devise excuses in order to weaken the opposition.

At that time, though there were many members of EPRP who realized Isaias' leadership was going out of line, they still considered themselves members of the secret party that was temporarily frozen but would soon be reactivated to lead. Therefore, they didn't move to form parties that would represent their views. It can be argued that the idea of forming parties was feared based on previous experiences in the EPLF when attempts to form parties were severelysquashed. The measures that the EPRP took in the journey of the "revolutionary" EPLF, was almost similar to the measures taken by the Ethiopian occupiers against the Eritrean people: perceived hindrances, be it Menka'a or Yemeen, be it Btsay Goitom Berhe or otherwise, had to be executed and eliminated.

It was under such circumstances that at the end of 1993 the congress of EPRP that was frozen since 1989 was convened in Valineki near Adi Nefas in the northern outskirts of Asmara. Suddenly, in the middle of that year information was circulated concerning the issues that should be discussed and that questions and agenda items should be registered in advance to assist in the preparation of the planned congress and election of delegates who would participate in the congress. The party that was frozen for years, was instantly given life just like butter that was frozen, and in a moment it thawed by the sudden rays of the sun. The entire episode was not healthy.

It was difficult to ignore the questions that were being raised by the fighters and the people in general. The maneuvers made to awaken the sleeping secret party was to pass over or to throw the unresolved issues to the party congress, thus to create a legitimacy cover so that Isaias would not be accountable on one hand and to create a ground work for the election of the leadership on the other, thus the new country can be directed according to his wishes. Many questions were raised in the meetings that were held to elect representatives to the congress, but since there was no one who could give an answer, the questions were simply listed to be raised and discussed at the forthcoming congress. The meetings offered an opportunity to raise many questions during which time almost all members of the party presented constructive ideas to enable the country to follow a correct pathand move forward.

The meeting was held based on resolutions that were passed on previous congresses. It was my conviction that the period of a one party dictatorship must end and the country should henceforth move towards a multiparty system of government. It is essential to create a conducive environment for freedom of expression and the free flow of information where parties can compete freely and present their respective programs to the people and work to advance the development of the country. I asked why so much time was wasted without parties being formed, and reminded the meeting that an environment where the activities of the government would abide by the congress resolutions should be created and these were the questions that I got registered. But since I was elected as a delegate to attend the congress and I thought that would give me an opportunity to present them again myself, I left for the Valineki congress equipped with my views and questions, and also those of the likeminded colleagues.

The Third Congress of the EPRP/ESP in Valineki was held secretly; it was convened in Mai Hutsa, Adi Nefas, in the northern outskirts of Asmara. Attendants travelled from Asmara and other places by night and reached the location under the cover of darkness to hide from the people who are the owners of the country and from the freedom fighters that ushered in independence. At that moment I started to ask myself, "What am I doing here?" The deteriorating situation in the country worried me. The expectations of the anxious attendants were to know the reason why the resolutions of the second congress were not implemented, and to know the future fate and direction of our journey. However, that was not the main purpose behind the convening of the congress and it soon became evident that the principal objective of the congress was to ensure that the interest of Isaias and his clique is protected.

As usual, the secret party congress was convened to prepare the ground for the EPLF congress that was planned for the beginning of 1994. The highlight of the congress was Isaias' statement, when he said that: "this leadership is rotten; the leadership has lost direction and couldn't lead, it couldn't implement its mission properly." etc. It was a lecture that belittled and attacked the other leaders of the organization, implying that they failed in implementing the resolutions of the second congress and therefore the past leaders should be replaced by the "new warm blooded individuals." Such belittling of the former leaders should have been a reason to raise the question of who the leadership was and to what extent does it apply to the Secretary General and how does it reflect on the leadership of Isaias himself. Sadly none of the other members of the leadership asked questions or challenged his statements.

When the party had been frozen for over four years for no apparent reason, to accuse his colleagues in the leadership of the party and of the EPLF of being the cause for non-implementation of congress resolutions is disrespectful and hypocritical. He disregarded them as if they didn't lead the struggle to liberate Eritrea and to make it politically and economically self-reliant and to confirm its recognition internationally. His accusation was either out of fear of competition or else of being confident that he had mobilized enough mass support. At the time when the former freedom fighters of the EPLF were actively involved in the military, social, and economic spheres to build the country, Isaias is believed to have been secretly engaged in forming a new party. The members of his new secret party appeared to be well organized when they came to Valineki; they consisted of those who listen to anything Isaias tells them without question plus those from existing members of EPRP whom he doesn't consider a threat and others who were not until that time members of the EPRP but according to Isaias are the "new warm blood."

The situation inside the secret party's congress was almost like what Btsay Goitom Berhe described was happening during the meetings he attended in Sahel and his observation that those who come from different backgrounds and who were organized by Isaias came out of the meetings with a common and identical position. Isaac

Rezene, who later became a member of the party that was formed by Btsay, had also observed that it was just similar to the old ways. The congress also had a good number of participants who were former members of the Eritreans for Liberation in North America (EFLNA) and Eritreans for Liberation in Europe (EFLE) whom Isaias considered "warm blood" because they were loyal to him. The outcome of the party congress was that Isaias and his "New Blood Boys" controlled the "Kingdom" and the aged camels were replaced by the young horses.

They tried to bypass the issue of assessing the second congress' resolutions and aspects of their implementation. Let alone to raise democratization topics and discuss them, they didn't even want to mention them at all. The fact that those topics were not raised and that there was no challenge or comment regarding what Isaias stated, 'that the leadership is rotten', worried the participants of the congress. However, when I saw that the questions I and my colleagues registered at the meetings for the election of delegates 'were being ignored, I again repeated my question: "why didn't we work to establish a multi-party system? And now, is there any plan regarding that?" My question was shelved after Beraki Gebreselassie who was the moderator of the congress replied that the questions I raised were important and in order to give them sufficient time for detailed discussion, we will come back to them towards the end of the congress. While we waited for the issues to be raised before the end of the congress the coordinating committee announced the conclusion of the congress. Petros Hailemariam, a member of the revolutionary school (Ministry of Education), intervened and said, "Tsegu's question was kept on a pending list to be discussed towards the end and now it is being forgotten. Since the question was not posed by Tsegu alone, but by many of us, let's give it time." He managed to have the question raised again.

Many constructive and different ideas were presented regarding the importance of the presence of multi-parties in building a democratic system. However, Isaias and his clique of new blood, I am convinced, had secretly founded a secret party along with others and dominated it until the day of liberation of Eritrea. Now in independent Eritrea, the issue of multi-party is not only a headache to Isaias, but it also causes him high blood pressure. Because of that, though he didn't like the divergent opinions and questions that were raised from different corners, he realized he could not give a negative reply and move on. At the end, he assessed the situation through his mouthpiece Yemane Gebreab "Monkey", who was his right hand man and his political adviser and who was manipulating and controlling the congress as Isaias wished it. Yemane noted that multi-party system is an important and big issue and efforts should be exerted to push for it, but it should be applied in slow steps so that it would not be affected by 'sub-national' sentiments. He concluded it by saying, a multi-party system should not be expected to grow overnight like a mushroom.

In February 1994, the Third Organizational Congress was held in Nakfa and based on the resolution of the EPRP/ESP Congress; it changed the name of the organization from EPLF to People's Front for Democracy and Justice (PFDJ). A proclamation was enacted providing for the formation of a Constitutional Commission that would prepare a draft constitution as a supreme law of the country. And in April 1994 a fifty-member Constitutional Commission was formed. In general, usually the assessment of the party congress was taken as the starting point and constituted an assessment of the performance of the organization during the last six-years. Based on the resolutions of the party congress the new central committee of the PFDJ was elected. Apart from Ali Saed Abdella, Alamin Mohammed Saed, and Mesfin Hagos, all those others elected as members of the Executive Committee of PFDJ at the Third Congress were all what Isaias termed as 'new blood'. On the other hand, Ramadan Mohammed Nur who fell out of favor of Isaias had to be removed from leadership through, as per the advice of his colleagues, a well crafted window dressing that made him declinestanding for election. To make his removal palatable to the fighters and the public he was advised by his colleagues to decline nomination, and citing his invaluable contributions his case was explained as a voluntary resignation from the leadership of the organization and the government to give room for the younger generation (new blood).

At the end, the congress participants were told the existence of a secret party during the liberation struggle that was instrumental in the achievement of the liberation of Eritrea, and that it contributed greatly but that from then on said the party will cease to exist. Isaias who as the Secretary General of the party announced its dissolution to all the attendants in his statements at the congress had sent shock waves to even the secret party members who were taken by surprise to learn about the dissolution of their party with the rest of the Congress participants.

There was nothing that was not done to freeze the party as per Isaias's wishes--to inject life in it and use it and in the end to dissolve it after obtaining what he needed through it. He was so prepared to answer questions that could be raised. Isaias froze the old party and formed a new party after he filtered in those he wanted and discarded those he didn't want, and he accomplished his design by preparing and presenting a ready-made alternative party.

What Isaac Rezene didn't want to disclose ahead of time was the existence of another secret party within the secret party. Just like the EPRP/ESP that operated inside the EPLF was disclosed at the Third Organizational Congress when it was time to do so, now it was time to expose the party that dissolved the EPRP/ESP from the inside.

More than Isaias was managing to use the party as he wished the fact that the other leaders of the party were not able to answer the question of why they were silently paralyzed, or why they didn't react and challenge Isaias bothered all caring Eritreans who didn't mind raising the questions on their own. But to clarify the picture it is better to explain it in relation to subsequent developments and where it all ended up.

Though at the Third Organizational Congress the organization promised to establish a democratic government system with the existence of multi-parties, it carefully controlled the political platform and prevented the rising voices of opposition from expanding by controlling and directing the media towards what the new party decided. In the meeting that the National Council held in March 1994 the issue of the press freedom was extensively debated and a committee was established and mandated to draft a press law.

Though the press law allowed all Eritreans to express their views freely and equally, when the Catholic Church addressed the laying off of workers (Mtsiltsal) that affected a large number of civil servants who lost their jobs, and published an opinion that opposed the action, the Church's newspaper was banned from being published. The content was prepared by Eritreans who had the right to express their views or criticize government policies and actions based on freedom of the press and the law that was enacted by the government. The newspaper that was printed by a religious institution was stopped when other newspapers were at that time publishing articles that criticized the government. When other citizens were writing for the rest of the private newspapers, though it was possible to overcome the Catholic newspaper problem by telling them to publish it in the non-religious newspapers in order to protect their press rights, a decision was taken as a show of power, to intimidate, to force them to tow the line and kneel down to the government's directives.

The PFDJ presented some of the corruption cases that were seen among the combatants as if they caused serious damages and announced the establishment of a Special Court. Knowing that such a court doesn't follow normal procedures, and doesn't allow appeals, and that it serves as a tool of oppression, and that such a court can only be declared in emergency situations only if the country is in danger, regardless, Isaias wanted to use such an illegal institution and put it as a pre-condition, and since he was unable to establish it in 1994, he postponed it to the following year.

In October 1994, a proclamation was issued from the Office of the President (OP) declaring that all Jehovah witnesses who refused to vote in the referendum and refused to engage in the national service of military nature, because their religious belief prohibits them from carrying arms, would be denied any government services including issuance of passports, commercial licenses and visa services. In short, gradually all the democratic rights of the people started to be violated.

In 1994, Isaias controlled the highest power in the government and the PFDJ and started to operate on different levels and directions. While on one hand preparations were underway to draft a constitution and improve administration of justice (including criminal justice), simultaneously preparations were underway to establish a Special Court. Again, he formed a new committee in order to put limitations to the press law.

In order to solve the issue of salaries, which was the reason for the mini-strike of the freedom fighters in 1993, the process of demobilizationof many fighters from service started, and thousands of fighters began to register with the ministry of labor to be expatriated overseas to work as domestic servants. The government tried to help the demobilized fighters leave the very country that they liberated. To make up for the shortage in military manpower the government introduced the program of compulsory national service as a cheap labor pool of the youth working without salary.

Then there was the case of the handicapped. After their complaints fell on deaf ears, the handicapped veterans left their place in Mai Habar moving on wheelchairs towards Asmara to demonstrate. Even if the peaceful demonstration was done without police permission, the police forces instead of controlling it to remain within bounds, sent a commando unit under the command of Brigadier General Fitsum "Wedi Memhir" to stop them, and they were shot on the Asmara-Massawa road. Worse still, instead of bringing those who shot and hit the handicapped veterans to face justice, Isaias embarked on a process of identifying and hunting the organizers of the movement, confirming that he sent the commando units to do the task. All the official government activities lost direction and became haphazard and directionless.

After the Third Organizational Congress, I was appointed as a Director in the newly structured Ministry of Internal Affairs. My senior bosses were Minister Ali Saed Abdella, and his deputy Naizghi Kiflu; the administrative responsibilities were directly under the deputy minister. I was in charge of human resources, logistics and finances of the ministry. Naizghi and I were never good bedfellows and we quarreled whenever we met and in spite of the fact that we were antagonists we were appointed to work together, always in conflict.

I was not the only problem of Naizghi, as it was his nature to quarrel with anyone; he was unruly by nature who wanted to do what he pleased, and if anyone has to work with him, he tries to make them submit to him even if it means using force. He is a dictator by nature who wanted to control people, a small mirror image of Isaias. And that is why Naizghi was given such a sensitive and high position to be a tool to get some delicate jobs done. Naizghi was a kind of a person who would obey if Isaias asked him to go out to handcuff and bring back the devil, though he knows he couldn't find the devil. Naturally, I do not accept directives that are outside the bounds of guidelines, or under duress, and that is why I was not accepting unreasonable and at times illegal directives from Naizghi. We never developed a harmonious working relationship during my time at the ministry.

When I was the Director of Administration of the Ministry of Internal Affairs, I was not limited to administering the "budget" of the ministry; since there was no institutional process, there was no properly allocated budget but a temporary operational expenses account. Even expenses related to the Muslim and Orthodox religious administration were kept outside the "budget" of the Ministry of Internal Affairs under the Deputy Minister. After independence, it was seen as a problem to have the religious institutions to continue to be financed, and to work under the Ethiopian Orthodox Patriarch. A special "budget" was created for that purpose to delink and free them from dependence on the Ethiopian Orthodox Church. The cooperation wouldn't have been a problem if it was based on the general principles--a nation for all but religion is a private matter--if the government served the people and the religious institutions served the spiritual needs of believers.

As it is provided in the draft constitution that religious rights and freedom of worship of anyone is guaranteed under the law, and for all to freely follow any religion of their choice, at a time when the Eritrean citizens were expecting to move freely without pressure, in July 1995 the government issued a proclamation banning any civic, developmental or political activity carried out in the country. Therefore, all development related project activities such as health, education, agriculture funded and implemented by Non Governmental Organizations (NGOs) and religious entities were stopped. The government only wanted the funds; therefore they restricted implementation of projects to government agencies. Thus all NGOs were required to register with the Eritrean Refugee and Relief Commission (ERRC) and reveal the source and details of their external funding. Thereafter, only government agencies were permitted to implement development and social service related projects.

Isaias doesn't trust any independent organization, be it religious, civic, political, association and non-governmental or any other type of organization to operate without governmental control. As if he didn't interfere in the affairs of the religious institutions, he banned them from getting involved on issues of political nature, or from participating in the development activities of the country. The government also banned the newspaper of the Catholic Secretariat. He tried to steer them as he wished, and thus reflected his true dictatorial tendencies.

In actual facts, the religious institutions did not interfere in government affairs; it was only the Jehovah Witnesses which, because they refused to take part in the referendum and military service, were denied all their rights as citizens of the country. And in regard to the Catholic Secretariat newspaper's banning, it demonstrates that there is no tolerance on those who expressed their constructive criticism on issues of national concern. He banned the newspaper. Isaias wanted to control the Muslim and the Orthodox religious institutions that represent about 90% of the population through financial contribution in order to steer them to his wish, and those he can't buy with money, he tried to intimidate and threaten and force them to come in line with his wishes.

On top of offering funds for the administration of the offices of the Muslim and Orthodox religious establishments that were assisted with Ethiopian birr 200,000 each, a large office was built in Tiravuolo for the offices of the Patriarchate of the Orthodox Church, and the government bought vehicles for their use. The President infiltrated these religious institutions by placing his own men inside the two religious institutions in order to closely monitor and steer their activities. The Mufti of the Muslims, Sheikh Alamin, who was appointed without elections, and those who were replacing each other in the structure of the Orthodox Patriarchate (except a few) were all chosen with the blessing of the President and were driven in the direction he wanted them.

In one instance, Naizghi called the members of the Synod of the Orthodox Christians and met with them at the Ministry of Internal Affairs and tried to resolve some minor issues of difference that arose among the members. He exploited the differences that he observed there and realized that some will not do what he wants them to do if they were elected. One of the Synod members, Abune Maqarios, was ordered to leave Eritrea by Naizghi who compelled him to go abroad. Naizghi exploited a comment made by Abune Maqarios, when he said, "in my age I can go to Israel to pray and write a book," in order to banish him to exile. He exploited that comment and wrote him an order stating: "as per your request, you are hereby relieved of your duty." Abune Maqarios (Petros) and the others approached him again and tried to persuade him to reverse the decision that he ordered the supreme leader of the religious institutions to go to exile, but their effort came to no avail. It was clear that Naizghi was following orders from Isaias.

Naizghi was given a free ride to do anything he liked on issues concerning the bishops. In the meeting that was held after Synod members left, someone asked Naizghi if what he did was not interference in the affairs of the church. Naizghi said, "He is a spy, he is a member of the Egyptian Synod, and we don't want him." However, it was not only Abune Maqarios who was a member of the Egyptian Synod, but also Abune Yacob of Ethiopia, and Abune Marqos have all been members of the Egyptian Synod. This was a result of the situations created by the occupation. Truly though, it was Abune Yacob who sided with Ethiopia and wanted to have the Eritrean Orthodox Church remain under the Ethiopian patriarchate. His Holiness Abune Antonios, who has now been under house arrest for many years, didn't like the way Naizghi behaved. He told him, "My son, Naizghi, please let us handle our affairs on our own." To which Naizghi replied, "Okay, then don't ask us for funds." However, the Orthodox institution faced financial difficulties and couldn't operate and they appealed to the Ministry of Internal Affairs to intervene and the governmental assistance was resumed. In general, the government had the power to control any eventuality and didn't allow any institution to operate outside its sphere of control. Every Eritrean was made to kneel down under the dictatorship of Isaias.

When I worked under Naizghi, we didn't get along well at all and I asked to be demobilized. However my request was rejected. Given the fact that it was well known Naizghi and I could not work together, I was transferred to work as a Secretary of Minister Ali Saed. Although my new position fell under the Minister, when the minister was away, Naizghi covered for him, and our confrontation was minimized but didn't stop.

PFDJ Economic and Political Hegemony

In February 1992, my second son Aman was born in Asmara. Since she was transferred from Sahel to the frontline of Adi Keieh, Almaz had stayed there after independence. Even after independence, work was given priority and a situation where spouses can stay together was not created and that situation was only gradually reached in several stages. It was after delivery of our son that she came to Asmara and we started to raise our children together.

The situation of the struggle didn't allow families to be together. In addition to the bad luck of children who were born in the field, as freedom fighters we did our best to help nurture our children in the best way possible and this we did with our meager resources and under the constraining circumstances. However, the limited resources at our disposal and the circumstances in the front had negative psychosocial effects on the children in the field. When compared with the children born in the cities those who were born in the field were unruly, temperamental and behaviorally outside the norms of our society when compared with those brought up in a peaceful environment under the tutelage of both parents and social safety nets.

My eldest son Pitias went to Kindergarten in Adi Keih and later in Asmara. Based on the relatively egalitarian life of the freedom fighterswhere he lived as a toddler, he had no notion related to money or private property. He tried to take anything he wanted and acted as he pleased. If he found a hindrance he wouldn't hesitate to use force. He would move to any neighbor's house and act as if it is his house until slowly he became integrated into the civil society. He became used to the city life and finished pre-school at Cathedral kindergarten. It took time for the children who grew up in the environment of the revolution to integrate with the society. But how about those of us who were used to hearing gun shots like it was music for a long time? Wouldn't it be difficult for us to integrate in a society without going through a post traumatic psycho-social rehabilitation for post traumatic stress disorder (PTSD)?

If a slave who grew up under a master is freed and joins a normal society, he would still behave in a manner of a slave-and-master relationship until he is psychologically fully emancipated and integrated into the society. The decision to have the fighters continue to work without salary was based on denying the fact that fighters worked without salary for many years to achieve equality of all citizens. Just as it takes time for a slave to integrate in a society, the leadership took a long time to administer the people by introducing a natural salary system for the fighters. When Isaias refused to listen to the wakeup call of the strike of the fighters, whohad fought for their people, and address their demands, he accused the fighters who tried to wake him up characterizing them as 'mutineers'. Instead of identifying the sources of the problem and seeking a satisfactory solution, he was quick to arrest his colleagues who became aware they had to leave the Sahel norms behind and move ahead by introducing an equitable salary system.

There were not enough administrative skills and knowhow within the EPLF, only a few departments depended on research and studies to carry out their tasks while the rest of the departments were applying trial and error method of work and correcting mistakes in the process. But that would not have been a problem under the unique circumstances of a liberation war. The problem arose during peace time when it was required to administer the entire population. In order to elevate the level of administrative skills studies were conducted by experts, including those experts brought in from abroad to fill the gaps; still, the administrative skill of the 'PFDJ'-led government was not satisfactory enough to meet the needs of the nation. The EPLF that had operated in harmony and co-existed with the people 'like water and milk' and was able to liberate Eritrea, was now categorizing the society into 'fighters' and 'civilians', us and them, and causing dissension and fragmentation in place of unity and making the relationship distinctly separated like 'water and oil'. Because of the PFDJ's policy and practice of mal-administration many experts left the country because they were unable to work under the precarious and difficult circumstances.

In the initial few years, the government adopted a policy that attracted investors among whom were many Diaspora Eritreans and foreigners from abroad. The trend during the first few years after independence exhibited an upward economic growth which was later reversed downward and especially after the 1998-2000 border war with Ethiopia. This was partly because of the nature of the government that continued to act and behave as a war time front and not as a peace time state. Starting from the eve of Independence Day until the Third Organizational Congress PFDJ proclaimed that the properties that were created by the contribution of the entire population and the properties and money that was snatched from the enemy by the muscles of the brave fighters belonged to the ruling party and not to the government of Eritrea. It was an indication that PFDJ was determined to dominate and monopolize both the economic and political field in the country before any other party that could compete with it is created. Since there were no competing parties and were also not allowed to operate later on, the economic competition was directed against the private investors. The PFDJ was the licensor and denier of everything, and the situation was not suitable for the local and foreign investors who came to compete and operate in what they thought were a free market economy. They were systematically pushed out and the PFDJ occupied the entire field of the economy and monopolized it.

Clearly the PFDJ that monopolizes the national economy and political power does not care much about the people it is supposed to govern and with whom it should establish a relationship of trust. But instead of assessing the situation and striving to develop the country, it is watching the national economy slide downward and the standard of living of the Eritrean people gradually deteriorate. Now, while Eritrea was heading towards disaster President Isaias and his cohorts did not appear to care less. It is in such a dire situation that critical questions and opposition on the undemocratic system of governance and administration started to appear in different corners of the country and abroad.

When I worked as a Secretary at the Ministry of Internal Affairs, one of my duties was to prepare a summary report about the departments that were under the Ministry, namely: police, prisons, immigration, religious affairs, and security, to be submitted to the Office of the President. Isaias received on a daily basis a condensed summary of the reports and data about prisoners who were jailed or released, the complaints and views of the people, the number of nationals who enter and exit Eritrea, and other information considered important. The daily report also covered the propaganda and rumors spread by his agents alleging that corrupt officials working under the President were responsible for the wrongdoing taking place without his knowledge. Such was a propaganda ploy by those who are cheerleaders in the camp of the President aimed at painting an innocent picture of him. The reports were presented to him stating that officials under him were engaged in corrupt practices without his knowledge. But there was nothing that went in the country without the President's knowledge. Let alone matters that concern the national security, he even knew details of all the transfer and replacement of officials in every ministry.

Most of the reports were about the people's grievances concerning the mismanagement of government affairs and poor delivery of services, starting with the leaders of the Ministry of Internal Affairs. The reports that were prepared by the Ministry of Internal Affairs addressed issues such as the ones believed to be negative practices committed by the leaders against the people. There were many people whose Identity Cards Naizghi would take during the nights when he was drunk, and the next morning they would come to the Ministry to claim their IDs. He would say, I found her drunk and prostituting, or, I suspected they were selling hashish, etc, matters that were not within the sphere of his responsibility. Police stations often called to ask what to do with prisoners who were placed in custody by Naizghi Kiflu, just like someone would entrust goods for safe keeping. Sometime he forgot that he placed people in the custody of the stations. In short, at night after Isaias went to sleep Asmara fell under the control of Naizghi. However, the senior leaders of the party and the government kept quiet though they knew everything aboutwhat Naizghi was doing.

The burning question is therefore, why is it that no action has been taken against him to remedy the situation? My hunch is that Naizghi knew a lot of secrets about the President and the secret party. In addition, there were specific sensitive missions that he was needed to carry out. It is worth noting that the archives of Halewa Sewra were in his hands and he had people who were appointed to him to do what he ordered them to do, and after we entered Asmara the sensitive documents, particularly those that concern Menka'a and Yemeen movements, were separately kept in his office. As long as he possessed the sensitive documents that could criminally implicate Isaias his unruly behavior and actions would not be sanctioned.

When I worked as Secretary of the Ministry, I once had an altercation with Naizghi and we were about to hit each other. He ran and stormed into Ali Saed's office. Ali was shocked and asked me what had happened, and I told him that we reached that stage because Naizghi wouldn't let me do my work; he interrupted our meetings and made disturbances, and he started to campaign among the fighters to implicate me in wrongdoings. Ali wanted to calm the situation. He asked Naizghi to stay in his office and said to me, "This boy is troublesome and everyone knows that, however, the man (meaning Isaias) has asked me to handle him in my way; whatever he says, I want you to ignore him, and update me about his situation regularly."

Naizghi was allowed to do whatever he wanted until he accomplished the mission that was given to him. Equipped with that confidence, during Tekhlay Hareka's wedding in Mendefera, after he drank enough alcohol, he expressed regionalist sentiments in front of his colleagues, members of the Central Committee Weldemichael Gebremariam and Weldemichael Abraha and other veteran freedom fighters; he stated that the government was dominated by people from Hammssen and Akele Guzai. The report about the incident had reached Isaias but no actions were taken against him. That is in contrast with many brave fighters who were accused of regionalism and of being members of Menka'a and Yemen and executed in the journey of the struggle as has been narrated. Instead of moving forward by giving leadership opportunities to citizens who had education and administrative skills to be able to correct the mistakes and improve in time, Isaias and his cohorts still chose to administer the country with their "Sahel state of mind," the archaic mentality that they refused to leave behind.

At a time when they were denied the free services of fighters, and when the administration of the new country required people with specialized skills who can move the country ahead, they didn't want the skilled people to take responsibility of managing the affairs of the state and instead they chose to meet the new challenges with the old militaristic mode of administration of Sahel. Based on the military administration that they knew very well, they marginalized any educated and skilled individual who stood in their way.

Isaias was not able to form the Special Court that would not be answerable to the justice department based on the proclamation of 1994, in time. In order to establish the system that he wanted, anything that he considered a threat should first be removed under the guise of corruption. According to Isaias, the Special Court was established to remedy the shortage of legal experts that he created himself and used as an excuse. It was presented as a court that was established to hasten the process of the corruption cases, as a replacement of Halewa Sewra, where the accused cannot have a lawyer, and can't appeal a ruling, a court that was outside the jurisdiction of the ministry of justice and administered and steered by the ministry of defense. It was a tool that he established to squash people he didn't like.

In 1996, news spread that senior officials of the party, including Naizghi, spent the night in Imperial Hotel and were fighting over women. I and my colleague Weldegabir Abraha (Wedi Roma) went to the surroundings of Cathedral to meet "Bla'a Ilwo", a pimp who knows the details of city gossip. We took him from bar Diana to the area of Cinema Croce Rossa to Bar Lemlem "Tre" and asked him to tell us the story. Naizghi along with an Eritrean businessman named Mikael Mussie, who through the intermediary of Naizgi had secured a lucrative contract from the Ministry of Internal Affairs to print Eritrean passports as commission agent of a European firm, came to the bar. By chance, Naizghi had seen my car outside and came inside and greeted us; he and his friend started to drink standing at the counter of the bar. A few days earlier, Naizghi and other senior officials had asked the pimp Bla'a Ilwo to bring them women and he brought them women. One of the women he brought for Naizghi didn't want to go with him and she escaped and left. Owing to that incidence Naizghi was uncomfortable when he saw the pimp sitting with us and chatting.

Naizghi wanted him out of the bar and ordered him saying, "Listen Bla'a Ilwo, why are you sitting with those dignitaries, they are not your equals, Get up and get out."

I replied, "No one came to your counter, it is better if you don't trespass on the tables of others, you will not touch this person who is sitting with us... don't spoil our evening."

Bla'a Ilwo didn't like the situation and wanted to leave but I told him to be quite and sit tight and not to respond to Naizghi.

"Boy, I am talking to you, are you buying them the drinks?" He then took the money from Bla'a Ilwo's pocket and told him to leave.

I returned him from the door, "He will not leave at all."

Naizghi started his threats and shouted, "Today we will spill blood."

"Whose pistol is longer for you to spill blood? You shoot us with an M14." I wanted to remind him that in one battle he threw away an M14 gun and ran away from the field of battle.

The situation became tense, Naizghi was using vulgar words and I was replying, and Bela'e Ilwao didn't like the situation and sneaked out and left. Mikael Mussie and Naizghi prepared to leave. On the way out, Naizghi said to Weldegabr Abraha, Wedi Roma, "Your friend is an imbecile but good night to you." Wedi Roma told Naizghi, "you disturbed us enough, just leave," Wedi Roma refused to shake Naizghi's hand and Naizghi slapped him. Instantly Weldegabr Abraha, Wedi Roma, jumped of his seat and hit him in the face. Naizghi sprawled under the table with his false teeth damaged. All the clients ran away from the bar. The next morning, the rumor went in town that we beat up Naizghi and put him in a fridge. It was an indication of how much people hated Naizghi. If it was rumored that we killed him, some people would even have celebrated.

The next day, he came to my office and asked where Weldegabr Abraha, Wedi Roma, was, and the three of us met and Naizghi wept a lot and said, "I made a mistake and pushed you to the edge let's keep the problem among ourselves." We settled the matter amicably and continued doing our work. After work while we were driving close by Nyala Hotel, a car hooted from behind us and we stopped. A person came out of the car and came straight to us and asked, "What happened yesterday evening?"

I replied, "Nothing happened".

"Naizghi was at the Office of the President complaining that you hit him."

We said, "Okay, thank you for the information." And we parted.

We are lucky the fighting was at a bar and many people witnessed it. Next morning at work, I explained what happened to the Minister, and he told me it was okay and not to worry about it but to go about my work. For two weeks nothing happened but after that Minister Ali Saed called and informed me that we will go to the chief of police and that we should hand over our work documents. The order came from the Office of the President. When we left our offices we found a car with private license plates and two security officers in civilian clothes in it. They took us to the chief of police.

The chief of police instructed us to go to the training camp and that we should not leave the place and our case will be investigated and we will be disciplined. Thus the case was totally reversed! Naizghi who threatened to spill our blood and who was hit as a response after he started using force was not sent to face administrative punishment, but we who defended ourselves from his attacks were sent to the police department to be punished. But we are lucky we were not sent to the Special Court. After spending two months in detention we were removed from the positions we held. In 1996, I was appointed to the Department of Religious Affairs as a Director and Weldegabr Abraha Wedi Roma was appointed to the refugee office as an Operational Officer. I was luckily removed from the sensitive place that I had constantly been requesting to be relieved from. The action we took against Naizghi, who used to get drunk and disturb the entire city of Asmara every night, pleased the residents of Asmara and as a show of solidarity countless people came frequently to the place of our detention to visit and entertain us.

I didn't' like my new job and again I asked to be demobilized and manage my personal affairs. However, the Minister of Internal Affairs told me that if I make that request again I will be put in jail. I had joined the revolution to help solve problems of the nation and here I was in a problem of my own that I couldn't solve and kept going in circles. Joining the revolution was my conscious decision and I had no regrets, but the journey that continued after the initial goal of independence that I aimed for was achieved, when like all the freedom fighters what I wanted was to follow the course that suits ones individual choices and beliefs. That was the bell of liberation ringing in our ears.

The Special Court was accusing and charging several former freedom fighters of corruption and sentencing them without due process of law and in March 1997 the Special Court jailed Ruth Simon, who was the first reporter for Agence FrancePresse in Eritrea, for citing a speech that President Isaias gave at the Municipality building where he spoke about supporting the opposition forces of the Sudanese government. Her report was distributed by Agence FrancePresse and Ruth was jailed being accused for revealing state secrets. As the Tigrigna saying goes, "you can't steal a camel and hide at the same time," Isaias shouldn't have given a speech revealing national security matter in public, and Ruth as an accredited reporter of a foreign press was jailed because she reported what was publicly stated. She was jailed for reporting what she was expected to as part of her professional duty for which she was paid.

Throughout his life in the front Isaias was hiding behind the Sahel Mountains in seclusion, where he was accustomed to do what he pleased. Thus, he is unable to function and live in a normal environment of openness among the people. He chose not to realize and correct his weakness so that he can move along with what the new world required. On one hand the constitution and the formation of parties and preparation for election. On the other hand, he caused the violation of basic rights of self expression by establishing a Special court outside the legal system and to imprison people. It must be that he has gone mad or the people who were following him were not okay; it is absurd.

The chaos has its source at the Valineki secret party congress; Isaias had not only prevented those he thought were disloyal to him from being elected to the executive body at the Third Organizational Congress, but also he froze and removed them from their government positions. Furthermore, they faced the fate of those they didn't try to protect, who were thrown in jail because they were not submissive enough or didn't get along with Isaias.

Chapter 7. THE "PEOPLE'S FRONT FOR DEMOCRACY AND JUSTICE" (PFDJ), AND RELIGION

In 1996, the Ministries of Defense and Internal Affairs evaluated all the experiences that the members gained during the course of the revolution and their educational backgrounds, and assessed the leadership qualities of each member and decided on the ranks they should be given. The distribution of ranks had some shortcomings because the evaluations covered many years. For ranking the military staff, the evaluators weighed the members based on their respective abilities and level of education. There wouldn't have been a problem if the assessment was based on examinations and timely evaluations from the early stage. The Eritrean revolution didn't offer salaries because the struggle was carried out by volunteers and it was not initiated for ranks, but ranking has to nevertheless be done after independence. The process followed established military norms and standards; however some degree of favoritism appeared.

Based on the training and experiences that were accumulated over many years there was not much that could be considered as shortcomings of the military skills of the freedom fighters. But there were many shortcomings in the adherence to ethics and protocols that needed to be corrected. We all went for training in the use of military uniform and code of conduct, salutes, and other training that goes with it. However, the way a soldier should dress cannot be learned in a short time, but could only be learned with time. After the assessment I was given the rank of a colonel and I started to work in the Ministry of Internal Affairs.

After I was released from disciplinary detention and transferred to the Religious Affairs Department of the Ministry, I didn't find it appropriate that military people should be involved in administrative affairs of religious institutions. In addition to that, I had misunderstandings within the Ministry and I asked again to be demobilized, but all was in vain. But after the administration of Religious Affairs was moved to the Ministry of Local Government, though I was not allowed to be demobilized, part of my question regarding the controversial issues of military personnel involved in matters related to administration of religious affairs and the bad feeling of the people towards that, was partly resolved. At the Religious Affairs Department, my rank and salary was handled as a civilian.

The religious institutions that were recognized by the government were Islam, the Orthodox Church, The Catholic Church, and the Evangelical Lutheran Church. The Jehovah witnesses were officially banned, but the rest of the small Christian denominations were neither recognized nor officially banned. These denominations fulfilled all government requirements with their followers participating in the national service and fulfilling their military obligations.

All the ones the Isaias regime didn't recognize, even the ones that were supposedly recognized didn't in reality enjoy full recognition. The proclamation that was issued regarding NGOs and religious institutions didn't allow them to get involved in activities related to education, health, and socio-economic development projects. Based on the above noted proclamation, the regime instructed the Religious Affairs Department, through the Eritrean Refugee and Rehabilitation Commission (ERRC), to stop all activities undertaken by the Religious institutions and compel them to hand over their project activities and resources to the government. The request was rejected until further studies were done because it was not based on thorough studies and adequate preparation.

The religious institutions operated elementary and middle schools for a long time and they had extensive experiences in it, some even had established schools for the deaf and the blind, institutions that the government does not possess the expertise to establish and manage. In alleviating the health status of communities and related challenges, though they were at times accused to be biased and leaning towards their co-religionists, they have nonetheless contributed in the provision of first aid services and distribution of basic medical supplies to sectors of the population.

The rationale given to stop these institutions from carrying out their educational and health activities were presented as an intention to have them operate within the national curriculum and standards which was not convincing andwas far from the truth.

To begin with, there was no entity that would readily take over and continue the activities of the religious institutions that we were instructed to stop. In addition, there was no skill pool that would run the specialized schools for the deaf and the blind. If there was a well thought out genuine intention to make qualitative transformation of the education and health services a detailed study and preparation should have preceded the decision in order not to disrupt the existing services and even further improve it. The actual conditions on the ground did not support the decision of the government to stop their activities.

Commissioner Werqu Tesfamichael, the now frozen former Commissioner of ERRC, rushed to implement the decision which she said she received from the Office of the President. She wanted to complete the handover process in a day, but she was told that public institutions are not commercial enterprises that can be opened and closed willfully without preparing alternatives. The Ministries of Education and Health were asked about the alternative arrangements that should have been in place to which both ministries stated that the matter was new to them and that they were given only one month to carry out the necessary studies. And though they tried, they informed the concerned authorities that it was undoable and the matter was temporarily stopped.

Isaias didn't want the non-political religious institutions to continue operating freely simply because he didn't like the fact that they were organized. Isaias was not afraid to go on stage and give a lecture and do whatever he pleases in any place that he fully controls. However, he doesn't have courage in any organized situation that he doesn't control.

It was time for the Orthodox Church--that was under the Ethiopian Patriarchate during the Ethiopian occupation--to have its independent Patriarchate and manage its spiritual functions independently on its own. In 1998, preparation was underway to find a candidate for the position of a Patriarch to head the Eritrean Orthodox Church. The topic regarding the source of the seat was controversial, but the elders of the Orthodox Church provided the historical explanation that when the faith entered the Horn of Africa, Abune Kessatie Berhan went to Ethiopia through Eritrea. Putting that into consideration and that Eritrea as a new country has become free and independent from Ethiopian control; all umbilical cords that connect it with Ethiopia had to be cut. Therefore, the seat of the Orthodox Church was brought from Egypt.

The election of the Patriarch had shortcomings, and in spiteof the push and pull, for anyone aware of Ethiopian intrigues, the election was relatively fair and just. But for those who didn't know, it created dissatisfaction and confusion; the process of the election exposed the struggle that was tied to the national question and interest. The Synod presented participants to the election based on their religious ranks and the service they provided after independence, but when it came to the views of the various candidates on Eritrea as a country it was not something one could confidently say were the same.

One group nominated a candidate who had not severed relations with Ethiopia and who had traveled to Egypt and argued that Eritrea was not self-reliant and it should stay under the Ethiopian Patriarchate (the candidate from this group had been serving in Ethiopia and only came to Eritrea when he was sure it was stable). There could be no religion without a country and in the absence of freedom of the faith there could be no democracy. The Orthodox religion was the official religion of state in Ethiopia and Eritreans were considered subjects and oppressed. Anyone who tries to return to that system of the era of Emperor Haile Selassie when Eritreans were denied their country cannot be an Eritrean religious leader--that would be against the wishes of the people. In a free country, a religious leader who doesn't have full faith upon the nation, and a national leadership which doesn't equally treat the religions of its people, should both be prevented from assuming positions of leadership until they develop full faith in the country and start to see the rights of all religions equally.

Earlier, substantiated evidences were presented about the views of the religious leaders who were nominated for the election and during the time I accompanied the Patriarch to Egypt where he was to be anointed, I brought along additional evidence in the form of audio recording of conversations held between the Ethiopian delegates and their Egyptian counterparts that fully confirmed the evidence we had regarding the views of some the Eritrean church delegates. It was ascertained that Abune Yacob had argued and advocated that because Eritrea was not self-reliant it should stay under the Ethiopian Orthodox Patriarchate. Before and after independence the leaders of the Eritrean Orthodox Church were either under the Ethiopian or the Egyptian Synods. Abune Maqarios and Abune Marqos were members of the Egyptian Synod whereas Abune Yacob was a member of the Ethiopian Synod. The view of Greater Ethiopia that was influenced by the colonizers was reflected on those with links with Ethiopian Synod and not on the members of the Egyptian Synod. The view of the first group was contrary to the national interest of Eritrea. Finally, Abune Philipos was elected as the first Patriarch of Eritrea.

WhenAbune Shenouda arrived dressed in the holy gown on the eve of the anointment he put the holy gown on Abune Philipos because no Patriarch will be accepted without the holy gown. Subsequently on May 8, 1998, in the presence of six Eritrean Bishops, 54 Egyptian Bishops, and 9 other Bishops invited for the occasion from Africa, Europe, America and Israel, and leaders of religious affairs, dignitaries, and 7000 members of the faithful, on St. Mark's Day, the first Eritrean Patriarch, Abune Philipos I was ordained by Abune Shenouda III at Saint Mark's Cathedral in Cairo. When the Abune was consecrated, Abune Shenouda put on the holy dress on Abune Philipos and handed him the scepter to shepherd the faithful and said:

> "Receive this scepter of shepherding from the hands of the Abune the Pope and Patriarch Shenouda, and shepherd the lambs of the lord; if you lose them, you will be answerable for their blood."

At the end, in the presence of members of the Egyptian and Eritrean Synods, religious affairs leaders of Eritrea and dignitaries, a protocol between the Egyptian Coptic Church and the Eritrean Orthodox Church was signed by Abune Shenouda and Abune Philipos. The protocol contained 15 articles that aimed to reinforce the relations between the churches of Eritrea and Alexandria at the level of Patriarchate and Synod. Considering that the Eritrean Orthodox Church was at the establishment stage and needed financial and educational support, in order to enable it to build a theological college in a short period of timeUS Dollars 100,000 was provided by the Egyptian Coptic Church for the design work for the construction of the intended college. After a reception at the residence of the Patriarchate in Egypt and the Embassy of Eritrea, most of the bishops and delegates of the government and dignitaries returned to Asmara to participate in the ceremonies of the patriarchal enthronement in Eritrea.

After the celebrations, Abune Philipos was accompanied by two bishops and went to the monastery of Aba Bishoy on the road between Cairo and Alexandria. His Holiness stayed there until he assumed his official seat on May 29. He carried the seat of the Orthodox Church that was acknowledged by presidential decree No 41/1998, signed by Egyptian President Mubarak, and left to Asmara together with Abune Shenouda and other bishops for his enthronement which was held between May 29 and May 31. While the celebration was going on, Abune Shenouda and his accompanying bishops went to the Asmara-Mai Nefhi road to the place that was allocated to the Orthodox Church to build the theological college and sprayed holy water on it. They concluded their visit and returned to their country.

Though there were plans to build a college and the project had secured initial financial support, it was never built. No one knows why it was not built. Could it be because the Church doesn't need a college? However, the Egyptian Coptic Church had promised to train Eritrean priests in Egypt until the time a theological college is built in Eritrea. We asked the Orthodox Church to prepare ten young priests/deacons who had linguistic proficiency and agreed with the Eritrean Embassy in Egypt for them to travel to Egypt for advanced theological education.

The Orthodox Church is one of the religious institutions that lacked talents and it should have cultivated its servants to a higher level, but in spite of the acute need the Church was not allowed to build the theological college. In addition, its financial standing was limited and it depended on the government's financial contribution. And based on the agreement that was reached, it could have received financial support from its sister Coptic Church of Egypt as it had received in the first meeting.

The two Eritrean religions of Orthodox and Islam that represent 90% of the population lack resourses. So the government exploits their resource constraints and throws at them meager support and doesn't want them to have any assistance from external entities. In the proclamation that was issued regarding NGOs and religious institutions, the government clearly required them to immediately report any foreign relation they had and particularly as concerns foreign funding. This was done to create an environment that would keep them dependents on the government and prevent them from becoming self reliant because in that way they will always remain under the tutelage and control of the government.

That is why the government seized the church property and transformed the plot of land at Enda Selassie in Edaga Hamus to a vegetable retail market. Later on it presented a cover-up claiming that it will build a youth entertainment center in the plot. And without the knowledge of the Orthodox Church, they gave the plot of land to the National Youth and Students Union (NUEYS). The Orthodox Church opposed the decision but the government threatened the Church that it will repossess the Mai Nefhi plot if the church objects to the transfer of the Edaga Hamus plot to NUEYS. Thus, in the end the college building project was hampered. Constraining the YMCA and the YWCA from carrying out their activities and hence paralyzing them was uncalled for, and moreover, building something that was not in the plan in a rush was simply stirring trouble. It was a plot intended to abort the college project. But that was not the only reason: Isaias wants to abuse and rule the people; the above case is also related to the closure of the Asmara University.

I didn't want to continue in such a situation and I wanted to stay away from the intrigues of politics. When an opening that matches my professional experience appeared in another government institution, the Bank of Eritrea, I was approached by the Governor and then I asked the Ministry of Local Government for my release. Deragon Hailemelekot, the then Director of the Religious Affairs Department, objected to my transfer explaining that the unit in which I worked will face problems if I was to leave and I had to stay for almost another year. Finally, I directly met Minster Mahmoud Sheriffo and explained to him that I was transferred to the Religious Affairs Department as a form of punishment, and that anyone else could do the work that I was doing. I asked to be transferred to a place that requires my experience and expertise. In the end, I was released and assigned to the Bank of Eritrea as a Director of Security of the Financial Institutions in the country. That way I was finally relieved from the Religious Affairs Department of said Ministry.

Chapter 8. PFDJ'S DOWNWARD JOURNEY

8.1 The War with Ethiopia and Its Consequences

The year 1998 was a year of madness in Eritrea. Though rumors of his madness was not new at all, in that year Isaias' madness hit the roof and he talked a lot about 'noisy empty barrels'. He had embarked on a mission to smear and sully the names of EPLF leaders who fought alongside him till independence and who were working hard to put the new country on a path of sustainable development and to erase whatever negative influence they cultivated on the people. When Isaias stated 'the leadership was rotten' at the secret party congress in Valineki, he was mainly targeting those patriotic leaders who were striving to ensure the development and progress of the country and the institutionalization of a constitutional and democratic system of governance in Eritrea.

One of the institutions that Isaias considered a threat to his regime, starting from the eve of theIndependence Day, was the Security and Intelligence Unit that was known as Unit 72 during the struggle era which contributed greatly to the revolution and was acknowledged internationally for its resourcefulness and effectiveness. He wanted to damage the popularity and good standing of its leader and replace him and its members with individuals loyal to him; hence Isaias wanted it so, 'to dry the sea in order to kill the fish'.

Petros Solomon, who led the Intelligence Unit 72 until the early years of independence, was an easy going, sociable, humble, and resourceful person who cultivated a close relationship with the ordinary fighters whose problems and difficulties he observed and for which he attempted to find solutions. He was an astute, farsighted, and flexible politician who introduced innovative systems to stay in tune with the new global developments and strived to elevate the preparedness of the unit members by providing them training courses both inside and outside the country. He in a sense became the father of new ideas in the field of intelligence gathering, analysis and application.

In a party organized by the Ministry of Defense held at Expo, where drunk generals of the Ministry massaged their egos and boasted that they brought independence, even the drunk Isaias told them point blank that it was not they who brought independence but Unit 72. My objective here is not to inflate the role of Unit 72 and belittle the role of the defense forces, but only to show the prominent role played by Unit 72 throughout the struggle for independence. Certainly the role played by the defense forces in bringing about the independence of Eritrea cannot be underestimated. Unit 72 was not the real threat to Isaias, but the real threat were Petros and his colleagues who held him in high esteem and respect. That is in my opinion why Isaias disbanded Unit 72, an institution which over the years evolved into a sizable and sophisticated intelligence institution acknowledged worldwide. Isaias wanted to dismantle it in order to remove the individual who caused him personal fear and anxieties.

Naizghi Kiflu, who acted as the principal instrument of Isaias in the dismantling of Unit 72 and who was later appointed Deputy Minister of the Ministry of Internal Affairs, began a character assassination campaign to defame Petros. He even bragged to his colleague Simon Gebredingel, the Deputy Commissioner of Police at that time saying, "It took us time to remove the Christian Highland organization that was led by the selfish Petros." Simon worked under Petros as Director of Signals during the era of the struggle but he didn't get along well with Petros in the post-independence time.

The sub-nationalist Naizghi, who has not come out of his peasant village mentality, defamed others who didn't boast of their skills, qualification and achievements, those brave freedom fighters who successfully led the EPLF to independence. Naizghi tried to prolong his time and that of Isaias, his boss, not knowing the fate that awaited him, and embarked on defaming well known patriotic leaders. It was in the middle of that crazy year that Isaias began to talk about the 'noises of empty barrels', in 1998 the year of madness.

Towards the end of 1996 and the beginning of 1997, the Eritrean-Ethiopian relations in the border areas were steadily deteriorating. However, no matter how sensitive the situation it didn't warrant a military confrontation between the two countries that came out of an extended period of warfare, and although it affected the relations between the border peoples of both sides such as merchants and local administrators of the area, it was possible to resolve it peacefully through dialogue. But it appears that the people-driven participatory process of drafting the constitution and related developments that could lead to democratization and rule of law worried 'President' Isaias, and he was not comfortable with it. He escalated the border problems that could have been solved easily through dialogue with the intention of holding the democratization process hostage, and transformed the border dispute into an unnecessary, costly and atrocious war.

In the meeting of the National Council held in September 2000, 'President Isaias in reference to the Third Offensive said it was concluded with the victory of Eritrea. Major General Berhane Gebrezgher responded, "Our borders have been violated, and the enemy has penetrated 100 kilometers deep into our territories, the lives of our people have been disrupted, it is unacceptable to consider it a victory." The 'government' of Eritrea, under the leadership of Isaias who couldn't think beyond protecting his power, dismantled Unit 72 that could have effectively monitored the military intelligence situation and seen the consequences ahead of time, and could have averted the disaster of the war and saved the country from incurring enormous human and material cost. Though Isaias came out of the war weakened, he felt he was powerful enough to force Ethiopia to kneel down. Using the war as a pretext, he held the approved constitution hostage and exposed Eritrea to great risks. Prior to the Third Offensive, thousands of Ethiopian troops and their pack animals quietly penetrated the Eritrean defense lines and were able to infiltrate deep into Eritrean territory. The defeat was clear, and he faced internal opposition, and finally he attempted to explain it in a confused double speech manner saying: "we were victorious, yet, we were defeated."

The troubles started after the constitution was ratified based on a consensus reached to draft one whether Isaias liked it or not. When the constitution drafting process was underway, though Isaias had appointed his loyalists in the Constitutional Commission with the intention to sabotage and derail the process from within--for example to object the existence of multi-parties--and he tried to steer it to his wishes, but failed. In the end, since he was opposed to a constitutional government system, he held the constitution hostage by presenting the border dispute as a serious problem and finally immersed the Eritrean and Ethiopian people into a costly and disastrous war.

In August 2000, Foreign Minister Haile Deru'e whowas heading the Eritrean Delegation in the international mediation efforts, explained, "the border issue should have been resolved peacefully, it was agreed in the meetings of May 27 - June 6 that the delegates consult their respective governments; the meeting didn't state that the process of a peaceful resolution has ended; the repercussion of not signing the agreement in that meeting led to unnecessary human and material losses-- we had shortcomings in handling the peace process." However, the war was ignited because it was needed to be ignited.

The constitution that was ratified in May 1997 touched many aspects of the people's lives. Based on it, the National Council formed a committee to draft laws that would regulate the formation and activitiesof political parties and resolved to hold a national election in 2001. But the noose was tightening on Isaias' neck, and he doesn't allow the existence of organizations or parties--that could be obstacles to his objectives of maintaining power. When all the means to derail the constitution making process failed he decided to ignite a war. The EPLF chairman, who later became "President" of Eritrea, customarily made assessments after every battle but unusually he chose not to assess the border war with Ethiopia. That is because the losses were enormous and visible and he wanted to avoid personal responsibility and accountability.

When the war ended, about a million people were displaced, the enemy controlled large swathes of populated areas, looted and destroyed properties and damaged the national economy, raped our women, and inflicted great psychological trauma on the psyche and pride of Eritreans:in short, it was an unwanted and destructive war ignited for narrow personal interests of the President.

After the war, appeals for resolving the dispute through peaceful means were made by the international community, and when the issue was on the right path for a legal resolution, Isaias declared that since there was no peace in our country the constitution would not be implemented and allowing the emergence of political parties would result in divisive politics causing risk to sovereignty –in short stating that the time is not ripe--and he started to drag his feet from handing over power to a popularly elected government. Advocating the opposite view point to that of the President, Foreign Affairs Minister Haile Derue, when the UN peace forces arrived in Eritrea, stated during a public meeting he held in Frankfurt, Germany, that we need now to attend to our internal issues and he urged for the implementation of the constitution, to allow parties to be established, and power to be handed over to a person duly elected by the people. Even though the implementation of the constitution as a supreme law of the land concerns all citizens, according to Isaias the constitution was simply just a paper, as he told the Los Angeles Times.

Instead of leading to understandings, the internal criticisms inside the National Council led to squabbles, mistrust, and mutual defamation, and attacks ensued. Isaias started to freeze those who rejected his views, and accused them of corruption.

When General Oqbe Abraha who was a close ally of Isaias started to tell the 'President' about the shortcomings that were appearing in the processes and raised issues of leadership deficiencies that must be corrected, Isaias sarcastically replied to him: "the accusations that you are presenting are to cover up to the accusations put forward against you regarding corruption going on within the Red Sea Corporation," known as Zero 9. But after the case against him was investigated it was verified that there was no wrongdoing that made General Oqbe accountable. The main reason why that was mentioned at that time is very clear and was intended to create an excuse to get Oqbe tried by the Special Court and get him sentenced. Moreover, in February 2000, Isaias informed General Oqbe Abraha by letter that he was stripped of his military rank of a general and relieved of his government responsibilities. He also stripped Major General Berhane Gerezgiher of his military rank and used General Sebhat Efrem, his Minister of Defense, to fire him from his job.

After Unit 72 was disbanded, Petros Solomon became Minister of Foreign Affairs for three years and then he was transferred to the Ministry of Marine Resources. The reason for transferring Petros, a highly rated expert in the field of intelligence, a person who sees himself as a military man and who diligently studies military science and intelligence, to the Ministry of Marine Resources was a decision only Isaias may be able to explain the rationale behind it. But the country that Isaias immersed in dangerous and trying moments denied Eritrea the benefit of Petros' experience and talents in its hour of need. Isaias worried more about maintaining power than the safety and security of the country and its people. He continued removing and freezing most of those experienced leaders on the Front who criticized him during the meeting of the National Council and challenged him to accept responsibility.

Berakhi Gebreselassie, the Minister of Information, had warned Isaias to stop meddling in the operations of the Ministry regarding the media campaign that he started in relation to the Ethiopian-Eritrean border disagreements because his meddling was illegal and out of bounds. Minister Berakhi had given him his views regarding the Rwanda-US peace proposal advising him that, "it's better to accept it while all our forces and dignity are intact and we can maneuver in its implementation." But Isaias who talked about 'noisy empty barrels' a lot considered the wise advice and farsightedness that foresaw the damage that lay ahead, and characterized it as cowardice. His aim was to hide behind the war in order not to hand over power to the people. He arrogantly replied, "We have no reason to be terrified or to surrender." It is paradoxical that Isaias who claimed not to be terrified when he ignited the war became terrified of an assessment on the impact of the war after the effect, and as if he didn't boast, "we have no reason to be terrified or to surrender." He was not willing to courageously accept responsibility as a leader and assess the defeat because he was terrified and humiliated. At the end, he removed Berakhi from the Ministry of Information and banished him far away to Germany as an Ambassador.

After Brigadier General Estifanos Seyoum was transferred from his position as Director of Finance at the Ministry of Defense, to the Ministry of Finance and Internal Revenue in 2000, he ordered an audit of the secretive and unrestrained commercial ventures of the enterprises of the PFDJ. But the illegal system of Isaias didn't want to have the accounting books and the contraband activities and commercial ventures of PFDJ that operated without paying taxes to the state, to be scrutinized and exposed by auditors. The Red Sea Corporation, which was hiding behind the system's curtains, imposing prices as it wished without paying dues and taxes, monopolizing the market by pushing out private investors and controlling the economy of the country, trusted Isaias' muscles and refused to cooperate with government auditors to be audited. That is when a confrontation ensued between Isaias and Brigadier General Estifanos Seyoum.

Saleh Kekiya had been Deputy Foreign Minister and later became the Minister of Transportation, Communication, and Posts. His questions and views almost summarized all the questions and criticisms of the other colleagues regarding various unethical and unprofessional actions and behaviorsof the senior leaders of the system. Some of his questions were as follows:

> "In the last ten years institutional work within the EPLF has digressed, the work manners of the field have continued--the executive branch does the work of the legislative branch, and that in turn doesn't have proper supervision over the executive branch, and the judiciary branch with all its weaknesses couldn't develop independently."
>
> "Corruption cannot be solved by a special court but only when there is a responsible rule of law, and corruption cannot be eradicated immediately, and the special court is a political stick."
>
> "The committee that was established to draft the party law finished its task but when it wanted to present it to the people for debate, the President stopped it. Abrogating the decision of the National Council without its knowledge is a dangerous dictatorial step."
>
> "Though the press law is provided for in the Constitution it was not implemented, it has to be implemented and developed. There were no delays in ratifying the Constitution; a constitutional government should have been established soon after it was ratified. If there was a wish to implement the Constitution, the 13th meeting of the National Council decided to precede its implementation, and a time was set for that, however, the ground for that was the party law which was not ratified, and also the election laws--elections should not be held for the sake of elections only."

Minister Saleh Kekya thus criticized Isaias; however, Isaias who is not receptive to advice and unwilling to learn from his mistakes in order to improve and develop, stripped the Minister from his responsibilities and in an attempt to banish him as far as he could, he transferred him as Governor of Asseb, but Minister Saleh declined the appointment, or rather demotion.

Based on his attitude of belittling those who challenge him and the wrong military intelligence he possessed about national security, Isaias underestimated the military strength of Ethiopia, and holding the constitution implementation hostage, he went to war over minor border incidents that could have been resolved peacefully. He appeared on television and said, "Badme falling to the enemy means the sun will not rise, the noise of Weyane (TPLF) is just like the noise of an empty barrel." He thus exposed more of his noisy empty barrel parlance! The Ethiopian government named its offensive, "the Sunset Operation." Finally, the sun did set on Isaias and Ethiopia penetrated as far as the strategic military garrison town of Barentu.

The experienced military and Intelligence leaders were either frozen or were transferred to civilian administration duties, and others were sent to fish farms. The experienced leaders, whose conscience did not allow them to watch in silence when their country was being invaded, made an effort to be by the side of the unfrozen colleagues and to help them. The camels, Isaias' allies during the long struggle era, his colleagues in good and bad times who led the struggle to victory and independence, were removed from their previous positions. And the warm blood horses, those who came from mass organizations in Europe and America, some of whom were removed from their position in America by the demand of the mass organization members, those who had no clue about war strategies and tactics, those who were drawing war strategies in gas stations in Washington, DC and other cities in America and Europe, became members of the committee that was established to lead the war and attend its meetings.

All the advices, criticisms and constructive challenges didn't find listening ears, and in order to prevent the criticisms and proposals from being discussed and resolved the meetings of the Central Council and the National Council were indefinitely postponed. Particularly the Cabinet of Ministers didn't convene for a year and half. After Isaias violated the law and ignored the questions and propositions of the members of the National Council and senior leaders, he characterized all the requests for holding meetings as coming from 'empty noisy barrels'. The Minister of Communication, Transportation and Posts said that such language is not expected from a President, it is sad to observe that the dictator's vocabulary has evolved from a jerry can to a barrel.

After observing the unfavorable situation that unfolded in Eritrea, a group of scholars later known as G13 met in Berlin to discuss the critical Eritrean situation, and upon the invitation of the President they went to Asmara to present their views that they thought would help resolve several outstanding issues, and met and talked to 'President' Isaias in an attempt to present and discuss alternatives of how to govern the country. These conscious and concerned Eritrean scholars and professionals met in Berlin and evaluated the Ethiopian-Eritrean border war and came to the conclusion that it was very destructive and had resulted in thousands of deaths and disabilities, displacements and deportation of hundreds of thousands of people, and wastage of scarce national resources. Furthermore, it has put the sovereignty of Eritrea that was achieved with so many sacrifices at great risk. As a result of the destructive war thousands of Eritreans were affected. They left their homes and became internally displaced or refugees outside Eritrea.

Over 75 thousand Eritreans and Ethiopians of Eritrean parentage that lived in Ethiopia lost their properties; they were imprisoned, humiliated, and finally deported. So many Eritrean refugees still remained in Sudan. The problems that the G13 presented as a priority, and committed themselves to help solve, were such issues. They praised the manner in which the Ethiopian citizens residing in Eritrea were treated during the war and encouraged to maintain such humane treatment. Referring to the international image of Eritrea, they stated that the world, including Africans, consider Eritrea a quarrelsome and irresponsible country, and they called for it to abide by international laws and standards of behavior and to properly handle the NGOs that are representatives of foreign countries and international institutions.

Though they mentioned that satisfactory developments were registered in the areas of infrastructure, education and social services, they stated that in the field of constitutional system of governance and democratization, Eritrea lacked the rule of law, democratic space and accountability and transparency, and because of that, the country lagged behind; they called for immediate correction of the wrong footing and direction the country has taken.

On national reconciliation and unity, they said that political views should be wise and nationalist without focus on differences, and that unifying views should be promoted in order to rebuild what was destroyed, and during the constructing of the nation, the PFDJ should create the platform for individual and group freedoms and that the Constitution should be implemented immediately.

They emphasized the fact that collective participation in leadership that was apparent during the struggle was discontinued after independence and noted that renowned and able veteran leaders were sidelined, and the leadership structure was monopolized by a one man autocratic rule that stifled the views of the established majority. The dictator who monopolized power and those who allowed that to happen are equally responsible for the malaise the country has fallen into and the G13 group recommended for its immediate rectification.

As far as the chaos in the leadership was concerned, they criticized the fact that the individual communications, the misunderstanding and opposition inside the meetings were not kept a secret but came out in public, widened the differences that existed within the leadership and in this connection they recommended that such issues should be handled with care and dialogue.

Referring to the political and economic role of the PFDJ, they observed that duplicating the government tasks and allowing two similar tasks to operate in parallel, and that in a small underdeveloped country like Eritrea, is a waste of resources and creates conflicts of interest between the public and private spheres. The G13 group expressed their concern and recommended that the party should not get involved in tasks that are in the realm of government and that affects peoples' trust and also works contrary to the government policy of encouraging development of the private sector and adherence to free market economy. The party's involvement in the economy could also promote corruption that pulls the country backwards. They recommended that the PFDJ rethink its position and evaluate its operations in detail and do the necessary corrections.

Finally, referring to the Constitution as the supreme law of the land, which was a culmination of the struggle for self determination, democracy, and social justice, they called for its immediate implementation and the institutionalization of a rule of law. They further underlined the fact that no one has the right to tell the people that the Constitution they debated and ratified does not belong to them. They also called for the abolishment of the illegal Special Court to give way for the rule of law, and for a proper judicial administration to take over all cases that were previously handled by the Special Court. They also called for the cases of all the people who were languishing in prisons to either be immediately brought to the regular courts for a fair and speedy trialor released if they have no case to answer.

As for the practice commonly referred to as "freezing" of public sector employees, an act that had psychologically affected many veteran fighters, an act which is contrary to the rule of law and which subjected brave freedom fighters to be unjustly punished and feel defeated and fearful. The act the G13 group argued is also an archaic type of punishment that doesn't aim at rehabilitation and correction of the persons concerned and is counterproductive. Therefore, they called for that to be stopped.

In General, the stage required for the leadership and the people to engage in an open dialogue and to expose the situation in which the people struggled to realize their rights. They called for the President to revise his stand and feel the heartbeat of the people, and be magnanimous to bring about a solution for the problems that unfolded.

After the G13 met the president in Asmara, I and a work colleague of mine and another who was a member of the Central Committee met Dr. Assefaw Tekeste, a member of the G13, around Nyala Hotel and tried to talk to him about the outcome of their meetingwith the President. Dr. Asefaw seemed to wonder how we dare ask him such questions in a country where presenting one's views or posing questions were punishable acts. Dr. Assefaw was almost not willing to reply to the questions we posed, and it was visible on his face that he was afraid of the looming danger in the air, that he was concerned about the possibility that he would not be allowed to exit the country.

Isaias was not interested in the free words of wisdom he received from concerned and wise Diaspora Eritreans. Instead of thanking them, and learning from the advice he received to correct mistakes committed, he considered them as if they were on a mission to undermine the interest of the country and he admonished them and belittled and ignored their advises. By then, Isaias who doesn't want to listen to any advice from anyone had reached the highest level of rejection of advises; that confirmed he can't listen to any advise and was unable to compromise.

8.2. The Jailing of G15 and of Journalists & Reporters

In August 2001, I and my work colleague Dawit Gedle from the Central Bank represented Eritrea and participated in the Fifth Conference on Economic Crimes of the East and Southern Africa Region in Johannesburg, South Africa. On our way back home from South Africa we stopped over in Nairobi to meet and exchange experiences with the Kenyans who were also participants in the conference. From Nairobi we flew through Khartoum to Asmara on September 11.

When we were about forty minutes away from Asmara we were told that the airplane had a technical problem and it was going to return to Khartoum. The airplane landed in Khartoum and refueled and after about an hour the flight to Asmara resumed again. Upon arrival at the Asmara airport the airport security officers informed us about the September 11 terrorist attack in the US and that all airplanes were instructed to return to where their flight originatedand that is the reason why we returned to Khartoum.

Starting on September 11, Asmara was unusually a beehive of activities. The security cars were busy monitoring the movements and following the senior Eritrean government members wherever they went. The conflicts within the government authorities was already out in the open and every once in a while the private newspapers were conducting interviews with the section of the authorities who were seen as reformers and were publishing divergent and constructive opinions that came from different corners. It was easy for the public to identify the divergent views and positions on critical national issues and know who is who among the leadership. However, the relation among the generals was not as close as it appeared to be from the outside.

General Oqbe Abraha, General Berhane Gebrezgher and General Sebhat Ephrem were longtime friends and appeared to be close to each other and spent their free days and evenings together. Considering the close friendship they had no one who knew them closely guessed that there could possibly be differences of opinion among them. However, in the end all the secret private meetings and chats carried out inside cars on the roads to Dekemhare and Mendefera did not appear to have brought the opinion of three on the same platform. General Sebhat Efrem from among the three friends did not sign the document that was issued by the G15, the group who asked for a National Council meeting to be convened in order to take stock and assess the military and socio-political outcome of the war and draw positive and negative lessons from it.

The terrorist attack of September 11 did not only affect the US but as the international media attention focused on the terrorist act in New York and ignored all other global news, on September 18, 'President' Isaias took advantage of the media blackout and jailed those members of G15 who were inside Eritrea. To implement the action, Isaias first held separate meetings with military commanders, senior leaders of the PFDJ and senior staff from national security. Following that, he convened a meeting for the cadres and leaders of the armed forces and senior members of government departments held in Embatkala in a series of rounds to assess the situation. A hunting squad was formed under the leadership of Abraha Kassa, the Director of National Security, and Simon Gebredingel, Head of Internal Security, to undertake the arrests.

The struggle that was waged to liberate and build a democratic system of governance in Eritrea was arrested when the senior government authorities who advocated for the establishment of a democratic Eritrea in place of the dictatorial regime of PFDJ under Isaias were collected from everywhere and were taken to prison in unknown locations. The jailed have now been in prison for over fourteen years without being charged or presented to a court of law. It is believed that some of them have died, and others are in the mid-eastern valley prisons of Ella-Ero where even their loved ones or friends cannot visit them; and where human right advocates, the Red Cross, or lawyers could not meet them. Their whereabouts are unknown to the public.

The kidnapping didn't end there, it reached the editors and reporters of the few emerging private newspapers that had become the voice of the people and were disseminating alternative views and opinions; they also faced the fate of the senior political and military leaders of the government who were imprisoned. Naizghi Kiflu, the then Minister of Information imprisoned the reporters, paralyzed the nascent newspapers and finally banned them. He then took over Sheriffo's position by assuming responsibility for the affairs of the local administration situated in the Office of the President. And as a reward for accomplishing his mission, Isaias sent him to Pakistan where he had a kidney transplant, after which he was sent as an Ambassador to the UK where he joined his family who resided in London while getting medical attention. However, the UK didn't accept the credentials because of his human rights violation records. Nevertheless, he stayed in the UK until his death in Feb, 2012.

Yemane Gebreab 'Monkey', the Director of the Political Department of PFDJ opened the meetings of Embatkala by stating: "It is natural for differences of opinion and views to appear in this meeting; we have to identify our problems in detail to be able to evaluate them in order to be able to find solutions, we have to express our views courageously without any fear. There will be no repercussion for asking questions in this meeting." This was done with the intention of assessing the political views of each participant. Those who didn't know how the PFDJ functioned, aired their views openly and frankly thinking they were contributing to the improvement of the unhealthy path of the PFDJ.

The martyr Isaac Wedi Rezene who gave his life for the liberation of Eritrea would have easily read the meanings of the political statements in the meeting. Nothing was new for those who were wise and knew the nature of the EPLF. While the wise discerned the situation and chose to say less and not to talk much, others took Yemane's assurance at face value and openly aired whatever was on their mind. The nature and character of those who spoke their mind in the meeting were scrutinized and evaluated and in the end some of them were accused of corruption and others for undefined charges and all were put in prison and their cases were brought before the Special Court whose decisions were final without recourse to an appeal.

Why did those who were advocating for the rights of the people and who spent half their lifetime in the struggle for national liberation and independence and to build a prosperous and democratic nation fall to such a low situation? How was Isaias able to do as he wished with the country? And why would the Eritrean people that fought a war of liberation for half a century and achieved independence against all odds be silent and remained docile spectators? Where are the freedom fighters who were offering their lives so that their comrades could survive? Such questions are only natural. Since Eritreans struggled in unison, such questions are equally of concern to all and every Eritrean should recognize that answering the questions is his/her individual duty and one should strive to find a solution.

In order to be able to assess the post-independence situation properly one needs to find answers to some questions: where were the G15 leaders when Bitweded Abraha, was detained and abused, when the victims of the 1993 veterans' movement, or the leaders of the movement of the handicapped veterans were killed and imprisoned? The tables turned on them and they faced the same fate. Mustafa Nurhussen the one who was the governor of the Southern Zone at the time he was imprisoned in connection with the January 21 Forto Mutiny, had replaced Bitweded Abraha as Governor of Asseb after independence, and to please the 'President' of the State of Eritrea he caused the imprisonment of Bitweded Abraha by manufacturing corruption charges. Another example of failure is Sheriffo, who at the time was the senior authority administering Dankalia and other areas, though he described the accusations against Bitweded as 'nonsensical talk', he didn't challenge the decision in order to correct it. Those who were instrumental in the imprisonment of the G15, starting with Abdella Jabir who was in charge of the Organizational Affairs of the PFDJ, Minister Ahmed Haj Ali, Governor Mustafa Nurhussen, etc… are now all in prison themselves. Even the remains of Naizghi Kiflu

214

who was Isaias' right hand man and served him throughout was refused entry for burial in Eritrea following his death in the UK. If all those who are currently cheering Isaias, his heartless lackeys, do not learn from the past history it would be inevitable that they will face the same fate when their turn comes.

In life's struggle it is natural to succeed or fail, to fall or spring up and in the end face life head on. But the worst journey in one's life is when a human being doesn't learn from history, which is akin to heading towards doom. The members of G15 had clearly explained that they made mistakes in the journey of the struggle but learning from their experience they were ready to acknowledge mistakes made in the past and work to build a prosperous and democratic society as reward to the people. They courageously challenged the President and did not blink when they faced the risks of prison and death. Though they didn't fully succeed in meeting their objectives they nevertheless left an important historical legacy of standing up against dictatorship for the people of Eritrea. They learned from the past and paid the price experiencing up being detained in undisclosed prisons. Isaias has not slept calmly for a single night since then.

The experienced leaders of the struggle were defeated not because they didn't know how to handle and confront the situation but because they took non-violent means choosing to avoid bloodletting. In the process of any struggle everyone aims for success; however, once the process begins only one side might succeed, or alternatively the protagonists may choose a win-win outcome by compromising, and there are also situations where the two sides lose. However, though these reformers knew the nature and character of Isaias very well as his colleagues of many years, the intriguing question is how did he manage to outsmart them? To answer this question we have to go back to 1989-1990during which time the secret Eritrean Socialist Party (ESP) was frozen.

ESP was not actually only frozen but also changed its image. As everyone was aboard the party boat it became a sifting machine that retained those Isaias needed and discarded those whose services he didn't need any more. Hence, many of the members of the old leadership were unloaded at different stations in the process of the struggle. Those who remained to the end were preoccupied with the final battles wedged to liberate the remaining towns of Asmara, Keren and Asseb. And after independence, because the honeymoon didn't end quickly most members of the leadership were preoccupied with

215

the referendum and designing and laying down the foundations for building the new nation. As was pointed out before, while the old leaders were engaged in all of that, Isaias was busy doing his homework setting up an alternative secret party and the remaining old leaders were officially made to disembark from the boat first at Valineki and then at the Congress in Nakfa early in 1994.

Isaac Wedi Rezene had seen that beforehand. He had seen the engine that was geared to personal gain. It is the diabolical machine designed by a cold blooded evil genius who is ruthless and single-minded by efficient. To vary the methaphore, the leaders were overtaken by the sharp blades of a saw which mercilessly removes anything it finds on the right or on the left of its path. Isaias did his homework ahead of time. He declared that parties are not mushrooms that grow overnight. He used the argument of the danger posed by the emergence of sub nationalist parties in order to prevent the formation of alternative political parties to PFDJ. He retained a few loyal "camels" that allied with him but brought in the "horses" that he baptized as the new blood and established himself as the undisputed President by using the PFDJ as an instrument for his power. He was thus able to control and dominate the political and economic spheres of Eritrea.

The PFDJ under Isaias had totally monopolized the political and economic life of the country. The structure of the PFDJ as an institution has a Secretary General and Directors for each of the four departments i.e., politics, economy, organization, and research and documentation. When seen from a wider angle the structure appears as if it was created for the administration of the party. However, the party is far from administering its internal affairs, but since it was able to control all the political and economic aspects of the government, it would have been appropriate to have a department that controls the social aspects. But, the party is not concerned about the interest of the people, only on how to maintain the seat of power. It is a party without conscience a fact that can be demonstrated by the sad reality of the people's livelihood.

The Organizational Affairs Department of PFDJ monitors the activities of the people by operating as an appendage of the national security apparatus. In short, the party is concerned with protecting the interests of a few people and would not tolerate anything that threatens those interests. The members of G15 have exposed the ugly face of the PFDJ; however they adopted a non-violent method of struggle to remove Isaias and his clique from power and they failed. In a word, they gumbled and lost. They preferred looking ahead and knowing that in the long run, the oppressor will eventually reach his downfall as the natural social process dictates. The vast majority of Eritreans now believe that the day when those who betrayed the G15 and stood against the democratic governance and development and the attainment of liberty, will very soon stand to face the law is not far.

***

At the beginning of 2000, I started my work by advising the National Bank of Eritrea and other operating banks that didn't have security units, including the Commercial Bank and the Housing Bank, to establish security units in their respective organizations. I wanted them to establish modernized security units and found out that it was important to first study the experience of other countries, and I started to implement that after I returned from Pretoria, South Africa, by applying the security courses that I took at the Reserve Bank in Pretoria in addition to my own personal experience. I organized and structured the security task, and as a first step I replaced the militia who used to guard the banks by employing professional civilians who had undergone military training.

Soon I received documents from the then Governor of the Central Bank, Tekie Beyene, who instructed me to review them together with the Inspector of the bank. The papers related to accounts that were borrowed in the thousands and millions from the bank that had defaulted. It was not clear to me who was in charge of such issues and I asked the Governor to pass it to the concerned parties. He tried to overlook my comment and told me to just look into it along with the inspector. The inspector was Berhane Wedi Abeba who was one of those cadres who actively participated to defend the Isaias regime at the Embatkala meetings that was moderated by Yemane Gebreab 'Monkey'.

When I found out that the Bank had lent money in the millions to demobilized fighters, I told the Governor that it was not appropriate for him to lend that money, but since it had already happened he bare the responsibility for lending that amount of money without collateral. I suggested that it would be nice if the demobilized former fighters, who were humiliatingly expelled from Ethiopia after their properties were taken, could work and repay their debts since taking them to prison would neither benefit them nor the Bank. When I told him that

217

he was out of line in lending the money, he told me that he acted on the telephonic instruction of the 'President' and that he didn't ask the instruction to be in writing. When I asked why he didn't keep a document, he told me there were also other similar incidents. During the time of the Eritrean-Ethiopian border war he was instructed by a telephone call to send a given amount of dollars to Naizghi Kiflu who was the Eritrean Ambassador in Russia at the time for procurement of armaments from Eastern European countries.

In addition to that, I was instructed by the Governor to put all Nakfa currency bills in sacks and burn them in May Dibnet, the place I used to meet with the members of the EPLF communication unit when I worked in clandestine cells. As I have observed how other countries handle that, I told him the bills should be destroyed in the presence of all concerned entities, that is: Ministry of Finance, Auditor General's Office, National Security and Police, and representativeof the Bank of Eritrea, who should destroy it after it was counted, and the bills should be destroyed, just as it is done in many parts of the world, after it was shredded and made into blocks because it has a nature of plastic and that it could not be burned. He accepted the first suggestion but not the second one. The machine that the Ethiopians were using earlier and which was wasting a lot of time, on top of the pollution it created, was out of order and they were not willing to buy a new shredding machine. The money was burned at the Gandini tools forge in the center of Asmara where some of the bills were burned but others were half burned and were blown out by the wind and scattered around.

The way in which they worked was astounding. Let alone at the level of a government, even in a household people count and take care of currency and bills. The Minister of Communication was right when he said our work is not institutionalized and that we were continuing the system of the guerilla days, and asked for that to be corrected.

The work of bank security provides an example of wrong practice and is very educational: knowing the security aspects of documents and currencies, to protect the country from counterfeit bills, to control theft and embezzlement, and protect the country from bank thefts, to transport money in a safe and efficient way, to guarantee the safety of the people who work in controlling safes and other aspects related to money, etc. However, the Eritrean bank system knows only how to collect money and doesn't understand that it can invest money and reap returns; only in that way could one protect the value of money by not letting it sit idly. The system was unwilling to replace the free service of the militia and hire paid and professional security officers. In the end the bank expelled the few officers who could have been trained.

When I asked for tools and instruments that were necessary for control of the banks of the country, I was told there was no money for that and the bank was not even willing to buy cameras to install in the rooms where the bills and notes were stored. After the security officers were expelled and replaced by militias, I complained that I cannot be responsible for a work that is run by people who have other bosses and who have no tools and that I cannot work in that manner, as a consequence the bank officials found a good opportunity to expel me without demobilizing me. I opened the door for them and they immediately froze me. But the good thing was at that time there was no war to send me to follow the trail of Isaac Rezene, thus I survived to tell the untold Isaac Rezene's story. Just like those who were frozen before me, my time was up and I was frozen following the freezing of my boss Tekie Beyene.I joined the non-existent zone that the combatants commonly refer to as 'The Seventh Zone'.

Chapter 9. **FREEZING AND ENTERING LIFE IN EXILE**

Between the last months of 2001 and the first few months of 2002, I stayed late in bed in the mornings since I did not have to report to work. Being 'frozen' became a good opportunity for me to follow up on the South African correspondence or long distance education. However, I was not only frozen from work but the government also stopped even my education with the pretext of a budgetary shortage though the project was funded by the UNDP. I couldn't understand the rationale at all.

After independence, Petros Solomon, the Security and Intelligence chief, wanted those who worked under him to continue their education. To that end, he made arrangements with Asmara University, the US Embassy, and other experts who prepared a curriculum for a degree program in information management. The US Embassy agreed to furnish qualified experts from the US to teach the courses. The classes went on for six-months before they were suddenly stopped. When we asked why it was stopped we were told that the order came from 'high up'!

Following that, in 1997-1998, the UNDP funded an MBA course through the Open University of England, but after a limited period of time that was also discontinued using the border war with Ethiopia as a pretext. All the reasons that were given for stopping several educational programs were not justifiable. Everything had beeb started after the necessary studies and preparations were made and the funding was obtained from foreign sources which literally cost nothing to the Eritrean Government.

The policy of the Eritrean Government on education was narrow and archaic. Those who are asked about why there is negative policy on education would meet Isaias and then they would say, 'Kelaam

Faariq' (nonsense). When I asked Brigadier General Abraha Kassa, the chief of National Security, why the South African education program was stopped, he parroted Isaias' words for a reply, "this education is Kelaam Faariq." It can only be explained by the fact that the authorities were uncomfortable with the study of law because legal minds may pose more resistance towards the unconstitutional Special Court and those who study journalism could be unwilling to work for the Ministry of Information unless there is press law that guarantees freedom, etc. Obviously, Isaias was not interested in an institutionalized system of governance because it imposes transparency and accountability and he also has aversion to educational institutions because he sees them as gateway to highest consciousness and emancipation. It is now abundantly clear that the reason for igniting the war with Ethiopia was because he did not want to implement the Constitution which would lead to establishment of a constitutional system of governance.

In 2002, I became a member of what is commonly referred to as the 'Zone 7', and had neither school nor work to attend to. But I received my salary and spent my days wandering around teashops until I was tired of that. In the beginning, receiving a salary without working touched my conscience and bothered me. Then I began to think of it as a compensation for the many years I served without pay but my conscience could not accept that. 'Frozen' individuals are not allowed to work and if they are found working somewhere it was considered a crime that could result in imprisonment.

To escape that situation, I used my father's name to establish a commercial venture. It took us so many months to get the business license. But after obtaining the license when I wanted to import the required machinery from abroad they asked me to deposit US dollars in my father's account. The irony of it makes one laugh it off. They demand deposit in US dollars as if they pay salaries in dollars. If you wanted to buy dollars with Nakfa the government would not sell you even a cent and if you wanted to buy dollars from the black market it was considered contraband and a violation of the law; those who have relatives abroad who could provide dollars were not allowed to buy the machinery and send it to their relatives in Eritrea. If one brings any amount of dollars and deposits it in the bank whatever remains of the amount after paying the cost of the Letter of Credit, could only be withdrawn in Nakfa at the exchange rate of 15 Nakfa to the dollar.

This is the same dollar that the PFDJ was collecting from the black market through their agents at 40 Nakfa to the dollar.

The IMF and the World Bank noted the high inflation rate of the Eritrean economy and recommended to the Bank of Eritrea to devalue the local currency, but their recommendation was not adopted. Beyond that, in an unbalanced valuation, all holders of hard currency that entered into Eritrea through the airport, seaports, and overland, must declare the amount and type of currency they were bringing to Eritrea; the exchange rates were set by the Bank of Eritrea. In the black market, the dollar topped 40 Nakfa—as this book goes to print it's around 50. The hard currency that flows into Eritrea became, as the local saying goes, 'as rare as a woman's beard', and the PFDJ itself resorted to contraband of buying dollars from the black market. Why all of that? Why beg for something that could easily have been in your hands? The vagabonds who used to work at the gas station in the US and who worked on a cash basis with salaries hidden from the tax collectors are running Eritrea in the same manner as a contraband economy.

Every avenue was closed to me. I had no employment and no educational program to follow. I spent my days in my office and around Nyala and other entertainment places. Even my children started to ask me, "Papa, aren't you going to work?" I wanted to be away from the situation and decided to travel abroad but I was denied an exit visa and permission to leave. After 16 years of a tough struggle, and over 10 years of an unsettled environment of struggle in 'independent' Eritrea, the stability and peace that all Eritreans expected was nowhere in sight. People were imprisoned simply because they dreamed to have and enjoy of good things in life and tried to achieve their dreams. Those who had constructive ideas were denied the right to express them because the liberation of Eritrea was highjacked, and I observed the country missing its bright future and going down the drain in chaos. I was denied the right to speak my mind and freely do as I pleased within the limits of the law, and my preferences and choices were also denied me. In order to avoid the fate that had befallen my comrades and friends who were suffering in prisons of the monstrous regime I was constantly living in fear of what could happen to me.

As if I didn't face the challenges of the mountains and plains of Eritrea during my long years in the struggle without complaints, my health began to deteriorate during the peace time when I was treated like a stable horse eating without working. I couldn't get the necessary

223

treatment in the almost nonexistent health services in Eritrea under the rule of the PFDJ regime. I was allowed to leave the country and travel abroad only after the medical board of doctors testified that I could only be treated abroad. The Medical Board recommends treatment outside Eritrea without delay only to those who have ties with Isaias' party, whereas the rest of the former freedom fighters do not get such opportunities. The charitable organizations do provide opportunities for the treatment of people without resources and I had to be on a waiting list for almost a year when my turn arrived and I was finally informed it was my turn to be treated abroad. I was worried that the appointment with death may arrive before the treatment day and all I needed was an exit visa. By depending on the good relations that I nurtured with the Catholic Church during the time I worked in the Religious Affairs Department, I was offered an opportunity to be treated in Italy. So off I went to Italy with great relief.

When I was under treatment in a hospital in Italy, Weldemichael Gebremariam, who was then the Minister for Water and Land, was in Firenze for a hip replacement operation, and Zemede Tekle, who was my work colleague at the Ministry of Zonal Administration and was at the time the Eritrean Ambassador to Italy, came to visit Weldemichael who told him where I was at a distance of less than five minutes walk. Yet he only talked to me over the phone before returning to Rome. It should not be surprising that the horses started to look at the camels from afar, with disdain; they thought oh their career and are not bothered by a thing called decency.

When I was frozen and I was roaming around without work I painfully tasted the bitterness of suffering. However, by that time Isaias had solidified his organization and spread his wings around by deploying spies everywhere and was doing as he pleased in Eritrea. When the members of 'Zone 7, (the frozen) met in Expo, Nyala and Cinema Roma, etc, to kill time and chat, Isaias once stated, "I don't understand where the gossip that is going on in Expo Hotel is heading."It didn't take much time for the frozen that frequented Expo to disperse in order to avoid being victims of the unrelenting slicing by the double edged sword of Isaias.

Eritrea has completely fallen under a dictatorship and because the objective conditions were not ripe I didn't see a possibility of helping in bringing any solution from inside the country at the moment. The middle level cadres who knew each other and were close to each other observed the political situation very closely. But they talked among themselves with extra caution. The Isaias group was operating secretly and the cadres were afraid of facing the fate of Btsay Goitom. Instead of staying in such a dangerous and unstable situation, I decided to stay away from it all; I chose to stay away from the country that I love, the country where I left my children and the children of my martyred friends and comrades, the country for which I gave my youth for its freedom. Instead of disappearing inside Eritrea I chose to take care of all of them from a distance waiting for the day when I will embrace my beloved children just like I embraced my parents.

Chapter 10. **CONCLUSION**

The phenomenon unfolding in Eritrean with the youth leaving their country en masse started a long time ago and is getting worse over time. Such a situation is not only a considerable and irreplaceable loss and disastrous to the national human resources pool of a tiny poor country, its ability to spring back and stand after such a situation is also becoming increasingly questionable. The youth are the backbone of any country; however, the situation prevailing in our country breaks the backbones, and there is fear that the attempts to force the youth to kneel down in submission might eventually lead to violent confrontations.

Isaias must be aware that historically no force can hinder the youth from struggling, or has he forgotten the potential power of the mass exodus of the youth? Is that why he has started to mock them? The reality is that Eritrean young people are not allowed to pursue higher education; they are prevented from getting married and raising a family or to taking care of their aging parents. The PFDJ policy of indefinite enslavement which ties them like farm bulls in endless slave labor under the guise of compulsory 'national service' is a historic crime, and he knows it. Some do however break free from the grips of the oppressors and escape from the yoke of those who repeatedly tell them, 'we brought you freedom; you have to serve us and obey our orders'. Many of the youth, the blooming flowers of the country, are fighting the calamities that befell them by staying in hiding until they see an opportune time to cross international borders into the unknown life of exile. But 'President' Isaias mockingly and shamelessly labeled their flight from the oppressive system of his rule as a picnic.

During the time of the third round of the Ethiopian offensive, the students of the University of Asmara didn't want to sit idle while the country was in dire straits. Without anyone asking them they called a meeting of the student body on their own and resolved to take part in the defense of their nation. They carried out a demonstration, stood along side their elder brothers and sisters in defense of the nation. After they returned from the tough war situation, in addition to attending their school, they keenly followed the developments through coverage in the media, and were well informed of all the emerging political frictions among the senior authorities, including the critical and educational interviews and opinions of the senior reformers and political critics of the regime. It didn't take long for the government to become aware of the potential force of the Asmara University Students in being proactive to change the prevailing national political situation.

During summer vacation, the University Students usually worked and saved money to spend on educational items that they needed. But when the national politics became chaotic, 'the government of Eritrea' realized the risk that those students pose and felt that they could exacerbate the situation greatly. Hence, it ordered them to disperse and sent them to different corners of the country to assist farmers in their harvesting activities and that way they kept them under close surveillance and observation by the members of the defense forces. And to avoid questions that might arise regarding salaries, it allocated a budget to pay a token allowance of 800 Nakfa per individual, which was diverted from the budget that was funded as development aid by the World Bank and the UNDP, funds that were intended for the post-war rehabilitation and reconstruction projects.

The students were not comfortable with the prevailing political environment in the country. Not only did they reject the call for the summer work program, but also during the graduation ceremony described the PFDJ summer harvest program as illegal and imposed on them without their participation and consent. They wholly rejected the summer program conveyed through the President of the University of Asmara Student Association. Their main criticism was that there were poor and inadequate facilities and equipment in the university and were protesting the interference of the government in the affairs of the university. It was under such a situation, that on June 31, 2001, the Isaias regime arrested Semere Kesete, the President of the Asmara University Students' Association, and put him in prison.

The students rejected the forced summer project and demanded that their Student Association President be released. On 9 July, due to the exerted pressure, the government presented the Student Association President to court. As the students entered the courtroom to attend the court proceedings, because the Attorney General had no legal grounds to charge the accused, the court deferred hearing the case for another time. At that time the regime deployed its soldiers and rounded up the students who were inside the court and around the area, picked up the students who were not at the court area from their dormitories, and further collected others from other towns and brought all of them to the Asmara stadium, from where it put them on buses and sent them to Wia'a on the Red Sea coast.

Following the arrest of the students, parents gathered in front of Asmara University to inquire the whereabouts of their children but they were forcefully dispersed by the police. The parents demanded that their children be either released or at least be removed from the malaria infested, arid and hot desert region of Wia'a. Weldeab Isaac, who lived in Social Democratic Sweden, where opinions are freely expressed, was the President of the Asmara University and a member of the task force that vetted and deployed manpower. He wanted to please 'President' Isaias and declared the student movement as illegal.

Wia'a is located in the eastern coastal plains about 40 kilometers south of Massawa. It is a semi-desert area where the port city of Massawa gets its water supplies from. In summer, its temperature goes above 40 degree centigrade and at times can reach up to 50 degrees. In Wia'a, let alone to stay under a tree or a makeshift shade even air-conditioned houses are difficult to live in. The students were sent there without any preparation for what would be their basic needs; there was no food, or water, or shades. Out of the 2000 students who were detained there two students died of heatstroke: Yirga Yosief died on August 14, and Yemane Tekie died on August 19, 2001, while a biology student lost his mind and became insane. Many others suffered from malaria infection.

On September 18, 2001, when the members of G15 were imprisoned, the private newspapers were closed, the journalists and reporters were arrested, and the security arrangements in guarding the detained students became harsher. The movement of the students was severely limited to the extent that those who had dysentery were having difficulties being moved to private and secluded areas. The soldiers were always on guard over them, all day, even when they went to the outhouse to relieve themselves or as they slept. The biology student who went insane on August 19 was sent to the military hospital; the available information is that he is not cured to this day.

Finally, after three months of excruciating detention, hard work and threats, Major General Grezgiher Wuchu (Wedi Itay) gathered the students and told them, "You are infected by the G15 virus just like the AIDS virus infection; you have committed a crime against the people and the government that knows what is better for you. Therefore, you just have to be able to obey it. But as long as you are criminals you are responsible for your actions." That night, they took away some students who were considered instigators, and asked the rest to sign papers confessing they were guilty in order to be released. They were returned to Asmara on November 7, 2001. The expectation and trust that the Asmara University students had on the government was erased for good and they started to look forward to the day when the darkness would be lifted.

The death of two students and the insanity that afflicted others, and the anxiety of the students and their parents, including the bad impression the incident left on the population, didn't have an effect on the PFDJ regime. With the bad impressions still there, the students were forced to return to school. However, the President of the student association was jailed for a year in the maximum security prison at the sixth police stationin Asmara. In the end, a member of the security guard team who was opposed to the PFDJ policy and practice cooperated with him and both of them escaped together from the prison taking along a Kalashnikov rifle and hand grenades. After walking for six-days without any food they were able to cross the border and enter Ethiopia.

Because of the protest and resistance of the students, the Asmara University, Formerly Santa Familgia, was closed as of 2006 and the building has become derelict. By stepping over the rights of the Eritrean people, and banning the right of independent education, the President informed the directors and deans of the university about the closure of the university through the Minister of Education. The university faculties were dispersed all over the place: the College of Social Science and Arts was relocated in Adi Keih; the College of Agriculture, to Hamelmalo; the College of Business and Economics, to Massawa; and the College of Natural Science, to Mai Nefhi. The scattering of the colleges to many places was done without any preparation or participation of the faculties concerned. It was carried out under the watchful eyes of soldiers where colonels became the deans of the supposed academic institutions.

That tactic is based on Isaias' Machiavellian views of divide and rule and it was an opinion he conceived after the students rejected the summer harvest project and were sent to Wia'a and Gela'alo to suffer under extreme heat and military oppression. The 'President' of the state of Eritrea showed the Eritrean people openly that he doesn't accept any institutionalized system of management or legal operation, and that he stifles the right of self expression, and doesn't tolerate any organized collective activity. Therefore, what is left for the Eritrean people to do is to come out in the open and declare 'Enough is Enough', but the voice can be effective only when it is firm and unified and comes from all corners, and prevent him from dispersing the students, some to Mai Nefhi and others to Hamelmalo, Adi keih or Massawa.

Isaias knows very well how independence was achieved and now he knows how to prevent and hinder the achievement of freedom and liberation and that is why he didn't want to establish institutions. A good illustration of this is that Unit 72 which as was already noted masterminded and managed one of the most efficient intelligence operations during the struggle era and was disbanded by Isaias out of fear. He followed that by destroying the university that was established in 1950 by the Catholic Mission operatives and had more than forty years experience in producing Eritrean graduates. Just like the Haile Selassie and Mengistu regimes attempted to divide Eritrea into sects and regions and attempted to destroy the culture and language of the country, Isaias is following the footsteps of his colonial predecessors undoubtedly, he will finally fail and fall like them.

To prolong his stay in power, Isaias didn't only try to control the university students but he also extended his reach and put high school students under military control, particularly the 12th graders who were rounded up and sent to school in the Sawa military camp. Proclamation No 82, of October 1995, was issued providing that every Eritrean citizen between 18 and 40 years of age was required to fulfill the national service requirement of 18 months.

The military control doesn't end there: to prevent the youth of the high schools, 9th to 11th grade, from engaging in demonstrations and strikes, each police station monitors the schools in its assigned duty area. They carry out surveillance and have the mandate to stop any student action before it occurs. If any student movement is started, the stations are ready to quell it. The PFDJ regime that doesn't have a firefighting engine to fight fires that might start in any place in Eritrea, has full disaster preparedness to quash any student or popular movement.

In the developed world, citizens feel uncomfortable even to leave their country to work or study abroad for a limited period of time let alone to be exiled. Then, what are we witnessing in Eritrea, the country that Isaias was boasting to transform to a level where it can compete with Singapore? Why are Eritreans leaving their country in droves every month? While some are shot under the PFDJ policy of shoot-to-kill, others escape that fate, or manage to sneak out undetected, and are flooding the neighboring countries and even far beyond.

Going back to the issue of the national service and Sawa, even if we consider the proclamation as workable, the service is supposed to be for 18 months out of which six months are for military training. But in practice, the 12th graders are taking combined military and academic training and it has been over eighteen years since the program started and there are many who have been in the service since the program began, in virtual servitude.

Considering their ages, what is the reason for taking the youth away from the warmth of their parents to remote areas to conditions they are not accustomed to, and forcing them to stay under military administration, without enough food, shelter, or medical attention? Could it be that Isaias believes they will be better educated if they are exposed to harsh conditions? Could mixing military training with academic schooling make them good soldiers? Or, could it be because it is difficult to make a distinction between academic education and military training? Could it be that the parents were unable to educate their children and government wanted to take care of that on their behalf? Or is it because there is no better place and choice other than Sawa?

Regardless of whether the students of Warsay Yekaalo School in Sawa are 18 years old or under, they go through the compulsory labor and military training in record times. One wonders if that is not because they are required to quickly translate Isaias' dream of transforming Eritrea into Singapore! The youth, however, seem to think it is easier to go to Singapore and bring the country to Eritrea instead of pursuing Singapore through Sawa and through slavery!

Those who went through the Sawa experience have their own individual explanations. They are given two choices in Sawa: those who pass the matriculation test after the 12th grade are sent to the military administered colleges that were set after the Asmara University was closed, while those who fail are destined to join the human resource pool that is engaged in several national service work projects. It is rumored that failing students were not allowed to retake the matriculation exam until the son of the 'President' failed to pass it. Since then retaking the exam was allowed. No one except Isaias knows when the service period ends or when the victims will be released. There are youth who have served in the national service for more than ten years, and when you ask these members they seem to have forgotten the idea of a time limit. Since the service was transformed into slavery, they say that only Isaias, who has become a slave master in an era of technology, can answer that question.

Women could not tolerate the conditions in Sawa and that resulted in mental agony for many women; some of them started to walk backwards instead of the usual walking, forward. An unknown illness had inflicted a considerable number of women. In addition, women were often raped by the trainers and commanders at the military camp. The place of work was about three hours walk away from the camps and every trainee was given a task that should be accomplished in a given period of time. Not accomplishing the assignment does not only result in military punishment, but also the trainees are beaten with sticks and made to roll over a muddy ground. Sometimes the legs and hands of the trainees are tied from behind, in a formation known as No. 8 and they are exposed to the sun for hours.

In Sawa, the trainees are expected to leave their religion at home and praying is not allowed, but sometimes the lenient trainers let them pray before eating. However, if the Pentecostals or others are found preaching they will be taken to prison immediately. There is absolutely no religious freedom in Sawa.

At times members of the national service, unknowingly and informally, were transferred to the ranks of the regular army. The only difference is in the salary paid to one group and not the other. While the armed forces receive regular salaries, members of the national service are given meager amount of pocket money from the national service budget. At this time, they are working in the Bisha private company gold mines without pay or being provided enough food or proper shelter. They are also assigned to work on infrastructural projects with construction companies owned by the PFDJ: like Segen, Rodab, etc.

It is not allowed to refuse to be deployed when ordered, or to ask for a decent salary, and beyond that, to ask to be allowed to continue education, or to leave to help aging parents, or to get married and start a family. Since members of the national service do not get a positive response for their leave requests, they sneak out and go on their own to look after their aging parents. In that case, they face rounding up and being caught, and if that happens they face imprisonment and suffer inside metal containers and fox holes.

If the regime fails to find the absconding members, their parents are required to pay 50,000 Nakfa as a punishment for things they didn't do. Ironically, instead of the parents asking the regime of the whereabouts of their children, they become responsible for their children's disappearance from the hands of the government. Estimates are that every month over2000 youth escape the shoot-to-kill orders of the PFDJ and manage to cross international borders. There are many unattended underage children among the escapees. According to the UN, in 2012, over 1100 underage children crossed the border and were sheltered in several Refugee camps inside Tigray, in Ethiopia.

But not everyone leaving Eritrea is doing so because of problems related to the national service. PFDJ has blocked the right of citizens to move freely and the economy of the country continues to get worse. Urban centers do not have adequate water and electricity supplies and are suffering. The livelihood of the people is so poor that people stay in lines all night to receive ration of bread a day, hence children and women alike could not handle that life and they are escaping leaving the country behind. The difficulties do not end there; even experts, or government envoys, football players, singers, artists, doctors, and pilots are leaving the country. It is common knowledge that only a negligible number of people return to Eritrea after staying outside for an assignment.

The difference is that there are those who the government trusts and leave legally on a mission, or for medical treatment, and those touring sports people and artists who do not return after reaching the place of their choice. On the contrary, the youth who escape through the border risk being taken down by PFDJ bullets or are arrested to end up imprisoned in metal containers. Even those who cross borders are facing the same fate. They choose refugee camps where they are held as aliens because they decided to escape the serious human rights violations at home where people are shot without being presented to a court and imprisoned in a place where lawyers and family members cannot visit them. They face sentences of solitary confinement in prison, beatings, humiliations, inhuman treatment, and indefinite national service.

Whatever other alternatives are available is a lot better than living under the oppressive regime of PFDJ. That being the case, Eritrean youth, mothers, children and the elderly are leaving the country in the thousands facing the risk of the PFDJ policy of shoot-to-kill while crossing international borders. According to the report of the UN Special Rapporteur for Eritrea, obtained through interviews of many Eritrean refugees in neighboring countries and beyond, the principal cause for migration is the massive violation of human rights prevalent in the country. The tremendous trials and tribulations faced by Eritrean refugees inside and outside their country is well documented by various credible institutions. Many Eritreans are kidnapped from inside Eritrea by members of the army and sold to Rashayda smugglers who in turn sell them to the Bedouins in Sinai. Huge ransom amounts are demanded and those who cannot afford the ransom suffer loss of body parts, like organs such as kidneys. Many Eritrean families are burdened with the payment of ransom to free their loved ones from such a predicament.

It is a widely held view that members of the PFDJ regime are involved in the acts of human trafficking. Many people crossed the Eritrean border by bribing senior military officers who take them on government vehicles all the way from Asmara or other places across the border to the Sudan. There are also some who bribed their way out of Eritrea through the Asmara airport.

Isaias, the cause of all the miseries, has not only armed the youth, but he has also ordained that everyone between the ages of 18 to 60 in the country is subject to periodic military service. This has damaged the basic foundation of the society and destroyed the family, which is the basic unit of society, by scattering its membersto all corners of the world.

The critical question now is why are the youth leaving the country where they were born and raised? The answer is easy. The youth of Eritrea, simply because they have no future in their own country are immigrating to foreign land to a life of exile. The harasses are many, it may cost lives or body parts and many are falling prey to the Bedouins and paying hefty amounts of ransom money to human traffickers to be released. We can only live in peace and security in Eritrea after we remove the oppressive regime that has denied the Eritrean people peaceful existence in their own country and the sooner the regime goes the better.

Questions may arise regarding the path and the method to be

followed. The issue is how to force the criminal regime to face the law though the methods might be different. People must allow others to think freely just like they themselves want to think freely. People live in a context of harmony and differences, unity without diversity is tasteless and people should tolerate each other. Individual views represent only the beholder and it should not go beyond the individual to be imposed on others. On a common issue, all must put their individual thoughts aside and be able to deal with common goals, in unison. Debates must not be carried out for their own sake. Anyone should present constructive views and be able to listen to the views of others, and accept other views when they are better. Everyone should influence the other and move ahead together so that we can move along with the pace of the world.

The goal should be to transmit the positive aspects of the history of the Eritrean revolution to the future generation of the nation as bearers of the torch of independence. The objective of freedom which should have gone hand in hand with independence was not consummated because Isaias and his party the PFDJ arrested the process of ushering constitutional dispensation, and now the Eritrean people are going through the second phase of liberation, but this time against a dictatorship in an effort to bring about constitutional order in Eritrea. In this new phase of struggle for democratic and constitutional governance the divisive and sectarian politics of the past must be discarded and the youth should be given a primary leading role in the focus to resolve the struggle. Only a process which employs modern ideas and mode of operation, as well as to allow the proactive participation of the youth, can take the sociopolitical struggle to its logical conclusion.

The generations that paid dear to attain independence, with thousands of martyrs and many ending up handicapped, the freedom fighters that spent their youth in the struggle, are now old and have children to care for. They are burdened by the responsibility of raising and sustaining their families though they are fatigued. But though they face similar hindrances like the youth do, they should tirelessly encourage the new generation and lend them valuable experiences and provide them with advice and guidance and in so doing the old generation fighters would be honoring the promise of their fallen comrades. The world has changed and we all now live in a global village. We should avoid divisive politics of the past and focus on constructive activities in order to be able to reach our goal of removing the dictatorial regime and replacing it with a participatory and democratic constitutional government.

In conclusion, once we achieve our goal of removing the Isaias regime we must pool all our resources and energy for the reconstruction and development efforts of the country in order to make our country prosperous and developed, and to enable the Eritrean people to become rightful owners of their country. What the Eritrean people want is peace, stability and prosperity which is the exact opposite of what the PFDJ regime has been doing for a quarter of a century. Isaias doesn't abide by the rule of law, nor has he been accountable and transparent to the Eritrean people. In the post Isaias Eritrea there should be guarantee for the protection of the rights of Eritreans to express themselves freely, to be economically active and participate in the growth of national wealth, to work and in return to earn a living, to be freed from fear, terror, and slavery, and to be able to participate in governance at all levels, to elect and be elected in leadership positions at all levels, etc. In short, it is to be governed under a democratic and constitutional system. To achieve these goals demands our proactive, unreserved and determined participation. Therefore, let's all go forward united and with determination!

POSTSCRIPT

Introduction

Since the publication of "The Hidden Party," in Tigrigna in 2014, there has been a flow of information, suggestions for correction as well as commendations from various readers. I would like, first of all, to express my heart-felt thanks to all those who, on the basis of their appreciation of the value of the book, made their recommendations and suggested corrections, urging me to expand as well as improve it. In accordance with such recommendations, I have made a number of changes, including the issue of reference of names and the narrative of detailed events.

Above all, considering the suggestion for me to provide additional explanations with respect to the title of the book, I have decided to add this Postscript in accordance with the comments and opinions expressed, on various occasions, by the founding members of the party as well as my own observations as a member of the party. This is in addition to the relevant information that is found in interviews conducted by Dan Connell with some founders of the party and his conversations with Eritrean political prisoners (Conversations with Eritrean Political Prisoners) as well as his work titled "Building a New Nation."

The main objective of this book stemmed from an earnest desire to reveal and explain the origin and character of the party, first known as the Eritrean People's Revolutionary Party, later changed to Eritrean Socialist Party, a party that operated secretly and as such successfully led Eritrea's struggle for independence. In my description and analysis of the role of this party, I have given due weight to the mechanism the party utilized in order to remain in power; I have also made an attempt to expose the new secret party that was conceived within and came out of the womb of the party, which is now leading the country to ruin.

Nonetheless, I found it necessary to provide this brief comment in the form of a Postscript in order to provide a clearer idea about the origin and overall general conduct of the Eritrean People's Revolutionary/Eritrean Socialist Party (EPRP/ESP).

Origin and Operations

We cannot appreciate the origin and character of the party under discussion without making reference to the Eritrean Liberation Front (ELF), out of which the Eritrean people's Liberation Front (EPLF) and thence the secret party emerged. The ELF was started by two different groups of Eritreans: one group being students plus a few elder statesmen/politicians living in exile in the historic Islamic University of Al Azhar in Cairo; the other being former Eritrean soldiers who were veterans of the Sudanese army. The most prominent among these was Hamid Idris Awate, the founding head and inspirational leader of the ELF. The two groups, though bound by the same nationalist sentiment and a common sense of grievance concerning the oppression of their people, nevertheless represented different social classes. The students represented a small number of educated elite in contrast to the vast majority of uneducated people in the country, while the veteran soldiers were closer to the general population and a few of them like Awate had received a modicum of education from Italian colonial powers. Most of them also spoke Arabic on the basis of their Elementary Quranic education as well as their experience in Sudan. Most of the veterans hailed from the Barca region, while the students came from both highland as well as Lowland Muslim families.

The fact that the ELF was based in the Barca region and that the most important leaders were from that region inevitably had an impact on the behavior of its leaders and their conduct of the affairs of the Front. The question arises as to what is the dominant ideology reigning in Barca at the time that had an influence on the behavior of the ELF leaders. The answer is that it was an ideology born in a conservative (not to say backward) region whose economy and society had barely been touched by the "modernizing" force of the European colonization that had affected much of the rest of Eritrea, particularly the highland region. The conservative or backward state of much of Barca's economy and society reflected the nature and stage of development of the society in the region at large.

Eritrea's liberation struggle was affected by this socio-economic condition; for even though we recognize the positive side of the struggle in mobilizing the Eritrean people along a nationalist liberationist struggle, there was an undeniable truth that the struggle went through many ups and downs with some negative effect on its development in which tendencies appeared including in particular actions on the part of the leadership that led to mutually inflicted damages—damages far above those inflicted by our alien rulers. This is an incontrovertible truth. The journey of Eritrea's struggle involved a backward feudal culture that inhibited progress, keeping us limited to a static structure, a heritage defined by narrow-minded loyalties devoid of the capacity for tolerance and social progress and breeding division and mutual hatred instead of unity and harmony.

As a manifestation of this condition the Eritrean liberation organizations were involved in the worst kind of conflict, namely "civil war", or rather inter-organizational war—a tragic situation that became known throughout the world. Even now as a function of that history we are bogged down in the primitive rut in which primordial loyalties override the urgent need of progress toward national consciousness that gives precedence to the higher object of the national interest.

The above remarks inevitably raise the following questions: Why was the EPRP/ESP created? Why were the secret parties of Labor and the Baath Party created in the ELF? Why were the parties that appeared within the EPLF created and then crushed? Why did all these secret parties emerge? And what is the aim of the various parties that kept appearing and disappearing? What was the problem that prevented the Eritrean people from setting aside their differences and to march united in the struggle? These and related questions need to be discussed and summed up and I will attempt to give a summary account concerning this matter.

Why the Secret Party was Created

The creators of the secret party (the EPRP) explain the reason for its creation in terms of the need to meet the challenges of the backward sentiments prevailing in the region with its tribal, religious and regional allegiances, challenges that had to be met principally by constructing a democratic system. Among the freedom fighters who were not able to correct the backward tendencies from within the ELF, and in particular Addis Ababa University students who had joined the struggle, student like Isaias Afwerki, Haile Duru'e and Muse Tesfamichael, made a solemn vow by swallowing small pebbles (a traditional form of vow) and swore a blood oath to create a party. Soon after the crisis had erupted within the ELF with its attendant hostility toward the educated elements, Abraham Tewolde, Isaias Afwerki and a few other fighters broke away from the ELF and established an organization called the Liberation Party in the Ala sub-region and later a organization called Eritrean Peoples' (or Popular) Forces appeared. Other fighters like Mahmud Sherifo, Ibrahim Afa, Mesfin Hagos, Maasho Embaye, Ali Said Abdalla, Hasan Mohamed Amir, save Abubakar Mohamed Hasan who came to the Eritrean field after the split from the ELF and others had abandoned the ELF in defiance of the hostile condition prevalent there and escaped to Sudan. From there they had proceeded to Yemen (South Yemen) and they later affirmed that they had the clear intention of creating a party.

Following their entry into Dankalia, the group known as the First Popular Part and the one known as the Second Popular Part (also known as the Ala group), from these two groups Isaias and Romodan were those who played the biggest role into an understanding to create the secret party, pursuant to the wish of the members. This happened in late 1970 and early 1971. The cadres of the two parts of the Popular Forces, that is to say, from among those that entered from abroad and those who were in Ala, namely Romodan Mohamed Nur, Isaias Afwerki, Mahmud Sherifo, Mesfin Hagos, Mohamed Ali Umaro, Abubakar Mohamed Hasan, Ibrahim Afa, Hasan Moahmed Amir, Measho Embaye, Ali Said Abdalla, Ahmed Tahir Baduri and Ahmed Alkeisi, met at Mount Ghedem, near Hirgigo, and formed the Eritrean People's Revolutionary Party (EPRP) on April 4, 1971. The founding principles (or the line) followed by the EPRP might have been aimed at opposing the erroneous guidance of the ELF that had been founded on sub-nationalist sentiment and replacing it with the establishment of an independent Eritrean nation as well as developing Eritrean national identity; however, its members were not free from the Leftist Ideology prevalent at the time. The principal leaders and especially Isaias, Romodan and Mesfin Hagos had been trained in China and were influenced by the ideas of Mao Tse Tung, and others were influenced by similar ideas garnered from Cuba and elsewhere. Accordingly, the party was monopolized by a nucleus of people bound by a common ideology—a group that excluded people embracing a differing ideology. In sum, the dominant line was one that was wedded to the idea of one vanguard party system and opposed to the idea of multi-party system.

There was basic difference between the initial idea born in the ELF and ideas that were embraced subsequently. The party that began with the intention of eliminating sub-nationalism and substituting it with the establishment of an independent Eritrean nation accompanied by a nationalist ideology was not limited by those aims, important though that they were. It went beyond that and was actually dedicated to the establishment of a communist system in an independent Eritrea. E. P.R. P. was indeed an organization dedicated to the (Marxist) idea of mobilizing all it members under the leadership of the Alliance of Workers and Peasants pitted against the capitalist and imperialist systems and thereby establish a communist system. To that end, the secret party as a vanguard aimed at forming a National Democratic Front embracing all the different social classes as well as the active members of the EPLF.

The party was led by a Central Committee first elected in 1976 at the party Congress. Its chain of command was structured with an initial unit of five or six members forming a secret cell transitioning to sub-branches and branches and eventually forming regional party committees The party members were selected in a manner consistent with the formation of the secret party and the Front (EPLF), and as such they led and supervised all activities of the Front. With the exception of three members namely Ogbe Abraha, Berhane Gherezgiher and Mahamed Said Bareh, all the members of the Political Bureau (Politbureau) of the Front (EPLF) were members of the Central Committee of the party. The crucial areas of responsibilities of the Front were controlled by members of the party.

The basic function of members of the party was collecting and transmitting information in both directions, regarding all activities conducted on the Front. At a minimum, once a month, all reports of members of the Front and the activities were summed up and transmitted up along the chain of command. And all orders on activities including awareness raising, are transmitted from the top and their implementation reviewed and accounted for. In sum, all the activities in the EPLF were monitored and reviewed meticulously by the secret party.

The process of recruitment for membership of the party was designed to enhance the capacity of the party. To that end, every member of the Front was reviewed in accordance criteria that are monitored and records are kept. The criteria are divided into three parts which are also divided into smaller parts as follows:

1. Democratic (character)
   1.a active
   1.b inactive
   1.c dependent
2. Undemocratic
   2.a active
   2.b inactive
   2.c dependent
3. Unreliable
   3.a harmless
   3.b inactive
   3.c dangerous

These criteria were also applied to the members of the Front as conditions for their entry into the Party. The criteria were applied strictly in terms of the patriotism of members, their readiness and commitment for martyrdom, and in their commitment to be engaged in social activities and above all their readiness to accept views about Marxism.

In consequence to the division of the criteria, those that attain grade 1.1 (active-democratic) are submitted as candidates for party membership. They are then sent to the School for Cadres, or assigned an appropriate party member as a mentor in order to raise the level of their Marxist understanding and opinions. And after a period of intense review they are made members of the party.

Members of the party are prohibited from revealing any matter related to the party or disclosing the existence of the party. Moreover once a fighter becomes a member he or she is not allowed to leave the party. Once in-never out! Opposition to the decisions of the party is not permitted; and it is obligatory for members to enforce party decisions. It is also prohibited to propagate opinions contrary to decisions of the party.

Turning now to what I characterized as a Machiavellian slogan, I beg the indulgence of the reader to allow me to offer some views. It is perfectly understandable to expect an organization created to offset the backward tendencies prevalent in the ELF, to work in secrecy. Nor was it contrary to reason, following the separation from the ELF, to continue to operate in secrecy pending the consolidation of the democratic forces. Operating covertly until you gain strength not only enables you to minimize your exposure to danger but it also prevents your enemy from knowing your activities. And to the extent that your enemy is not able to know and control your activities, you are able to perform your tasks effectively. However, once you have overcome your enemy and reached a position of superiority the need to continue working secretly does not arise.

But EPRP continued its secret existence long after the EPLF had grown to be powerful and self-reliant having passed the danger point. To perpetuate such secrecy in the context of a common struggle inside a national Democratic Front can only be described as motivated by the special interest of a clique at a time when all members were engaged in a struggle paying the ultimate sacrifice for the common cause in equal measure.

Even though this conduct of affairs seems to signify (or glorify) the Leftist line mentioned before, nonetheless EPRP had revised its Leftist ideology proposing in its place a multi-party system based on social justice and changing its name from EPRP to ESP (Socialist Party of Eritrea). Yet the leadership of EPRP was not willing to fulfill its promise of change. Indeed, due to its reluctance to make the change, having realized the future potential for challenges and problems of meeting such challenges, it abandoned the party thus forestalling the challenges. More ominously, it was at the time when the party had become "frozen" that Isaias created a new (another) secret party having selected those elements that he had identified as unquestioningly obedient cadres and new disciples he called "new blood." It is with this new party that Isaias is leading Eritrea to ruin and its people to unprecedented misery and despair. This closed secret mode of operation stems from a deep sense of inadequacy, lack of self confidence and an inability to administer people, masquerading as dedication to the cause of the oppressed when in reality it is a diabolical deceptive program pitting the oppressed against the oppressed, its hidden motive being the promotion of one's aim of pursuit of power and the accumulation of personal wealth.

Let me reiterate my earlier reference to the Machiavellian axiom that, 'the end justifies the means' to help explain the constantly changing behavior of Isaias who changes his color, Chameleon-like, at times becoming a revolutionary Marxist or a Maoist, and when it suits him becoming a democrat, always claiming that there is no one who

245

cares for the Eritrean people like him—all this in order to stay in power and accumulate wealth. But it is clear now that after all his supreme acting (worthy of Hollywood), all this deception and its tragic consequences on a helpless people, the game is up. His days are numbered and he knows it, judging by the desperate moves he has been making. He has seen the writing on the wall; so have his captive ministers and other servants. The game is up and Eritrea will be rid of this cancer.

INDEX